Woman's Own
COOKBOOK

A New Complete Guide to Family Cooking
by Alex Barker

TREASURE PRESS

First published in Great Britain in 1981 by
The Hamlyn Publishing Group Limited

This edition published in 1988 by
Treasure Press
Michelin House
81 Fulham Road
London SW3 6RB

Reprinted 1989

Line illustrations by Richard Jacobs (page 8 Marilyn Day)

ISBN 1 85051 316 3

Produced by Mandarin Offset
Printed and bound in Hong Kong

Contents

Useful Facts and Figures

Notes on metrication

In this book quantities are given in metric and Imperial measures. Exact conversion from Imperial to metric measures does not usually give very convenient working quantities and so the metric measures have been rounded off into units of 25 grams. The table below shows the recommended equivalents.

Ounces	Approx g to nearest whole figure	Recommended conversion to nearest unit of 25
1	28	25
2	57	50
3	85	75
4	113	100
5	142	150
6	170	175
7	198	200
8	227	225
9	255	250
10	283	275
11	312	300
12	340	350
13	368	375
14	396	400
15	425	425
16 (1 lb)	454	450
17	482	475
18	510	500
19	539	550
20 ($1\frac{1}{4}$ lb)	567	575

Note: When converting quantities over 20 oz first add the appropriate figures in the centre column, then adjust to the nearest unit of 25. As a general guide, 1 kg (1000 g) equals 2.2 lb or about 2 lb 3 oz. This method of conversion gives good results in nearly all cases, although in certain pastry and cake recipes a more accurate conversion is necessary to produce a balanced recipe.

Liquid measures The millilitre has been used in this book and the following table gives a few examples.

Imperial	Approx ml to nearest whole figure	Recommended ml
$\frac{1}{4}$ pint	142	150 ml
$\frac{1}{2}$ pint	283	300 ml
$\frac{3}{4}$ pint	425	450 ml
1 pint	567	600 ml
$1\frac{1}{2}$ pints	851	900 ml
$1\frac{3}{4}$ pints	992	1000 ml (1 litre)

Spoon measures All spoon measures given in this book are level unless otherwise stated.

Can sizes At present, cans are marked with the exact (usually to the nearest whole number) metric equivalent of the Imperial weight of the contents, so we have followed this practice when giving can sizes.

NOTE: **When making any of the recipes in this book, only follow one set of measures as they are not interchangeable.**

Oven temperatures
The table below gives recommended equivalents.

	°C	°F	*Gas Mark*
Very cool	110	225	$\frac{1}{4}$
	120	250	$\frac{1}{2}$
Cool	140	275	1
	150	300	2
Moderate	160	325	3
	180	350	4
Moderately hot	190	375	5
	200	400	6
Hot	220	425	7
	230	450	8
Very hot	240	475	9

Notes for American and Australian users
In America the 8-oz measuring cup is used. In Australia metric measures are now used in conjunction with the standard 250-ml measuring cup. The Imperial pint, used in Britain and Australia, is 20 fl oz, while the American pint is 16 fl oz. It is important to remember that the Australian tablespoon differs from both the British and American tablespoons; the table below gives a comparison. The British standard tablespoon, which has been used throughout this book, holds 17.7 ml, the American 14.2 ml, and the Australian 20 ml. A teaspoon holds approximately 5 ml in all three countries.

British	*American*	*Australian*
1 teaspoon	1 teaspoon	1 teaspoon
1 tablespoon	1 tablespoon	1 tablespoon
2 tablespoons	3 tablespoons	2 tablespoons
$3\frac{1}{2}$ tablespoons	4 tablespoons	3 tablespoons
4 tablespoons	5 tablespoons	$3\frac{1}{2}$ tablespoons

An Imperial/American guide to solid and liquid measures

Imperial	*American*	*Imperial*	*American*
Solid measures		**Liquid measures**	
1 lb butter or	2 cups	$\frac{1}{4}$ pint liquid	$\frac{2}{3}$ cup liquid
margarine		$\frac{1}{2}$ pint	$1\frac{1}{4}$ cups
1 lb flour	4 cups	$\frac{3}{4}$ pint	2 cups
1 lb granulated or	2 cups	1 pint	$2\frac{1}{2}$ cups
castor sugar		$1\frac{1}{2}$ pints	$3\frac{3}{4}$ cups
1 lb icing sugar	3 cups	2 pints	5 cups ($2\frac{1}{2}$ pints)
8 oz rice	1 cup		

American terms
The list below gives some American equivalents or substitutes for terms and ingredients used in this book

British/American
Equipment and terms
deep cake tin/spring form pan
double saucepan/double boiler
flan tin/pie pan
frying pan/skillet
greaseproof paper/wax paper
grill/broil
loaf tin/loaf pan
piping bag/pastry bag
stoned/pitted
Swiss roll tin/jelly roll pan

British/American
Ingredients
aubergine/eggplant

bicarbonate of soda/baking soda
biscuits/crackers, cookies
cocoa powder/unsweetened cocoa
cornflour/cornstarch
courgettes/zucchini
cream, single/cream, light
cream, double/cream, heavy
essence/extract
flour, plain/flour, all-purpose
glacé cherries/candied cherries
icing/frosting
lard/shortening
shortcrust pastry/basic pie dough
spring onion/scallion
sultanas/seedless white raisins
yeast, fresh/yeast, compressed

Introduction

I think you will find that this book is not just one to refer to for a specific recipe, but that it contains advice and information for all sorts of occasions. Whether you are a new cook looking for something simple and economical, or have been an expert cook for many years and are looking for just that something special for a dinner party, you will find a suitable dish here. There are reference charts to help you with freezing, preserving and catering for large numbers, plus many helpful tips when it comes to deciding the type of joint to buy, choosing the right equipment, creating exotic ice creams and puddings, making the most of leftovers or coping with disasters.

If you, like so many, have to cook two meals a day on a shoestring and find it incredibly boring and time-consuming, I hope this book will help make it easier and maybe even more enjoyable. Cooking can be fun, and should be for the amount of time and money many of us put into it. However, it never will be if you cook the same things every day, have disasters at the crucial moment and find budgeting a constant battle. For this reason I have included as many everyday family recipes as possible, that have been popular over the years in *Woman's Own*. There are recipes that can be made up in minutes; ideas for cheaper meals and ways to stretch your more expensive foods; dishes that can be made from storecupboard ingredients and leftovers; or dishes to which you can add your own favourite touch. Enjoying cooking so much myself, I like to think that other people can do so too. I hope that this book will help you.

Alex Barker

Soups

Soup has long been a British favourite, although its original name was taken from the French, *soupe*. Then it was a broth-like mixture containing, in more wealthy homes, meat and game which was either pounded to a paste or left whole. Poorer people poured thinner broth over bread or toast.

Although we have become far more adventurous with our choice of soup, it is still just as important to our diet, both as a warming, tasty start to the meal, or a filling, nourishing meal in itself.

Use the many cans and packets available to form the bases of your soup. Don't forget the importance of leftovers – vegetables, meat bones, a few spoonfuls of sauce or gravy – which can all be used to help you make more interesting and economical soups.

Stock

A good stock can make all the difference to the flavour of your soup. Whenever you can, make up a few pints, either to freeze (in ice cube trays to transfer to polythene bags for easy storage) or to keep in the refrigerator. Meat stock will keep for about 3 days in the refrigerator, but without one, reboil it daily and it should keep for a couple of days. See page 24 for Fish stock.

Meat Stock

450 g/1 lb or more beef, lamb, veal, game or poultry bones, either fresh from the butcher or left over from a roast or boned joint
$\frac{1}{2}$ teaspoon salt
1–2 carrots
1 onion
1 bouquet garni

Trim the bones of as much fat as possible. Put them in a large pan with 1.75–2.25 litres/3–4 pints of water and the other ingredients. Bring to the boil, skim off any fat or froth occasionally with a large metal spoon, and simmer, covered, for 2–3 hours. Strain and use as required, or clear the stock to use in consommé (see below).

If, like many cooks, you don't have time to make fresh stock, cubes are a very good substitute. But you could try combining these two ways and get the best of both worlds. Place the cube and recommended amount of water, plus 300 ml/$\frac{1}{2}$ pint extra, in a large pan. Then add the juice of half a lemon, a few sprigs of fresh herbs or the outer skins or leaves of carrots, celery, lettuce and other vegetables. Simmer for 20–30 minutes before straining.

Vegetable Stock

25–50 g/1–2 oz butter
450 g/1 lb mixed root vegetables, sliced or chopped
1 bouquet garni or fresh or dried herbs
salt and pepper

Melt the butter in a large saucepan and sauté the prepared vegetables until just turning golden. Add the bouquet garni or herbs with 1.75–2.25 litres/3–4 pints of water and the seasoning. Simmer for about 1$\frac{1}{2}$ hours. This stock does not keep for more than 1 or 2 days, even in the refrigerator. As an alternative to this type of stock, use the water from boiling vegetables. Always save this if possible and store in the refrigerator.

To Clear Stock

For a good consommé, stock should be crystal clear, but this does take time. Strain the stock, then bring it back to the boil. Add one egg white, then whisk hard until it froths. Remove from the heat and leave to settle. Place a large sieve over a bowl, and cover it with a thin clean cloth (double muslin or a jelly bag is ideal). Pour the stock in slowly and leave until it all drips through. Do not disturb, or the result will be cloudy. This stock can then be flavoured with many other ingredients to make consommés and clear broths.

Mint and Lamb Consommé

(Illustrated on page 17)

450 g/1 lb lamb bones
1 small onion, quartered
2 cloves
1 stick celery, coarsely chopped
salt and pepper
1 sprig thyme, rosemary, parsley or basil, finely
chopped
1 bunch mint, finely chopped
to garnish
1 sprig fresh mint, chopped
1 orange, sliced

Roast the lamb bones in a hot oven (220°C, 425°F, Gas Mark 7) for about 1 hour. Put into a large saucepan with the onion, cloves, celery, seasoning, herbs and mint and 900 ml/1½ pints water. Bring to the boil and simmer gently for about 1 hour. Cool, strain to clear and chill. Garnish with the chopped mint and orange slices. **Serves 4**

Consommé of Spiced Fruits

(Illustrated on page 17)

50 g/2 oz dried apricots
juice of 1 orange
100 g/4 oz peaches, sliced or 1 (213-g/7½-oz) can
juice of 1 lemon
3 cloves
pinch each grated nutmeg and ground cinnamon
¼ teaspoon yeast extract

Soak the apricots overnight in a large pan containing 900 ml/1½ pints of water. Add the rest of the ingredients, bring to the boil and simmer gently for 30 minutes. Remove the cloves. If wished, strain at this stage. Chill or serve hot. **Serves 4–6**

Orange Soup

(Illustrated on page 17)

3 oranges
450 ml/¾ pint chicken stock
salt and pepper
150 ml/¼ pint natural yogurt
3 tablespoons cream
pinch grated nutmeg
1 tablespoon chopped parsley to garnish

Grate the rind and squeeze the juice from the oranges. Reserve a little orange rind to garnish. Put the remaining rind and juice in a pan with the stock and seasoning. Bring to the boil and simmer gently for about 15 minutes. Allow to cool and chill. Store like this for up to 2 days in the refrigerator. When required, mix in the yogurt and cream, check the seasoning and stir in a pinch of nutmeg. Serve garnished with the remaining rind and chopped parsley. **Serves 4**

Watercress and Yogurt Soup

3 bunches watercress
900 ml/1½ pints chicken stock
50 g/2 oz walnuts
600 ml/1 pint natural yogurt
salt and pepper
to garnish
few sprigs watercress
4 tablespoons natural yogurt

Wash and trim the watercress, add the stock then bring to the boil and simmer for 15 minutes. Liquidise or sieve with the walnuts and cool. Add the yogurt, season to taste and chill thoroughly. Serve garnished with sprigs of watercress and a swirl of yogurt. **Serves 4–6**

Vichyssoise

4 leeks, sliced
1 onion, sliced
50 g/2 oz butter or margarine
salt and pepper
1.15 litres/2 pints chicken stock
2 potatoes, sliced
200 ml/7 fl oz cream
to garnish
chopped chives or extra sliced leeks
sliced boiled potato

Wash the leeks and fry gently with the onion in the butter or margarine for about 10 minutes until transparent. Add the seasoning, stock and potatoes. Bring to the boil, cover and simmer gently until the vegetables are soft. Cool. Sieve or liquidise the soup and then stir in the cream. Chill.

This can be kept for up to 2 days in the refrigerator in an airtight container. When required, check the seasoning and garnish with the chives or leeks and boiled potato slices. **Serves 4**

Creamy Tomato Soup

(Illustrated on page 17 and on the jacket with a garnish of parsley and a swirl of fresh cream)

450 g/1 lb tomatoes, peeled or 1 (425-g/15-oz) can
1 onion, chopped
2 carrots, chopped
1 teaspoon sugar
450 ml/$\frac{3}{4}$ pint chicken stock (use only 300 ml/$\frac{1}{2}$ pint if using canned tomatoes)
salt and pepper
150 ml/$\frac{1}{4}$ pint milk
150 ml/$\frac{1}{4}$ pint double cream
1 tablespoon shredded coconut to garnish

Simmer the tomatoes, onion, carrot, sugar, stock and seasoning together until tender. Pass through a sieve or liquidise and return to the pan with the milk and cream. Heat through and garnish with shredded coconut. Serve with French bread. **Serves 4–6**

Artichoke Soup

(Illustrated on page 17)

350 g/12 oz Jerusalem artichokes, roughly chopped
2 tablespoons lemon juice
450 ml/$\frac{3}{4}$ pint chicken stock
150 ml/$\frac{1}{4}$ pint dry white wine
150 ml/$\frac{1}{4}$ pint milk
salt and pepper
pinch grated nutmeg
few sprigs tarragon to garnish

Put the artichokes in a large pan with the lemon juice, stock, wine, milk, seasoning and nutmeg. Bring to the boil and simmer until very tender. Then liquidise or sieve. Reheat and garnish with tarragon before serving. **Serves 4**

Avocado Soup

2 medium avocados, stoned and peeled
900 ml/1$\frac{1}{2}$ pints chicken stock
1 tablespoon grated onion
salt and pepper
1 tablespoon chopped chives
2 tablespoons cream

Sieve or mash the avocados and whisk into the stock with the onion. Bring slowly to the boil. Season to taste, sprinkle with chives and stir in the cream before serving. **Serves 4**

Split Pea Soup

50–75 g/2–3 oz bacon, chopped
175 g/6 oz yellow split peas, soaked and drained
2 large onions, sliced
few sticks celery, chopped
2–3 leeks, sliced
1 clove garlic, crushed
25–50 g/1–2 oz butter
300 ml/$\frac{1}{2}$ pint tomato juice
300 ml/$\frac{1}{2}$ pint beef stock
salt and pepper
1 bouquet garni
900 ml/1$\frac{1}{2}$ pints water
50 g/2 oz cheese, grated

Place the bacon, peas, onions, celery, leeks and garlic in a large saucepan with the butter. Fry quickly to brown the onion. Add all the remaining ingredients except the cheese. Bring to the boil and simmer for about $1\frac{1}{2}$ hours – adding extra water if necessary. Remove the bouquet garni. Mash slightly when the peas are well cooked. Top with the cheese. **Serves 4–6**

Celery and Spinach Soup

(Illustrated on page 17)

25 g/1 oz butter
1 tablespoon oil
450 g/1 lb spinach, chopped
2 tablespoons chopped spring onion
1 head celery, chopped
1 clove garlic, crushed
salt and pepper
1.15 litres/2 pints chicken stock
150 ml/$\frac{1}{4}$ pint single cream
slices of onion and mushroom to garnish

Melt the butter with the oil and fry the spinach, spring onion, celery, and garlic for 10–15 minutes until softened. Add seasoning and the stock and simmer for 20 minutes. Liquidise or sieve then return to the pan and reheat. Stir in the cream. Garnish with the onion and mushroom. **Serves 4–6**

Curried Onion Soup

(Illustrated on page 17)

25 g/1 oz butter
2 onions, sliced
$\frac{1}{2}$ teaspoon curry powder
750 ml/$1\frac{1}{4}$ pints beef stock
salt and pepper
100 g/4 oz mushrooms, chopped
50 g/2 oz walnuts, chopped

Melt the butter in a saucepan and fry the onion until dark brown. Stir in the curry powder, stock and seasoning. Simmer for about 40 minutes. Stir in the mushrooms and walnuts, reserving a few of each to garnish. Serve hot or cold, with the mushrooms and walnuts.

To make a more substantial supper dish, add 225 g/8 oz minced beef when frying the onion and add 100 g/4 oz rice with the stock. Serve with fried bread croûtes. (Illustrated on page 86). **Serves 4**

Stilton Soup

Stilton need not be at its best for soup, so it's a good way to use up any which is beginning to dry. Other blue cheese, or a mixture may be used.

25 g/1 oz butter
1 small onion, finely chopped
1 clove garlic, crushed
225 g/8 oz Stilton, crumbled
225 g/8 oz Cheddar, grated
75 g/3 oz plain flour
$1\frac{1}{2}$ chicken stock cubes
1 bay leaf
900 ml/$1\frac{1}{2}$ pints water
300 ml/$\frac{1}{2}$ pint double cream
6 tablespoons dry white wine

Melt the butter in a large saucepan and cook the onion and garlic until softened. Add the cheeses and flour. Cook, stirring, for 1–2 minutes. Remove from the heat and gradually stir in the remaining ingredients. Return to the heat and whisk continuously until it boils. Simmer for 5–10 minutes, whisking. **Serves 6–8**

Cock-a-Leekie Soup

1.25–1.5-kg/$2\frac{1}{2}$–3-lb boiling fowl
450 g/1 lb leeks, sliced
2–3 carrots, sliced
1 onion, sliced
few sprigs parsley, chopped
salt and pepper

Clean and truss the chicken. Place in a large pan with enough water to cover and simmer for about $1\frac{1}{2}$ hours. Skim off any froth and check the water occasionally. Add the leek, carrot and onion to the pan with some of the parsley. Simmer for a further 20 minutes. Remove the chicken from the pan. Pull off some of the flesh and add to the soup (use the rest for another dish). Season to taste and garnish with parsley. **Serves 4**

Bacon and Brown Rice Soup

A very substantial soup – almost a meal in itself.

300–600 ml/½–1 pint bacon stock (the more salty it
is, the less you need)
75 g/3 oz brown rice
few sprigs parsley
½ red pepper, seeds removed and sliced
50 g/2 oz button mushrooms, sliced
2 sticks celery, sliced

Add enough water to the stock to give
900 ml/1½ pints, pour the mixture into a
saucepan and bring to the boil. Add the rice and
parsley. Simmer for 30 minutes. Add the
pepper, mushroom and celery to the soup.
Simmer for another 5–10 minutes, until the
rice is cooked, remove the parsley, then serve.
Serves 4

White Fish Chowder

1–2 rashers bacon
350 g/12 oz coley, huss or cod, skinned weight
25–50 g/1–2 oz butter
4 medium potatoes, diced or grated
2 onions, finely chopped
600 ml/1 pint milk
1 (227-g/8-oz) can tomatoes
salt and pepper
6 slices toast

Dice the bacon and fry in its own fat until crisp;
remove from the pan. Cut the fish into neat
pieces. Heat the butter in a saucepan and toss
the fish until golden, but do not overcook. Add
the potato and onion, and mix with the fish.
Add the milk, tomatoes and bacon. Simmer
gently for 15–20 minutes and add seasoning to
taste. Put a slice of toast into each soup bowl
and top with the chowder. **Serves 6**

Mackerel Saffron Soup

(Illustrated on page 36)

1 onion, chopped
1 clove garlic, crushed
2 sticks celery, chopped
450 g/1 lb tomatoes, peeled and chopped
1 bay leaf
2 tablespoons chopped parsley
salt and pepper
little saffron, or 2 teaspoons turmeric
grated rind and juice of 1 lemon
1 whole smoked mackerel
600 ml/½ pint mussels or 1 (150-g/5¼-oz) can,
drained
2 egg yolks
3 tablespoons double cream

Put the onion, garlic, celery and tomato in a
large saucepan with the bay leaf, parsley,
seasoning, 1.15 litres/2 pints water, saffron or
turmeric and the lemon rind and juice. Simmer
gently for about 30 minutes. In the meantime,
cut off the mackerel head, tail and fins and
remove the skin and backbone. Clean the
mussels and discard any which do not close
when tapped. Cut the mackerel flesh into small
pieces and add to the soup with the mussels.
Bring back to the boil and simmer until all the
mussels open. Check the seasoning and take
out a little of the liquid. Mix the egg yolks and
cream with this, return the mixture to the pan
and cook the soup gently, without boiling until
it thickens slightly. **Serves 4**

Although soups are a very quick and easy way to begin a meal, light starters, mousses, pâtés, fruit or fish cocktails may suit your plans better. Many can be made in advance or frozen to avoid last-minute work, and many are suitable for light lunches, snack entertaining or picnics. Remember when you are planning a menu that the starter should not be too heavy, or so overpowering in flavour that you ruin the total effect of your meal.

Liver Pâté

450 g/1 lb lamb's or calf's liver
350 g/12 oz chicken livers
2 tablespoons oil
1 clove garlic, crushed
1 onion, chopped
salt and pepper
pinch dry mustard
2 tablespoons stock, brandy or whisky
100 g/4 oz butter
to garnish
gherkins
basil leaves

Wash and trim all the liver and cut into small pieces. Heat the oil and cook the liver very slowly until it is firm but not browned. Remove from the pan then fry the garlic and onion until tender. Then either blend the liver, onion and garlic in a liquidiser, or pass them through a fine sieve. Beat in the seasoning, mustard and stock, brandy or whisky. Pack the mixture into a pâté dish and chill in the refrigerator until firm.

Garnish with gherkins and basil leaves. For better and longer keeping, any pâté or terrine can be topped with a layer of clarified butter (see page 184). **Serves 8**

Duck and Orange Pâté

1 small duckling
1 large onion
225 g/8 oz duck livers (if available) or chicken livers
grated rind and juice of 1 orange
2–3 tablespoons brandy
salt and pepper
2 tablespoons cream
1 egg
2 tablespoons sliced olives
pinch dried rosemary
pinch dried marjoram

Remove all the flesh from the duckling and mince half with the onion and livers. Stir in the orange rind and juice, brandy, seasoning, cream, egg, olives, rosemary and marjoram. Spoon half the mixture into the base of a pâté dish.

Tear the remaining duck into strips and arrange over the minced mixture. Top with the remaining mince. Cover, sealing well and cook in a bain-marie in a moderate oven (180°C, 350°F, Gas Mark 4) for about $1\frac{1}{2}$ hours.

Drain off any excess liquid and chill well. **Serves 6–8**

Quick Cheese Mousses

1 (298-g/$10\frac{1}{2}$-oz) can condensed consommé
75 g/3 oz cream cheese
3 tablespoons natural yogurt
3 tablespoons chopped spring onion stems
pinch grated nutmeg
salt and pepper

Beat all the ingredients together until the mixture is smooth. This is most easily done in a liquidiser, but if you do it by hand it makes no difference to the end result. Divide the mousse between four individual serving dishes, ramekins or glasses. Chill until set then turn out just before serving if you wish. **Serves 4**

Hot Mackerel Terrine with Tomato Sauce

225 g/8 oz white fish fillet
3 tablespoons white wine
salt and pepper
1 tablespoon chopped parsley
2 tablespoons oil
175 g/6 oz button mushrooms, thinly sliced
1 bunch watercress
450 g/1 lb mackerel
½ clove garlic, crushed
1 very small egg

Skin the white fish and cut the flesh into strips 1 cm/½ inch wide. Marinate for about an hour in the wine, seasoned with salt, pepper and parsley. Meanwhile, heat the oil and fry the mushrooms. Blanch the watercress in boiling water for 1–2 minutes, then drain. Skin and bone the mackerel and mince or liquidise with the salt, pepper, garlic, watercress and egg. Line a terrine, or 1-kg/2-lb loaf tin with greaseproof paper, fill with a 5-mm/¼-inch layer of mackerel mixture, a layer of the drained white fish, then a layer of mushrooms. Add a layer of mackerel, the remaining white-fish and mushrooms and finish with a layer of mackerel. Pack down well, cover with a sheet of foil and a weight, and cook in a bain-marie (or roasting tin half full of water) in a moderately hot oven (200°C, 400°F, Gas Mark 6) for about 50 minutes. Turn on to a heated serving dish and serve hot with Tomato sauce (see page 188). **Serves 6**

Salmon Mousse

25 g/1 oz butter
1 shallot or 2 spring onion bulbs, finely chopped
200 ml/7 fl oz fish stock, or stock made from chicken and herb stock cubes
7 g/¼ oz powdered gelatine
2–3 tablespoons dry vermouth or sherry
225 g/8 oz salmon, cooked or canned
salt and pepper
pinch grated nutmeg
150 ml/¼ pint double or whipping cream

Melt the butter in a frying pan and gently cook the shallot or spring onion until just trans-

lucent. Add the stock and simmer for about 10 minutes to reduce. Remove from the heat and sprinkle the gelatine over. Stir, then leave until the gelatine has dissolved and the mixture is clear. Add the vermouth or sherry. Meanwhile, pound or liquidise the salmon to make a paste, then beat in the liquid and seasoning and nutmeg to taste.

Chill until just beginning to set. Lightly whip the cream and fold into the mixture. Turn into one large or four small moulds and chill. Serve with plain or Green mayonnaise (see page 183). **Serves 4**

Grilled Curried Prawns

100 g/4 oz butter, melted
16 whole prawns
1½ teaspoons curry powder
1 lemon, quartered

Butter a small ovenproof serving dish. Add the unpeeled prawns, sprinkle with the curry powder and pour a little melted butter over the top. Grill for 5–10 minutes on each side, turning once. Add more butter and baste occasionally. Serve with the lemon quarters. **Serves 4**

Prawn Cocktail Salad

2 small grapefruit, peeled and segmented, or 1 (227-g/8-oz) can
1 firm avocado
175 g/6 oz peeled prawns or 1 (212-g/7½-oz) can
4–5 tablespoons thick mayonnaise
salt and pepper

Place the grapefruit segments in a bowl, reserving the juice from the can. Peel and chop the avocado and add immediately to the grapefruit. Add the prawns (drained if canned), mayonnaise, a little canned grapefruit juice, if you wish, and seasoning. Chill before serving. **Serves 4**

Artichoke soup (see page 12); Consommé of spiced fruits (see page 11); Orange soup (see page 11); Curried onion soup (see page 13); Celery and spinach soup (see page 13); Mint and lamb consommé (see page 11) and Creamy tomato soup (see page 12)

Mixed Bean Salad

100 g/4 oz sliced green beans, fresh or frozen
1 (141-g/5-oz) can baked beans
1 (212-g/7½-oz) can butter beans, or 75 g/3 oz
dried butter beans, cooked
1 small onion, thinly sliced
1 tablespoon chopped parsley or chives
2 tablespoons vinegar
1 tablespoon lemon juice
salt and pepper

Cook the sliced green beans in boiling salted water until tender. Drain and cool. Drain the baked beans and butter beans, reserving the liquid. Mix the beans, onion and parsley together. Mix the vinegar and lemon juice with a little of the bean liquid; season well and stir into the beans. Chill before serving. **Serves 4–5**

Italian Salad

(Illustrated opposite)

100 g/4 oz strawberries, hulled and sliced
175 g/6 oz Mozzarella or Fetta cheese, diced
7.5-cm/3-inch piece cucumber, sliced
26 black olives
4 tablespoons Vinaigrette dressing (see page 183)
½ teaspoon chopped mixed herbs

Toss the strawberries, cheese, cucumber and olives in the dressing. Arrange on a serving plate and sprinkle with the herbs. **Serves 2–4**

Savoury Pear Cocktail

2 large ripe pears
150 ml/¼ pint natural yogurt
salt and pepper
few drops Worcestershire sauce
50 g/2 oz mild cheese (Lancashire or Edam),
grated
25 g/1 oz hazelnuts, chopped
paprika to garnish

Peel, halve and core the pears. Mix the yogurt with the seasoning; enough Worcestershire sauce to make it tangy; the cheese and the nuts. Spoon the mixture into the core cavity of the pears. Sprinkle with paprika and chill before serving. **Serves 4**

Mulled Melon

1 small Ogen melon
½ Honeydew melon
½ Lavan, or 1 small Galia melon
3 tablespoons lemon juice
3 tablespoons honey
½ teaspoon ground cinnamon
½ teaspoon ground cloves
1 teaspoon curry powder (optional)

If you wish to use the skins of Ogen and Galia melons as serving bowls, keep them in neat halves. Remove all the seeds from the melons and cut the flesh into bite-sized pieces. Heat the lemon juice, honey, cinnamon, cloves and curry powder in a small pan until well mixed. Pour this over the melon and leave to marinate for 1 hour, stirring occasionally. If you wish, heat before serving. **Serves 6**

Strawberry Appetiser

225 g/8 oz strawberries, hulled and quartered
½ cucumber, diced
4 frankfurters, sliced
½ teaspoon chopped mint
2 teaspoons grated onion
salt and pepper
1 (142-ml/5-fl oz) carton soured cream
few sprigs mint to garnish

Mix together all the ingredients except the soured cream and mint. Chill thoroughly. Just before serving, gently toss in the soured cream and check the seasoning. Garnish with sprigs of mint and serve with melba or hot toast. **Serves 6**

Italian salad (see above)

Grapefruit Cocktail

2 grapefruit
2 ripe figs
crushed ice
2 tablespoons gin
2 sprigs mint to garnish

Cut each grapefruit into eight segments, nearly through to the base, and open out. Loosen the flesh from the skin with a sharp knife. Cut the figs in segments and arrange in the centre of the grapefruit. Sprinkle with crushed ice and gin just before serving. Garnish with a sprig of mint. **Serves 2**

Tangy Avocado

This delicious, creamy avocado mixture can be more than just a starter. Serve it as a dip with raw vegetables; as a dressing for lettuce; or with hot toast for a substantial snack.

1 ripe avocado
finely grated rind and juice of 1 lime or few squeezes bought lime juice
1 teaspoon grated onion
100 g/4 oz cream, curd or cottage cheese
1 stick celery, finely chopped
salt and pepper

Halve the avocado, discard the stone and scoop the flesh from the skin. Mash or liquidise the flesh with the remaining ingredients. Chill before serving. **Serves 2–3**

Cucumber Fritters with Dill Sauce

1 large cucumber, peeled
salt
1 teaspoon dried dill
1 (142-ml/5-fl oz) carton soured cream
freshly ground black pepper
75 g/3 oz plain flour
2 tablespoons olive oil
150 ml/¼ pint tepid water
1 teaspoon baking powder
oil for deep-frying

Cut the cucumber in 5-mm/¼-inch slices, place in a sieve and sprinkle with salt. Leave for 1 hour. Rinse and drain on absorbent kitchen paper. Pour 1 tablespoon boiling water on to the dill and leave to infuse for a minute to bring out the full flavour. Strain the dill, mix with the soured cream and seasoning and chill.

Sift 50 g/2 oz of the flour into a mixing bowl with a pinch of salt. Add the oil. Gradually beat in the water, beating until smooth, then add the baking powder. Toss the cucumber in the remaining flour then dip into the batter using a skewer. Heat the oil to 190°C/375°F, or until a cube of bread turns golden in 1 minute. Deep-fry the fritters until puffed and golden. Drain on absorbent kitchen paper. Serve with the dill sauce. **Serves 4**

The British have never gone short of fish and, although it is gratifying to be internationally known for our fish and chips, it's a pity we couldn't also be credited with having invented some of the more imaginative fish dishes which have become classics.

As far back as the sixteenth century we were combining mackerel with gooseberry sauce, so that the acid fruit would counteract the oiliness of the fish. We occasionally use white wine when cooking fish, but other than that, our fish-eating habits have hardly changed since the beginning of this century.

The more expensive fish, such as plaice, cod and haddock, are still by far the most popular despite their escalating prices. Sadly, the increasing variety of alternative fish available is not yet fully appreciated and we are missing out on some very tasty meals at very reasonable prices.

From childhood we are all told that fish is good for us, but how? All fish contain good quantities of essential minerals; vitamins A and D are found in cod and halibut liver (hence the importance of cod liver oil), and fish roe is a very good source of vitamins B and C. The protein content of fish is almost as high as that of most of our favourite meats; with the exception of oily fish there is little carbohydrate in fish so it is ideal for slimmers, and even the fat from oily fish such as mackerel has a very low cholesterol content.

Fish also has all the qualities a modern cook needs – speed, economy, versatility and convenience, and the range of fish products on the market now can, if you wish, eliminate all the preparatory tasks. Above all, our fishing and freezing methods now produce fish that is, in most cases, exceptionally fresh.

To understand how to prepare and deal with fish you need a brief explanation of the main types of fish. Flat fish, on the whole, are almost flat, like plaice and sole, and produce four thin fillets. There is no need to skin them unless you particularly prefer to. Round fish are long, rounded and much more fleshy round the tummy. When filleted they give two generous fillets, for example mackerel and herring. They are not usually skinned but they do have a scaly coating which needs removing.

Buying Fish

Most of the fish bought nowadays from a fishmonger will have been cleaned and frozen at sea and will be in its freshest state. That's why the fish you buy as 'fresh' may often be still partially frozen. But that doesn't mean to say you don't need to check the fish first of all, or that every fishmonger has the best. Fish should always look moist and shiny, with bright colourings and should still be quite firm.

A good fishmonger will fillet and prepare the fish for you, if you give him enough time or choose a slack time of day. If you can't see what you want, or the price has suddenly soared, ask his advice for an alternative but do tell him what you want to do with it, or else be guided by him. Remember to take away the bones and skin (you have paid for them) to make a good fish stock (see page 24) or to add flavour to the dish you intend to make.

Cleaning Fish

Although most fish is sold gutted and cleaned, you may occasionally find you have to do it yourself. Be sure to do this thoroughly, or you can taint the flavour of the fish.

Flat fish: to cook whole, leave the head, fins and tail on. Make a slit behind the head and gills and scrape out the innards. Rinse very

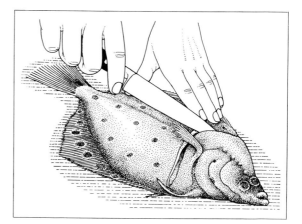

thoroughly and dry. If you intend to fillet the fish, remove the tail and fins first, then clean out as above.

Round fish: first you need to remove the scales. Holding the tail end firmly in your left hand with a damp cloth, scrape down towards the head end with the blunt side of a knife. A wire brush can be used for the larger, firmer fish.

With a sharp pointed knife, slit the fish down its belly from head almost to the tail. Remove the innards and rinse out very thoroughly. This is now ready to cook whole or stuffed, but if you prefer, cut off the head, tail and fins with scissors.

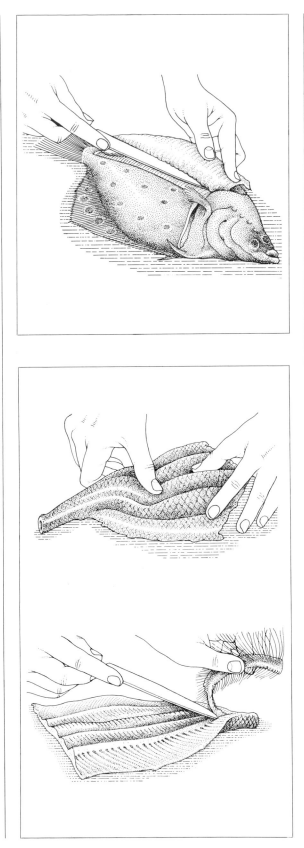

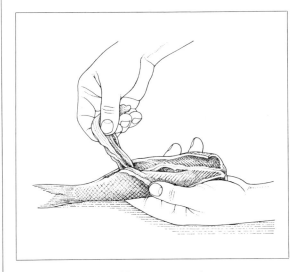

Filleting Fish

Flat fish: place the fish flat on a large board. With a long, thin, very flexible filleting or boning knife, make a slit down either side, as close as possible to the backbone. Work from the head to the tail in long sweeping movements down one slit, keeping the knife almost flat on the bone, so you leave as little flesh on the bone as possible. Repeat for the second fillet on that side, then turn over and continue.

Round fish: after cleaning, remove the head, tail and fins. Continue the slit under the body right down to the tail. Put the fish down, belly side open, on the board and press with your fingers all the way down the backbone until the fish is almost flat. Turn it over and gently ease out the backbone all in one piece. It can, of course, be stuffed and cooked whole like this, or cut all the way down the backbone into two fillets.

To Skin Fillets

Place the fillet, skin side down, on a board. Cut under the flesh at the thin end until you can take hold of the first bit of skin. Then holding the fish firmly (a generous sprinkling of salt will give a better grip) scrape the knife along the skin, at the same time pushing away the flesh.

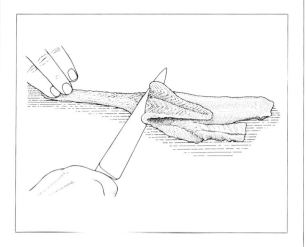

Frying Fish

Shallow frying the fish should be well dried and the coating applied evenly and thoroughly. The fat (butter and oil mixed is the best) must be really hot to seal the outside quickly and prevent food from becoming soggy and greasy. Don't use too much fat – about 5 mm/$\frac{1}{4}$ inch should be sufficient.

Drain the fried coated fish on absorbent kitchen paper or crumpled tissue paper then serve as quickly as possible.

Deep-frying don't fill the pan more than half full with oil and don't cook too many pieces at once. Heat the oil to 190°C/375°F, or until a cube of bread turns golden in about 1 minute. If the fat is too hot, allow it to cool before frying.

Meunière (the French way) ideal for trout, white fish and prawns or scampi. Heat 75–100 g/3–4 oz butter in a large pan and fry the seasoned fish, or fish coated in seasoned flour until tender. Remove and keep warm. Add $\frac{1}{2}$–1 tablespoon lemon juice or vinegar to the butter, together with 1 tablespoon chopped parsley or capers and serve with the fish.

Fish in brown butter fry as above then brown the butter a little before adding the extras.

Fish in black butter fry as above but allow the butter to turn dark brown before adding the extras (not really as black as the name suggests).

Dry frying excellent for oily fish such as herring or mackerel. Sprinkle the pan with salt and fry the fish (coated with unseasoned flour or oatmeal) over a gentle heat, turning occasionally.

Oven frying the term may not be strictly correct but the results are excellent. Coat the fish in seasoned flour or egg and crumbs, but don't use batter. Place the fish flat on a hot greased baking tray and sprinkle with melted oil or butter. Cook in a moderately hot oven (200°C, 400°F, Gas Mark 6) for 15–20 minutes.

Coating Fish

Coatings are used to protect the soft flesh from very high temperatures, but this is not as important for meunière frying or for whole firmer fish such as trout and mackerel. For the best results, always toss the fish in flour first, this makes the coating stick well.

Egg and crumbs coat the fish in flour, then in beaten egg (add 1 tablespoon water to make it go further) and then crumbs. One egg and about 50 g/2 oz crumbs are sufficient for four to six pieces of fish. Use any type of bread for crumbs you like, although the finer the crumbs the better the fish will look. Give extra flavour to the fish by adding a little grated cheese, grated onion, chopped herbs or curry powder to the crumbs; or use oatmeal or crushed crisps instead. (For speed, put the dry coatings in a plastic bag and toss the fish in this.)

Batter coating coat the fish in seasoned flour, then dip into the batter and drain off any excess before lowering into hot fat. For four to six portions you will need 100 g/4 oz plain flour, a pinch of salt, 1 egg and 200 ml/7 fl oz milk and water mixed. Reduce the quantity of liquid if you want a thicker batter. Add extra flavour by using tomato, lemon juice or other flavourings in place of some of the liquid.

Grilling Fish

Brush the grill pan and both sides of the fish with melted butter, sprinkle the fish with salt and pepper or other seasonings if you wish, and cook under a medium heat. Turn once and baste occasionally. Fillets will need 3–4 minutes each side, more if very large or thick; whole fish will need 4–10 minutes each side. Allow at least an extra 5–7 minutes if the fish is stuffed.

Poaching Fish

For dieters and invalids this can be the best way of cooking fish, but if only milk is used the result may be rather tasteless. Use as little liquid as possible, preferably milk, milk and butter or fish stock (see below) and then add a bay leaf; a sprig of a fresh herb; a piece of onion or celery; a few black peppercorns or other fish seasoning; or pieces of lemon or orange rind. Add the fish when the liquid is boiling, then cook slowly to avoid breaking up the fish, allowing the time given for grilling. Remove the fish with a draining spoon and, wherever possible, use the liquid to make a very tasty sauce.

Fish Stock

fish bones, skin and trimmings
3 tablespoons lemon juice or white wine vinegar
2–3 carrots, chopped
1 onion, chopped
1 sprig parsley
1 sprig thyme
1 bay leaf
black peppercorns
$\frac{1}{2}$ teaspoon rock salt

Place all the ingredients in a large saucepan and add enough water to cover. Simmer for about 1 hour. Any fish may be poached in this liquid. If necessary, strain the liquid and freeze.

Bass (*Sea Perch*)

A round fish, grey-blue black in colour. It has a particularly delicate flavour and is usually cooked whole, whether poached, fried or grilled and is often served with a butter sauce.

Bream (*Sea*)

A plump and pretty round fish with a red tail and fins, weighing 900 g/2 lb on average. A delicately flavoured fish, it can be filleted, grilled whole or stuffed. It is often served with a butter sauce.

Brill

A flat fish which is similar to turbot, but smaller. Cook as for turbot, plaice or sole. Although rarely seen, it should be available all the year round.

Clams, Cockles and Winkles

Three types of very small shellfish which are all quite well known to seaside areas and the East End of London. They can be eaten raw, when young and very fresh like oysters, or cooked as for mussels. Clams are available from September to April – only the months with an R in. Cockles are generally best during the spring and summer, winkles in winter.

Crayfish and Crawfish

They may sound similar but there can be no confusion when you see them. Crayfish are tiny shellfish, which look like little lobsters and are usually only 75–100 g/3–4 oz in weight. Crawfish are large, the size of lobsters, but without the large claws. Both are delicacies, very rarely available in our fish shops. Best during the summer months.

Cod

A large, round fish with firm, white flaky flesh, often weighing up to 36 kg/80 lb. It is usually sold in pieces, fillets or steaks, in fresh, frozen or smoked form. Cod's roe is especially good smoked and used in pâtés and the Greek speciality, Taramasalata (see page 26).

Cod Thermidor

225 g/8 oz mashed potato
275–350 g/10–12 oz cod, poached
150 ml/¼ pint double cream
1 egg, beaten
1 teaspoon French mustard
salt and pepper
1 tablespoon grated Parmesan cheese
1 egg yolk
black olives to garnish

Pipe the potato around the edge of two individual dishes or scallop shells, using a large star tube. Break up the cod with a fork and mix it with the cream, egg, mustard and seasoning. Spoon into the dishes or shells and sprinkle with the Parmesan. Brush the potato with egg yolk and put a few olives on top of each dish. Bake in a moderately hot oven (190°C, 375°F, Gas Mark 5) for 20–25 minutes until golden. **Serves 2**

Hot Fish Mousse

675 g/1½ lb white fish, skinned and filleted
¼ teaspoon salt
freshly ground black pepper
3 large egg whites
600 ml/1 pint double cream

Pound or mash the fish with the salt and pepper until really smooth then sieve. Whisk the egg whites until stiff, then fold into the fish. Whip the cream and fold into the fish mixture. Spoon into a 1.75-litre/3-pint mould and place in a bain-marie or a roasting tin with cold water to reach half-way up the sides of the mould. Cook in a moderate oven (180°C, 350°F, Gas Mark 4) for about 35 minutes. Leave to settle for 5–10 minutes before turning out and serving. **Serves 6**

Goujons of Cod

4 cod steaks
25 g/1 oz seasoned flour
1 egg, beaten
1–2 tablespoons white breadcrumbs
oil for deep-frying

Cut the cod into 5-cm/2-inch long narrow strips. Coat in the flour, then in egg and breadcrumbs. Heat the oil to 190°C/375°F, or until a cube of bread turns golden in 1 minute. Deep-fry the goujons for 10 minutes until crisp and golden. Drain on absorbent kitchen paper and serve with Tartare sauce (see page 183). **Serves 4**

Baked Herby Cod

450 g/1 lb cod steaks
1 (99-g/3½-oz) packet stuffing mix
juice of ½ lemon
1 teaspoon prepared mustard
40 g/1½ oz butter
50 g/2 oz cheese, grated

Place the cod in a buttered ovenproof dish. Mix the stuffing with the lemon juice and mustard and add enough hot water to make quite a stiff mixture. Spread over the fish and top with butter and grated cheese. Bake in a moderately hot oven (190°C, 375°F, Gas Mark 5) for 30–35 minutes until the cheese is golden. **Serves 4**

Cheesy Fish Pie

350 g/12 oz cod
300 ml/½ pint milk
25 g/1 oz butter
25 g/1 oz flour
1 teaspoon prepared mustard
salt and pepper
75 g/3 oz cheese, grated
1 (370-g/13-oz) packet puff pastry, thawed
1 egg, beaten (or milk)

Poach the cod in the milk for about 7 minutes. Drain, reserving the liquid. Melt the butter in a saucepan, stir in the flour and cook for 1 minute, stirring. Gradually add the fish liquid and mustard and season to taste. Stir in the cheese. Do not reboil but heat to allow the cheese to melt. Flake the fish, add to the sauce and spoon into an ovenproof dish. Roll out the pastry to cover the dish, trimming the edges and using any extra pastry to make decorations. Glaze the pie with egg or milk and bake in a hot oven (220°C, 425°F, Gas Mark 7) for about 25 minutes until crisp and golden. **Serves 4**

Taramasalata

1 slice white bread
1 (198-g/7-oz) can smoked cod's roe
1 cooked potato
1–2 cloves garlic
juice of 1 lemon
few sprigs parsley
1 tablespoon olive oil
freshly ground black pepper
black or green olives to garnish

Make the bread into breadcrumbs. Using a liquidiser, blend the breadcrumbs, cod's roe, potato, garlic, lemon juice and parsley together until smooth. Switch the liquidiser to low speed and gradually add the oil. Blend to a smooth mixture, or beat the ingredients in a bowl until smooth. Add pepper to taste. Serve piped on to biscuits, topped with an olive on each. **Serves 4–6**

Coley (*Also called Saithe or Coalfish*)

Very like cod in appearance with a slightly stronger flavour, but coley should be much cheaper. However, its flesh often has a slightly greyish colour so it is best served with sauces and in colourful dishes. It can be used instead of cod or haddock in many white fish dishes.

Herbed Fish Cakes

450 g/1 lb coley, cooked and bones removed
225 g/8 oz mashed potato
2 tablespoons chopped herbs
1 small onion, finely chopped
2 tablespoons tomato ketchup
salt and pepper
75 g/3 oz seasoned flour or egg and breadcrumbs

Flake the fish or put it through a mincer if you like a finer texture. Mix the fish with the potato, herbs, onion, ketchup and seasoning to taste. Mould the mixture into cakes or rissoles and dip in either seasoned flour or egg and breadcrumbs to coat. Fry carefully in shallow fat, turning once and allowing about 5 minutes on each side. **Makes 8**

Chillied Fish Stew

(Illustrated on page 86–7)

2 tablespoons oil
100 g/4 oz long-grain rice
1 onion, sliced
1 red pepper, seeds removed and sliced
1 (396-g/14-oz) can tomatoes
salt and pepper
½ teaspoon chilli powder
2 teaspoons curry powder
150 ml/¼ pint dry cider
450 g/1 lb coley
225 g/8 oz courgettes, thinly sliced

Heat the oil in a saucepan and fry the rice, onion and pepper until golden. Add the tomatoes, seasoning, chilli and curry powders and cider. Cut the fish in pieces and add to the pan. Simmer gently for 15 minutes or until the fish is just cooked. **Serves 3–4**

Crab

Crab is usually sold cooked, and sometimes ready-dressed, but this is rare. It is at its best from April to July. When buying, check it has all its claws and legs and is heavy for its size – this is a sign that it has lots of meat. Normally a 1.25–1.5-kg/2½–3-lb crab, when dressed, will serve two people adequately.

If you have to cook the crab yourself, wash it well and place in a large saucepan with plenty of cold water, with 1 tablespoon lemon juice, a few parsley stalks, 1 bay leaf, salt and a few peppercorns. Cover and bring to the boil slowly. For a 1.25–1.5-kg/2½–3-lb crab allow only 15–20 minutes cooking time. Cool the crab in the cooking liquid.

To Prepare a Crab

Place the cooled crab on a clean board. Twist off the claws and legs and set aside to remove the flesh later. Push the main part of the body away from the shell in one piece (see illustration 1). Remove the grey feathered gills, known as 'dead men's fingers', and any other greyish matter attached to body and shell (see illustration 2). Cut the body into four pieces to enable you to pick out all the white flesh in the thin shell.

Push part of the shell, just above the eyes, until it comes out in one piece (see illustration 3). discard this entirely. With a teaspoon, scrape all the remaining flesh out of the shell, keeping the light and dark meats separate. Using a hammer, crack the shell along the dark lines on the outside (see illustration 4). Remove the pieces and then wash and scrub the remaining shell to use as serving dish.

To Dress a Crab

Mix the dark meat with 1–2 tablespoons fresh white breadcrumbs salt, pepper and lemon juice to taste and a few drops of Worcestershire sauce.

Mix the light meat with salt, freshly ground black pepper, cayenne pepper to taste and 2–3 tablespoons creamy mayonnaise.

Put the dark meat in the centre of the shell and arrange the light meat around it. Garnish with chopped hard-boiled egg, paprika and chopped parsley.

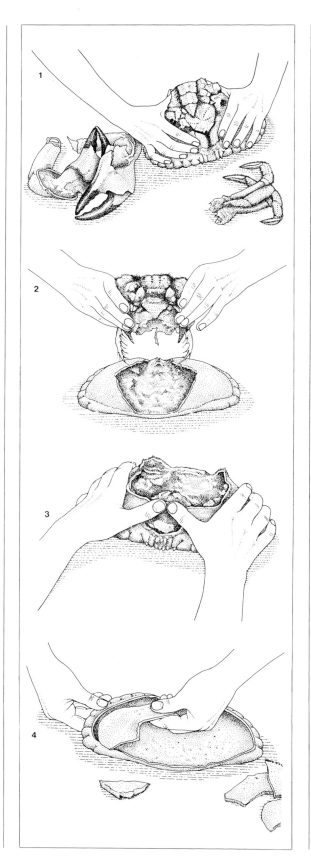

Eels

Although only found in fish shops in certain regions of Britain, especially around London, there is no shortage of eels. They are usually kept in tanks and sold very fresh, either whole or cut in slices or pieces. The whitish-grey flesh is very firm and dense, with a good strong flavour. It is often smoked, too, and is very good to use in smoked fish pâtés.

To skin, grill quickly until the skin blisters and can be removed easily. Eels can be fried, grilled or stewed to use in pies and casseroles.

Smoked Eel Fritters

225 g/8 oz smoked eel fillet
150 ml/$\frac{1}{4}$ pint Batter (see page 153)
oil for deep-frying

Cut the fillets into bite-sized pieces. Dip these in batter. Heat the oil to 190°C/375°F, or until a cube of bread turns golden in 1 minute. Deep-fry the eel for 2–3 minutes until crisp and golden. Drain on absorbent kitchen paper and serve hot. **Serves 4**

Haddock

Haddock is one of the cod family, though smaller, and can be used in just the same way. The flesh is firm and white, but with a more delicate flavour than cod. When smoked it will keep well for several days. Available fresh, frozen or smoked.

Cream of Haddock Mousse with Mussels

175 g/6 oz haddock
300 ml/$\frac{1}{2}$ pint milk
300 ml/$\frac{1}{2}$ pint Fish stock (see page 24)
25 g/1 oz butter
25 g/1 oz flour
freshly ground black pepper
15 g/$\frac{1}{2}$ oz powdered gelatine
2 tablespoons hot water
2 egg whites
1 (150-g/5$\frac{1}{4}$-oz) jar mussels
watercress to garnish

Keeping the fish in one piece, place it in a large pan with the milk and fish stock. Cook gently for about 10 minutes until tender. Remove the fish and set aside. Make a white sauce (see page 185) with the butter, flour and cooking liquid.

When the fish is cool enough skin, bone and mash it. Add the fish to the sauce. Season to taste with black pepper. Dissolve the gelatine in the water in a small bowl over a pan of hot water. Stir the gelatine into the fish mixture. Whisk the egg whites and fold in gently, using a metal spoon. Add half the drained mussels. Spoon into a 1.25-litre/2-pint mould or dish and chill until firm. Garnish with the remaining mussels and watercress. **Serves 4**

Haddock and Celery Crumble

350 g/12 oz smoked haddock fillet
1 (141-g/5-oz) can condensed celery soup
225 g/8 oz cooked carrots, chopped
100 g/4 oz cooked peas
salt and pepper
100 g/4 oz fresh white breadcrumbs
2 tablespoons chopped parsley
50 g/2 oz cheese, grated

Cut the fish into small pieces. Heat the soup gently and stir in the fish, carrots and peas. Bring to the boil, cover and simmer for about 5 minutes. Season to taste. Pour into an oven-proof dish and top with the breadcrumbs, parsley and cheese. Bake in a moderately hot oven (190°C, 375°F, Gas Mark 5) for about 15 minutes until the top is golden and crisp. **Serves 4**

Creamed Haddock Pudding

450 g/1 lb smoked haddock fillet
2 eggs
2 tablespoons double cream
2 tablespoons fresh white breadcrumbs
salt and pepper
300 ml/½ pint Parsley sauce (see page 185)

Mince or finely chop the fish and mix with the eggs, cream, crumbs and seasoning. Spoon into a greased 1.25-litre/2-pint pudding basin. Cover with greased foil and steam for 2 hours until just firm. Turn out and pour the sauce over. Serve immediately. **Serves 4**

Haddock Pâté

450 g/1 lb haddock fillet
1 (142-ml/5-fl oz) carton soured cream
salt and pepper
grated rind and juice of 1 orange
few sprigs parsley
slices of orange

Poach the haddock quickly in very little water. Remove the skin and any bones. Flake the fish and stir in the cream, seasoning and orange rind and juice. Garnish with the parsley and orange slices. Chill well and serve with hot toast. **Serves 4**

Fish in Lemon and Oil

(Illustrated on page 45)

All smoked fish, and many white fish such as haddock, cod and whiting, can be marinated for long enough for no actual cooking to be necessary. The oils and acids tenderise the fish. This is the same principle that the Swedes have used for many of their classic fish dishes over hundreds of years.

225–350 g/8–12 oz smoked fish fillet (cod, haddock, mackerel or kipper)
1 small onion, sliced
1 clove garlic, crushed (optional)
grated rind and juice of 2 lemons
3–4 bay leaves
1 tablespoon mustard seed
about 300 ml/½ pint salad oil

Arrange the fish on a large flat dish with the remaining ingredients. Turn the mixture frequently for a minimum of 24 hours. Serve the fish chilled and drained for a starter with hot bread or toast. **Serves 4**

Hake

In France it is often called merlan (whiting) colin (cod) or saumon blanc (white salmon). It has tender, white, flaky flesh, a good flavour and is easy to digest. Use as for cod.

Halibut

A very large, flat fish, usually sold portioned into fillets and steaks. It has a very firm, flaky texture and a delicious flavour. It can be poached, fried or grilled and is mainly served with Hollandaise or other butter sauces.

Huss (*Dogfish, Rockfish*)

A round, very long fish with a large head. It is always sold portioned. It has a moist but firm flesh and a distinctive flavour. It is delicious battered and deep-fried but is best for made-up dishes where chunks are required.

Herrings

Herrings are oily round fish with bluish scales and silvery sides. Usually 25–30 cm/10–12 inches long, they will serve one person each for a main course. Best fried, grilled or baked.

Kippers are herrings that have been lightly smoked. They can be grilled, fried or baked to use in mixed fish dishes.

Bloaters are herrings that have been slightly salted, then smoked until very lightly cooked. These should be eaten within 1 day of purchase.

Soused Herrings

8–12 small herrings
1–2 onions, chopped
150 ml/¼ pint malt vinegar
150 ml/¼ pint water
½–1 teaspoon pickling spice
generous pinch salt
freshly ground black pepper
pinch ground allspice

Remove the herring heads and split the fish down the underside. Discard the intestines but keep the roes. Open the fish and take out the bones (see page 22); roll up neatly. Put the herrings and roes into an ovenproof dish; add the onion and remaining ingredients (use a little more vinegar and water if the fish is not covered). Put a lid or foil over the dish and cook in the centre of a cool to moderate oven (150–160°C, 300–325°F, Gas Mark 2–3) for about 1 hour. Chill well before serving as an hors d'oeuvre or use for the following recipe. **Serves 8–12**

Herrings with Tomato and Cucumber Sauce

25 g/1 oz butter
4 medium tomatoes, peeled and sliced
4 Soused herrings (see previous recipe) plus
150 ml/¼ pint fish cooking liquid
5-cm/2-inch piece cucumber, peeled and diced
salt and pepper

Melt the butter in a saucepan and fry the tomato until soft. Add the herring liquid, cucumber and seasoning. Continue cooking for a further 2–3 minutes. Place the herrings, plus some of the cooked onion and roes, on a serving dish. Top with the thick tomato sauce and serve with boiled potatoes. **Serves 4**

Herrings with Lime and Mustard Sauce

This sharp, spicy sauce goes well with any oily fish.

4 herrings
2 tablespoons seasoned flour
6 tablespoons oil
grated rind and juice of 2 limes (use lemons if limes are not available)
4 tablespoons olive or vegetable oil
1 clove garlic, crushed
1 teaspoon dry mustard
½ teaspoon salt
¼ teaspoon freshly ground black pepper
1 teaspoon chopped parsley

Ask your fishmonger to clean and trim the herrings. Coat in seasoned flour. Heat the oil in a large frying pan then fry the herrings, turning once, until cooked (about 10 minutes). Meanwhile, mix together the other ingredients thoroughly and heat through to serve piping hot with the drained fish. This sauce is also very good to serve cold with smoked fish. **Serves 4**

Jansson's Temptation

(Illustrated on page 36)

450 g/1 lb potatoes, parboiled
2–3 tablespoons oil
2 small onions, sliced
450 g/1 lb smoked fish (haddock, kippers, mackerel)
grated rind of 1 lemon
salt and pepper
150–300 ml/¼–½ pint milk
50 g/2 oz butter

Slice the potatoes thickly. Heat the oil in a frying pan and fry the onions until browned. Remove the head, tail and backbone (see page 22) from the fish and cut into long strips. Layer the strips in an ovenproof dish with the potato and onion. Sprinkle with lemon rind and seasoning. Pour the milk over the top and dot with the butter. Cook in a moderately hot oven (190°C, 375°F, Gas Mark 5) for about 50 minutes until cooked and golden brown. **Serves 6**

Kipper and Caper Pie

450 g/1 lb kipper fillets
50 g/2 oz butter
50 g/2 oz plain flour
600 ml/1 pint milk
40 g/1½ oz capers, drained
salt and pepper
450 g/1 lb Shortcrust pastry (see page 136)
2 hard-boiled eggs, sliced
1 egg, beaten

Simmer the fish gently in water for 7 minutes; drain and flake with a fork. Make a thick white sauce with the butter, flour and milk (see page 185). Add the fish, capers and seasoning. Leave to cool. Roll out the pastry to a 30-cm/12-inch square and spread the cooled fish mixture in the centre. Arrange the sliced egg on top. Brush the pastry edges with water; bring the corners up and over the filling to join, pinching the edges to seal. Decorate the top with leaves made from the pastry trimmings and glaze with beaten egg. Bake in a hot oven (220°C, 425°F, Gas Mark 7) for 30 minutes. Serve hot or cold. **Serves 6–8**

Kipper Pâté

350 g/12 oz smoked kipper fillets, or mixed smoked fish
1 teaspoon grated lemon rind
1 teaspoon lemon juice
salt and freshly ground black pepper
pinch garlic salt
25 g/1 oz butter, melted
2 tablespoons soured or double cream

Skin the fish and remove any bones. Put the flesh into a bowl and pound or mash thoroughly (you could use a liquidiser, but it's hardly worth it), adding the remaining ingredients. When completely smooth, turn into one large or four smaller dishes. Chill for 2 hours. Serve with hot brown bread. **Serves 4**

Lobster

Lobster is nearly always sold ready cooked and, as for crab, should be heavy for its size. Lobster is best fresh during the summer. Uncooked lobsters are very dark bluish-black in colour. The female lobster, still carrying its eggs, is supposed to have the sweetest flavour. To cook a lobster, place it in a large saucepan filled with boiling fish stock, bring back to the boil then simmer gently for 20–30 minutes. Cool in the stock.

Mackerel

A deep blue-black fish with a silvery white underside. It is a round, oily fish, with soft, well-flavoured flesh which is darker than that of most fish. Usually larger than herrings, they provide generous individual servings. Best fried, grilled or baked. Available from August to March. They can be bought fresh, smoked or soused or frozen in fillets.

Fried Stuffed Mackerel

(Illustrated on page 36)

4 medium mackerel
50 g/2 oz chopped walnuts
75 g/3 oz fresh breadcrumbs
1 small onion, finely chopped
salt and pepper
½ teaspoon French mustard
2 tablespoons oil
2 tablespoons lemon juice, or white wine vinegar
few sage leaves
¼ cucumber, chopped

Wash and gut the mackerel, keeping the heads on. Dry them well. Mix the walnuts, breadcrumbs, onion, seasoning and mustard together and pack firmly into the mackerel, still keeping their shape. Heat the oil and lemon juice or vinegar in a frying pan and fry the mackerel gently for about 10 minutes. Turn, sprinkle with more seasoning, add the sage leaves and cucumber, then cover. Cook gently for another 10 minutes and serve immediately **Serves 4**

Smoked Mackerel Soufflé

450 g/1 lb smoked mackerel
3 eggs, separated
1 clove garlic, crushed
salt and pepper
1 tablespoon grated lemon rind
150 ml/¼ pint double cream

Skin and bone the mackerel (see page 22). Beat or pound the flesh well with the egg yolks, garlic, seasoning and lemon rind. Lightly whip the cream and mix into the fish. Whisk the egg whites until very stiff and gently fold into the fish mixture using a metal spoon. Turn into a greased 1.25-litre/2-pint soufflé dish and bake in a moderately hot oven (190°C, 375°F, Gas Mark 5) for about 50 minutes, until well risen and almost firm to the touch. Serve immediately. **Serves 4–6**

Scandinavian Pickled Mackerel

(Illustrated on page 36)

2 small mackerel
2 teaspoons sea salt
1½ teaspoons sugar
1 teaspoon freshly ground black pepper
2 tablespoons dry sherry or brandy
1 tablespoon fresh dill weed or 1 teaspoon dried
slices of lemon to garnish

Wash and gut the mackerel; remove the head, tail and fins. Remove the central bones (see page 22), then cut the flesh into thin strips. Mix all the other ingredients and spread a quarter of this in the bottom of a shallow dish. Lay the pieces of mackerel, skin side down, on top of it and cover with another quarter of the mixture. Continue layering until all is used up. Cover with greased greaseproof paper and place weights on top. Leave in a cool place for up to 5 days (but for not less than 12 hours), and turn the fish in the marinade once a day. Serve with a well-flavoured mayonnaise or use in a salad. **Serves 4–6**

Mackerel Pie

2 aubergines, sliced
450 g/1 lb leeks, sliced
1 (425-g/15-oz) can tomatoes
900 g/2 lb mackerel, filleted
1 (370-g/13-oz) packet puff pastry, thawed
beaten egg to glaze

Mix the aubergines, leeks and tomatoes together. Cut the mackerel into chunks and mix with the vegetables. Put in a pie dish. Roll out the pastry thinly on a lightly floured surface and cut a strip to fit the rim of the dish. Brush the rim with egg and press on the pastry top. Flute the edges and cut a hole in the centre to allow steam to escape. Glaze with beaten egg. Cook in a hot oven (220°C, 425°F, Gas Mark 7) for 15 minutes then reduce to moderately hot (190°C, 375°F, Gas Mark 5) for a further 15–20 minutes. **Serves 6–8**

Monkfish

A very large ugly fish that fortunately you will rarely, if ever, see whole. Only the tail piece is sold in fish shops and it is becoming more expensive as the restaurant trade use it more and more as a cheap alternative to scampi. Its very white firm flesh masquerades well as scampi, or lobster, and is delicious and rather similar in flavour. It is also good for fish stews and mixed dishes or to serve in salads.

Mullet

Grey mullet has white, slightly fatty but very digestible flesh with a delicate flavour. Red mullet, despite its name, is only red skinned, the flesh being pale pinkish-white in colour. It has similar qualities to the grey mullet. Both are usually grilled and served with a butter sauce.

Mussels

Mussels should be bought very fresh and still alive. They are always cooked in their black shells first, before continuing with any other recipe. Available only in months with an R in, that is from September to April. They are occasionally available cooked, shelled and frozen, or fresh but cleaned and scrubbed, which will save you a lot of time. Usually allow 600 ml/1 pint per person when serving them as a starter.

To Prepare Mussels

Keep the mussels in cold water until required. Discard any that are cracked or open. Scrub the shells very thoroughly and remove the tiny hairy 'beard' where shells meet (see illustration). Wash thoroughly in running water.

No liquid is necessary for cooking mussels as they will still have water in their shells, but a little butter, or wine, onion and seasoning will give a good flavour. Always cook in a covered pan for as little time as possible or they become tough. Usually 3–5 minutes over a strong heat is enough. If any shells have not opened, discard these mussels.

To serve cold, allow to cool in their own liquid, then remove from their shells if necessary.

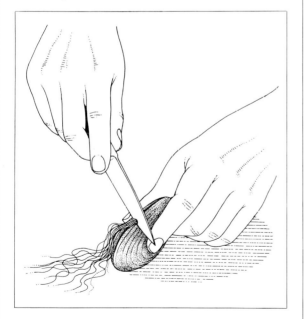

Moules Marinière

2.25 litres/4 pints mussels
300 ml/½ pint dry white wine or cider
1 small onion, chopped
1 small clove garlic, crushed
1 sprig parsley
1 sprig thyme
1 bay leaf
salt and freshly ground black pepper
2–3 tablespoons double cream
1 tablespoon chopped parsley

Clean and prepare the mussels according to the instructions to the left. Bring the wine or cider to the boil with the onion, garlic, parsley, thyme, bay leaf and seasoning. Add the mussels, cover and cook for about 5 minutes. Discard any that are still closed. Transfer the mussels to a serving dish. Reduce the cooking liquid by half by brisk boiling, strain and reheat with the cream. Pour the sauce over the mussels and sprinkle with parsley. **Serves 4**

Oysters

Buy from a good fishmonger and use as soon as possible, for they should be eaten very fresh. Available from September to April. To eat them raw, keep them very cold and serve on a bed of ice. You will need a strong sharp implement to prize open the shells. Sprinkle with lemon juice or a good herb vinegar, and sprinkle with black or red pepper. Many people believe you should not chew oysters, just swallow them whole, but that is a personal choice.

Oysters can be poached and served hot. Carefully remove them from their shells, with their own liquid, bring to the boil then remove from the heat. They can then be used in other recipes or returned to their shells and baked very quickly with cheese or mixed butter, garlic and breadcrumbs as a topping.

Sardines

Very small round fish, like tiny herrings, fished mainly off Sardinia. They should be eaten very fresh. Clean then grill quickly with butter, lemon juice and garlic. Fresh sardines are really only available in the early summer months. Sardines canned in oil or tomato sauce are best used for salads, hors d'oeuvres and made up dishes as they don't keep their shape well.

Plaice

Flat, slightly diamond-shaped fish, sold whole or filleted if you ask the fishmonger. The flesh is very soft and delicately flavoured. It can be fried, grilled, poached, on or off the bone, and cooked in most other ways. (Dab is a very similar but smaller fish.) Also available frozen in fillets.

Plaice Mornay

8 medium fillets of plaice
salt and pepper
50 g/2 oz butter
100 g/4 oz Edam or Gouda cheese
½ tablespoon oil
2 leeks, sliced
100 g/4 oz button mushrooms, quartered
juice of 1 lemon
150 ml/¼ pint dry white wine

Skin the fish (see page 22); season and spread with a little of the butter. Cut the cheese into eight fingers and put one on each fillet. Roll up firmly and secure with wooden cocktail sticks. Heat the remaining butter and oil in a large frying pan and fry the leeks and mushrooms. Then add the fish rolls and fry for 8–10 minutes turning several times. Add the lemon juice and wine towards the end of the cooking time. **Serves 4**

Stuffed Plaice

2 plaice
½ onion
1 bouquet garni
225 g/8 oz mushrooms, finely chopped
3 shallots, finely chopped
75 g/3 oz butter
salt and pepper
3 tablespoons flour
2 tablespoons double cream
2 tablespoons dry vermouth or Sambuca
lemon wedges to garnish

Fillet the plaice (see page 22) and reserve the trimmings and bones. Put the fish trimmings and bones in a saucepan with 600 ml/1 pint water, the onion and bouquet garni. Bring to boil, cover and simmer for 15 minutes. Strain the stock. Meanwhile, heat 25 g/1 oz of the butter in a small pan and cook the mushrooms and shallots until tender – about 10 minutes. Season, then spread the mixture over the fillets. Fold the fillets in half and arrange in an ovenproof dish. Add 150 ml/¼ pint of the reserved fish stock, cover the dish and cook in a moderately hot oven (190°C, 375°F, Gas Mark 5) for 20 minutes, or until the fish is tender. Just before the fish is cooked, make a white sauce with the remaining butter and flour (see page 185). Stir in the remaining stock, made up to 300 ml/½ pint with water. Bring to the boil, stir in the cream and vermouth or Sambuca. Boil rapidly for 3–5 minutes. Adjust the seasoning and strain the cooking liquor from the fish into the sauce. Stir quickly and pour over the fillets. Garnish with lemon wedges. **Serves 4**

Savoury tartlets (see page 140)

Prawns, Scampi and Shrimps

These all look very similar but differ vastly in size and price. Pacific prawns are the largest, 13–15 cm/5–6 inches long, and, of course, the most expensive. They are only available ready cooked and frozen but have the sweetest flavour. Dublin Bay prawns (scampi) are the best British variety and are available fresh only in the summer, or frozen most of the year. Smaller prawns are available frozen in their shells, or peeled and prepacked, throughout the year. Shrimps are available fresh in their shells in localised areas, or occasionally frozen. They are also available potted or in brine. Usually sold by the pint in their shells, or by weight if peeled.

All these shellfish can be cooked and used in the same way, either in their shells or peeled. To remove the shells, pinch off the head and tail. Then remove the feelers under the stomach and peel off the shell. The large prawns have a thick black vein down the back which should be removed; slit the back with a sharp knife and gently pull out the vein.

Chinese Pancake Rolls

These can be filled with any number of savoury ingredients, but this combination of prawns and beansprouts is the most popular. For convenience they can be partly cooked in advance and then refried for a couple of minutes in very hot fat just before serving.

1 spring onion, finely chopped, or 1 teaspoon finely chopped onion
1 stick celery, finely diced
50 g/2 oz button mushrooms, diced
50 g/2 oz peeled prawns, chopped
6–8 canned water chestnuts, chopped
50 g/2 oz beansprouts
1 tablespoon sherry
2 teaspoons soy sauce
1 tablespoon cornflour
salt and pepper
1 tablespoon oil
8 thin pancakes (see page 153)
1 egg, beaten
oil for deep-frying

Mix the onion with the celery, mushrooms, prawns, water chestnuts and beansprouts. Mix together the sherry, soy sauce, cornflour and seasoning. Heat the oil in a frying pan and lightly toss the vegetable mixture. Then stir in the liquid mixture and stir until slightly thickened.

Place a little filling on each pancake. Roll up and tuck the ends in like an envelope, sealing the corners with beaten egg. Turn the pancakes over and allow to rest for 5 minutes, while the egg seals the joins.

Meanwhile, heat the oil to 190°C/375°F, or until a cube of bread turns golden in 1 minute. Cook two or three rolls at a time for 3–4 minutes, until crisp and golden. Drain on absorbent kitchen paper while cooking the rest. Serve immediately. **Serves 8**

Mackerel saffron soup (see page 14); Scandinavian pickled mackerel (see page 32); Jansson's temptation (see page 30) and Fried stuffed mackerel (see page 31)

Prawns Provençale

3 tablespoons oil
2 onions, sliced
2 cloves garlic, crushed
1 red pepper, seeds removed and sliced
1 (425-g/15-oz) can tomatoes
4 tablespoons tomato purée
1 bouquet garni
225 g/8 oz frozen peeled prawns
salt and pepper
4 whole prawns to garnish

Heat the oil in a frying pan and fry the onions, garlic and pepper until golden. Add the tomatoes, purée, bouquet garni and 300 ml/½ pint water. Simmer for 20 minutes. Stir in the prawns, season and reheat. Garnish with the whole prawns and serve with plain boiled rice. **Serves 4**

Seafood Pastry Shells

300 ml/½ pint milk
1 bouquet garni
25 g/1 oz butter
25 g/1 oz flour
100 g/4 oz prawns, peeled
100 g/4 oz cooked white fish, flaked
175 g/6 oz cooked long-grain rice
salt and pepper
350 g/12 oz Puff pastry (see page 146)
1 egg, beaten

Simmer the milk with the bouquet garni for 10 minutes, then remove the bouquet garni. Make a sauce with the butter, flour and milk (see page 185). Cool the sauce slightly and add the prawns, fish and rice; season to taste. Roll out the pastry thinly. Cut the pastry in half and use half to line four floured, empty scallop shells (or metal or china shell moulds). Freeze for 10 minutes, then turn out, so that pastry holds the shape of the shells. Use the rest of the pastry to line the shells again. Divide the filling among the shells, brush the edges with a little beaten egg and use the frozen pastry shells to form lids. Seal well, brush with the egg and bake in a moderately hot oven (200°C, 400°F, Gas Mark 6) for 15 minutes. Turn the pastry shells out of the moulds, turn them over and return them to the moulds, uncooked side uppermost. Brush with egg and bake for a further 15 minutes, or until the pastry is golden and flaky. **Serves 4**

Salmon

A large, round, fresh- and sea-water fish with deep pink, fatty flesh and a delicate flavour. Usually weighs between 4.5 and 6.75 kg/10 and 15 lb and is mainly sold whole or cut into steaks for grilling, frying or poaching. Salmon trout are trout with pink flesh. Salmon are available fresh from February to August or frozen throughout the year. Smoked salmon can also be bought frozen.

To Cook a Whole Salmon

You will need a fish kettle or very large pan, or a covered roasting dish might just be big enough. Clean the salmon and wrap tightly in greased greaseproof paper. Place in the cooking dish, the paper edges underneath. Cover with water or use part white wine or fish stock if you wish (see page 24). Cover and bring to the boil. A small salmon (2.75 kg/6 lb) doesn't really need to cook, just turn off the heat and leave to cool in the water. Larger salmon should have 10–20 minutes gentle simmering, then cool as above. (If you have a freezer, keep this stock for poaching fish in the future.)

Salmon steaks can be poached in fish stock, preferably using wine, or in milk with a few herbs. They can also be fried gently or grilled with butter. Serve salmon steaks with Hollandaise sauce, a herb sauce or one of the other sauce ideas given on page 185.

Koulibiac of Salmon

(Illustrated on page 235)

450 g/1 lb Puff pastry (see page 146)
1 egg, beaten
filling
50 g/2 oz long-grain rice
pinch saffron or turmeric
25 g/1 oz butter
100 g/4 oz spring onions, minced
2–3 tablespoons milk
1½ tablespoons tapioca
1 egg yolk
3 tablespoons cream
350 g/12 oz fresh salmon steak, poached or 1
(320-g/11½-oz) can salmon
3 tablespoons ground almonds
pinch ground cumin
pinch paprika
1 teaspoon chopped dill or ½ teaspoon dried
cayenne pepper
salt and freshly ground black pepper
3–4 tablespoons vodka (optional)
3 hard-boiled eggs, sliced

First prepare the filling. Cook the rice with the saffron in boiling salted water until just tender, about 12 minutes. Rinse under cold water, drain well and set aside. Heat the butter in a frying pan and cook the spring onion until soft. Bring the milk to the boil, add the tapioca and stir to make a smooth paste. Lightly beat the egg yolk and cream into the tapioca. Skin and bone the salmon and flake or liquidise the flesh. Mix the salmon with the spring onions and tapioca paste. Add the almonds, the cumin, paprika, dill and cayenne and season well. Add the vodka if liked. Reserve a little pastry, then roll the remainder into a large oblong. Spread half the rice over half of the rolled-out pastry lengthwise, leaving a 2.5-cm/1-inch border. Spread half the salmon filling on top of the rice. Layer the remaining rice and salmon mixtures. Arrange the hard-boiled egg on top. Glaze the pastry with egg and fold the pastry over the filling, making an oblong. Use the reserved pastry for decoration. Place on a baking tray, glaze and bake in a hot oven (220°C, 425°F, Gas Mark 7) for 15 minutes. Lower to moderately hot (190°C, 375°F, Gas Mark 5) and bake for a further 25 minutes until the pastry is browned. Cool. **Serves 4–6**

Scallops

These are highly-prized shell fish, quite a lot larger than oysters. Scallops are always eaten cooked. A scallop consists of two parts, the white flesh and the bright red coral, joined together and both edible. The shells are often saved for serving individual portions of food in, or for other uses around the home – but they should be very well boiled before using as serving dishes as they are porous. Scallops are sometimes available prepared and frozen, but mainly they are available fresh from November to March.

To Prepare

Wash and scrub the shells thoroughly, then place, rounded side down, in the oven. Cook for only a couple of minutes in a very cool oven (120°C, 250°F, Gas Mark ½) until the shells open. Gently scoop out the flesh and cook lightly in fish stock before using as required in the recipe.

Skate (*Ray*)

A large flat, almost diamond-shaped fish with a long thick tail. It has white, soft, flaky flesh but can be slightly indigestible. It is usually sold skinned in fillets or wings. Large wings should be lightly poached in seasoned liquid before using in a recipe. Small, very tender wings can be fried and served with Black butter (see page 184).

Sole (*Dover, Lemon and Witch*)

Dover sole is by far the best of all these flat fish. It has firm, delicately flavoured flesh which is easily digested; it can be cooked whole or filleted, and can be fried, grilled or poached. Lemon sole is slightly smaller and more elongated, witch is smaller still and thinner and is a particularly economical substitute for sole in many recipes.

Sprats

A little smaller than a sardine and very similar in most respects except that the flavour is not quite as good. Sprats can be cooked in the same way and are sometimes smoked and salted. Available fresh from October to March.

Squid (*Calamare*)

A very small mollusc that looks like a small octopus. It has chewy, tender white flesh (which soon becomes rubbery if overcooked) with a very delicate flavour. Once cleaned, it is usually cut into thin strips and lightly fried, poached or battered and deep-fat fried. It is used in many Spanish and Portuguese dishes. Quite frequently available now in British fish shops either fresh or frozen.

To Prepare

Both fresh and frozen squid will require cleaning in the same way. Be sure to allow frozen squid to thaw thoroughly before cooking or it will be tough. Holding the squid with one hand at each end, firmly pull the tail end away from the head and tentacles (see illustration). Remove the grey-black ink sac from the tail section (this is used for the Spanish speciality – *calamares en su tinta* – squid in its own ink) and discard unless used in the recipe. Cut the tentacles off just above the eyes and keep. Discard the rest of the head. Pull the thin transparent feather-shaped bone out from the centre of the tail-piece and discard. Then peel off the pinkish outer skin and discard. Wash well and slice or use as directed in the recipe.

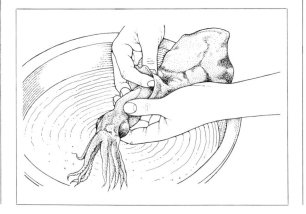

Calamares Provençale

900 g/2 lb prepared squid
2 tablespoons olive or corn oil
1 large onion, sliced
1–2 cloves garlic, crushed
1 tablespoon flour
1 (793-g/1 lb 12-oz) can tomatoes
salt and pepper
225 g/8 oz courgettes, sliced
1 teaspoon dried oregano

Prepare the squid (see left) and wash thoroughly. Cut into rings. Heat the oil in a frying pan and fry the onion and garlic until soft and transparent. Stir in the flour and cook, stirring for 1–2 minutes. Gradually stir in the tomatoes and bring to the boil.

Season to taste and pour into a casserole. Add the squid and the remaining ingredients and cook in a moderate oven (160°C, 325°F, Gas Mark 3) for 2 hours, or until the squid is tender. Serve with boiled brown rice and herby bread rolls. **Serves 4**

Trout

There are two different types of fresh-water trout – brown and rainbow – each weighing 175–400 g/6–14 oz. The speckled brown trout can be scarce, though they are the true British trout. Rainbow trout, originally introduced from Canada, are now extensively farmed and readily available fresh or frozen. Trout are usually sold whole and are traditionally served with the heads on. Smoked trout, now also readily available, is sold whole or in two fillets.

Plain 'n' Simple Trout

4 trout
3 tablespoons oil
50 g/2 oz butter
1 tablespoon chopped herbs
few peppercorns
2–3 bay leaves

Wash and gut the trout (see page 21). Pat dry and remove the fins and tails. Heat the oil and butter in a large frying pan and add the trout.

Sprinkle with the herbs, peppercorns and bay leaves. Fry over a medium heat, turning once, for about 5 minutes on each side or until cooked. Serve with some of the pan juices poured over and with fried potatoes and carrots. **Serves 4**

Trout in a Parcel

A wrapping of pastry keeps in all the natural juices of the trout.

25 g/1 oz butter
1 small onion, finely chopped
100 g/4 oz chopped frozen spinach
2 tablespoons soured cream
salt and pepper
2 trout
1 (370-g/13-oz) packet frozen puff pastry, thawed
milk to glaze

Melt the butter in a frying pan and cook the onion gently until soft and transparent. Add the spinach and leave over a low heat until all the liquid has evaporated. Stir in the soured cream and seasoning. Leave to cool slightly. Clean and gut the trout (see page 21) and divide the mixture between the trout, spreading it into the cavity left by the bone. Fold the trout back to their original shape.

Roll out the pastry on a lightly floured surface and cut two rectangles large enough to enclose the trout. Put the trout in position, moisten the pastry edges, fold over the trout and seal. Transfer to wetted baking tray, glaze with milk and make a hole in each pastry case to let steam escape. Bake in a hot oven (220°C, 425°F, Gas Mark 7) for 15 minutes or until the pastry and the trout are cooked. Serve with a salad. **Serves 2**

Trout with Mushroom Wine Sauce

6 trout, cleaned
150 ml/¼ pint dry white wine
150 ml/¼ pint chicken stock
50 g/2 oz butter
1 small onion, finely chopped
100 g/4 oz button mushrooms, sliced
1 tablespoon flour
1 teaspoon tomato purée
juice of ½ lemon
salt and pepper

Gut the trout (see page 21), wash and pat dry. Put in a pan with the wine and stock and bring to the boil. Simmer gently for 5–10 minutes until cooked. Melt the butter in a saucepan and cook the onion and mushrooms until soft and transparent. Stir in the flour and cook, stirring, for 1–2 minutes. Remove the cooked trout from the cooking liquor and keep warm. Gradually stir the liquor into the flour mixture and add the remaining ingredients. Bring to the boil and simmer for 5–8 minutes until cooked. Serve the sauce with the trout with boiled potatoes. **Serves 6**

Tunny Fish (*Tuna*)

A very large round fish caught mainly off the coast of Sicily and Portugal. When fresh the flesh is a dark pinkish red, very firm and oily. The fresh fish is very different from the canned variety, fresh tuna is strong-flavoured and meaty with a slight resemblance to veal. It is usually cut into steaks and grilled slowly. Fresh tuna is rarely, if ever, available in Britain but canned tuna can be used in nearly all recipes.

Turbot

A large flat fish with firm, white flesh and an especially good flavour. Usually sold in steaks or portions, it can be fried, grilled or poached to serve with butter sauces. Available most of the year.

Redfish

This bright salmon-red round fish is now quite readily available. It usually weighs 1.5–2.25 kg/3–5 lb and is ideal for stuffing and baking whole. The flavour is not very strong but it is good for soups and well flavoured dishes.

Whiting

A long round fish, usually 25–40 cm/10–16 inches in length, with pale silvery-brown skin. A very attractive fish to serve whole, it is traditionally cooked curled round with its tail in its mouth. It has a light flaky texture, a very good flavour and is easy to digest. Whiting makes a good substitute for sole or cod and is very much cheaper. Available frozen as fillets too.

Bread and Butter Fish Pie

350 g/12 oz whiting fillet
5–6 slices buttered bread
pepper
2 tablespoons chopped parsley
1 egg
150 ml/¼ pint milk

Cut the fish in bite-sized pieces and layer with bread in an ovenproof dish, seasoning the layers with pepper and parsley. Beat the egg with the milk and pour over the dish. Cook in a moderate oven (180°C, 350°F, Gas Mark 4) for 30 minutes. **Serves 4**

Whiting in Herb Sauce

2 large whiting
50 g/2 oz butter
1 tablespoon chopped mixed herbs (parsley, chives, dill, tarragon, sage) or 1 teaspoon dried
salt and freshly ground black pepper
150 ml/¼ pint dry white wine
few drops lemon juice
2 teaspoons cornflour
150 ml/¼ pint water
2–3 teaspoons double cream

Wash and gut the whiting (see page 21). Remove the head, tail and fins and fillet the fish. Melt the butter in a large pan and fry the fish very gently until just cooked. Then stir in the herbs, seasoning, wine and lemon juice and bring to the boil. Remove the fish from the sauce. Mix the cornflour with the water and stir into the sauce. Bring to the boil and stir until thickened. Stir in the cream. Arrange the fish on a serving dish and pour over the sauce. **Serves 4**

Chinese-style Whiting

2 whiting
2 tablespoons sherry
4 tablespoons soy sauce
3 tablespoons vinegar
2 tablespoons sugar
1 tablespoon tomato purée
½ green pepper, seeds removed and sliced
½ red pepper, seeds removed and sliced
rind and juice ½ orange
2 teaspoons cornflour
2 (269-g/9½-oz) cans beansprouts

Clean, gut and fillet the whiting (see page 21). Simmer the fish in a little water flavoured with the sherry for 8–10 minutes. Drain, reserving the liquor and keep hot. Make the liquor up to 450 ml/¾ pint with water. Add soy sauce, vinegar, sugar and tomato purée. Stir well and add the peppers, orange juice and rind. Simmer for 5 minutes. Mix the cornflour with a little water, add to the sauce and cook, stirring until thick. Heat the beansprouts and drain. Serve the fish on a bed of hot beansprouts, topped with the sauce. **Serves 4**

Whitebait

These young herrings are usually only 2.5–3.5 cm/1–1½ inches long and should be eaten whole while very fresh. They can be bought frozen. Either lightly shallow-fry, or, more traditionally, toss in seasoned flour with a pinch of curry powder or cayenne pepper and deep-fry.

Meat

Buying meat is likely to be our biggest food expense of the week, and the most risky. Meat and the way it is sold has changed so much recently that we can no longer be sure what to look for and where. The colour of meat varies according to how recently it was cut, how it was stored and the age of the animal, so colour is no longer a clear guideline to freshness or tenderness. Fewer and fewer people want to buy fatty joints – sadly people seem to think they are buying waste – so buying a joint without fat on gives you even less indication of its quality – and for that matter more likelihood of a dry result.

If you buy from a supermarket where everything is neatly packaged, you often cannot really see properly what you are buying, and the chances are that you and the meat attendant will both be in too much of a hurry to discuss your purchase. If you buy from a butcher, you may well be one of the many who are embarrassed to show him just how ignorant they are about meat. But the fact is that you must ask advice to be sure of a good buy.

My butcher always tells me that buying the cheapest or the most expensive cut is rarely wise meat buying. There is no such thing as cheap meat, for it will usually be tough – even tasteless – and after hours of preparing, cooking and adding taste, what advantage have you gained? The most expensive will no doubt be tender and tasty but your butcher may be able to suggest an excellent alternative which is much cheaper on that particular day. So ask him first.

Search your area for a good and reliable butcher, keep moving until you find one, and when you do, take advantage of his specialised knowledge. Remember, he can only advise if you have an idea of what you plan to cook, a roast or a casserole, for instance, and for how many. He may of course come up with other suggestions for you to try.

Beef

Beef is still our most popular meat, even though it is usually more expensive than other meats. Apart from market fluctuations, there are two important reasons for this. The first is that beef should be allowed to hang in cold storage for about 10 days to help to flavour and tenderise the meat. But cold storage of the size needed to keep a sufficient stock is very expensive. Secondly, there is only about 50% of saleable meat and bone on an average carcass, but someone besides the butcher has to pay for all the rest.

If you look at the charts on pages 44, 50–1, you can see the different cuts of meats most frequently used. It is helpful to remember that the front of the animal does the brunt of the work – hence it is lean and has very strong muscles. So most cuts from the 'forequarters' need long, slow, moist cooking to be tender and not dry. The back and rump however are well layered or marbled with fat, so from here come most of the best cuts.

Cuts of Beef

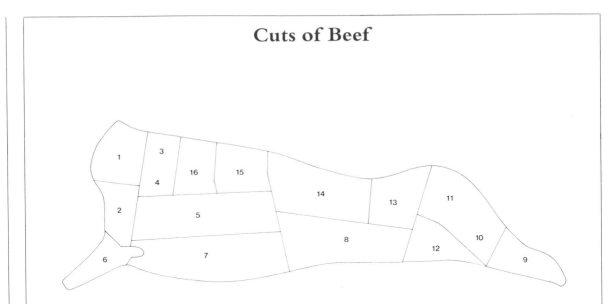

1. Neck or sticking piece: usually sold cubed or minced. Needs long, slow, moist cooking but is tasty and economical.

2. Clod (gullet, vein or sloat, clod and sticking): usually prepared as the neck. This cut also contains marrow bone.

3. Chuck: sold either sliced as braising steak or cubed for stewing. Needs long, slow, moist cooking.

4. Blade: usually cut into slices or pieces for braising. Tasty lean meat but needs slow cooking.

5. Top rib: often divided into thick and thin rib, or otherwise known as runner, flat rib, or leg of mutton cut. The front end makes a good boneless cut for slow roasting (leg of mutton cut) or for braising steaks. The back is layered fat and meat, suitable for braising and mincing.

6. Shin, leg or hough: has marrow bone in it and long thick sinews. Cut across the grain for braising or mince.

7. Brisket: a long joint, thickly layered with fat with coarse-grained meat. Very tasty after long slow braising. Usually cut into small joints and boned and rolled.

8. Flank, or thin flank: very coarse textured meat, usually cubed or minced. Skirt, flank steak and goose or rump skirt come from this part of the animal too; the best is goose skirt but there is so little it is rarely available. These are suitable for quick careful grilling, or, if you want well-cooked meat, for braising or casseroling.

9. Topside: a lean cut, good for slow roasting or pot-roasting.

10. Silverside: is coarse-grained and most frequently seen salted, but it makes a good slow roasting or braising joint.

11. Top rump, round or thick flank: usually slow roasted or braised but can also be sliced and braised or carefully fried.

12. Rump, hip bone, Pope's eye or pin bone: is thickly cut across the grain to give excellent steaks.

13. Sirloin: a large section of very tender meat on the bone with the prime fillet on the underside. It can be roasted on or off the bone or cut into steaks. At the fore-end are the porterhouse steaks; at the hind end, T-bone steaks which include the fillet. Sirloin steaks are boneless.

14. Forerib, rib roast or chine: the prime two or three rib roasts come from this part. They are very tender and are best fast-roasted on the bone. Ask for them to be chined for easy carving. Single ribs are best grilled.

15. Back rib: this makes a more economical rib roast. It is usually boned, rolled and cooked slowly.

Right: Fish in lemon and oil (see page 29)

Overleaf: Roast beef (see page 54)

Veal

Veal comes from very young calves. In France, Holland and Britain they are mainly milk-fed to produce very pale flesh, whereas in Italy they are grass-fed so the flesh becomes redder. Veal should be eaten very fresh and most cuts are very tender. However, it lacks fat so needs careful preparation.

The best cuts for roasting are shoulder, leg, rump, loin, breast and ribs. These can be slow-roasted as for breast of lamb. For frying and grilling, choose chops or steaks from the loin, best end or rump, or escalopes from the leg or rump.

For casseroling, the neck, shoulder and rump are best, or for a very slowly cooked dish, such as the traditional Italian *osso bucco*, knuckle and shin can be used.

Lamb

We are lucky to have a good and constant supply of lamb in this country. We import frozen lamb of high quality from New Zealand (though slightly smaller in joint sizes) through-out the year to supplement our fresh supplies.

New British lamb comes on the market in March when it is very young and very expen-sive. By early summer there is usually a good supply at better prices and, to my mind, this is a tastier product. The British season tapers off by November, for lamb has to be less than 1 year old.

Mutton, unfortunately, has lost its popularity here, mainly because it is more fatty, strongly flavoured and needs long slow cooking. How-ever, it is not totally unavailable and although most goes to the catering trade, your butcher may be able to order it for you if you plan ahead.

Lamb is probably the most versatile meat in the various ways it can be cut. Very few joints need really long slow cooking, and it improves with storage; four days is usually sufficient, so ask your butcher before you buy.

Chops

Loin, best end and chump chops naturally make perfect single-portion quick meals but can be cut in different ways. Both loin and best-end chops can be used for noisettes, the loin producing the larger and more meaty pieces. Your butcher will be able to prepare these for you but they are not difficult to do yourself. Once the bone is removed from the single chop, curl the long piece of flesh round the 'eye' to give a circular piece of meat, then tie with string or secure with a cocktail stick.

As one chop is often not sufficient for a hungry man, you could cook two together.

A double chop is two best-end chops cut in one piece and does enable you to keep the middle pink, if you like it that way.

A butterfly chop (Barnsley chop) is cut across the saddle giving two adjoining chops. The bones are trimmed so the thin piece of meat can be curled round and tied during cooking.

Pork

Most of our pork is home produced. It does not keep as well as lamb or beef, so it should rarely be hung, but should be eaten as fresh as possible. Also it should not be too fatty, although it is by nature more fatty than other meats. Try to make sure the rind, if you buy a joint with rind on, is quite pliable. Hardened rind is a sign of age and it will not 'crackle' successfully. Pork should never be undercooked.

Oxtail stew (see page 73)

Cuts of Lamb

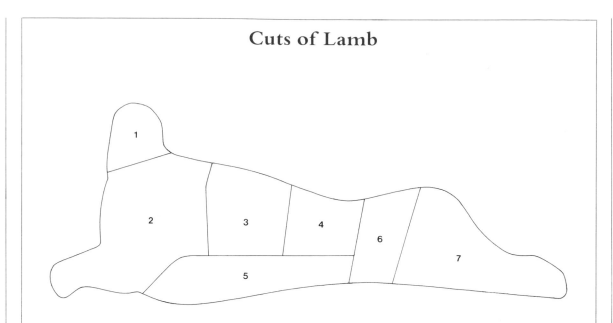

1. Neck, scrag: have irregular-shaped bones but can be cut into chops. Best for stews and casseroles.

2. Shoulders: this can be divided into two pieces, known as half shoulders – blade or knuckle (runner or shank) end. It can be roasted whole or in smaller cuts, or may be boned and stuffed. When asking for a shoulder to be boned, be sure you know what the butcher will do, either the leg bone can be left in place and just the flat front blade bone removed (see the diagram for how to do this yourself), or both bones will be removed. The shoulder can also be cut into pieces for kebabs and casseroles.

3. Best end, single loin, fine end loin, best end of neck: these are easily recognisable by the long thin chops (usually six to seven bones on one best end) which are traditionally called cutlets. It can be boned, rolled and stuffed for easy carving, or it can be roasted on the bone. (Be sure to ask your butcher to remove the chine bone or 'chine it' for you.) The best known roasts from a best end are: rack of lamb and carré d'agneau – the bones and meat are trimmed in slightly different ways. These are usually plain roasted, or coated in crumbs, or in parsley and garlic. The 'crown roast' and 'guard of honour' – these take their names, not surprisingly from their appearance. The crown (illustrated on page 178) is formed from two best ends, chined and placed skin sides facing each other. Once tied at each end, it can be pushed out into a round shape. Traditionally, it is filled with stuffing and topped with cutlet frills to finish off the crown.

The guard of honour differs only in that the two joints are placed with the bone sides facing each other. Once tied, the trimmed ends of the bones are interleaved like crossed swords. The middle of this joint can be filled with stuffing but it's slightly fiddly. The bones can be topped with cutlet frills, tiny tomatoes, cherries or onions.

Many butchers will be happy to prepare these special joints for you – if you give them time and due warning. Only with experience, the right equipment and a strong right arm would you manage yourself.

4. Loin, double loin or middle loin: is cut down the backbone to give two joints. If it is left whole this is called the saddle (the double loin). This is the best joint for roasting on the bone, or it can be boned, rolled and stuffed. It can also be cut into loin chops.

5. Breast, flank, lap: is the fattiest part but gives very tasty meat. It is usually boned, rolled and stuffed for slow roasting, or it can be braised. The breast, on the bone, can be cut into individual bones to use as an alternative to Chinese spareribs.

6. Chump, gigot: is perfect for frying, grilling and barbecuing or can be cut up for kebabs and fondues. Leg (chump) chops come from here and also lamb steaks.

7. Leg: is often divided into two joints, the gigot or fillet at the fore-end and the shank or knuckle. The whole leg provides a very good large joint but often just the half leg is sufficient. Either can be roasted on the bone, or boned and stuffed, or the gigot can give good frying or grilling meat.

Cuts of Pork

1. **Blade bone, sparerib, shoulder:** these can be boned and rolled for roasting or braising or can be cut into awkwardly-shaped chops known as the American spare-rib chop. These can be grilled, barbecued or casseroled.

2. **Shoulder, hand or hand and spring:** this is usually sold pickled or salted ready for boiling on the bone. It can also be boned and rolled for roasting or braising. It is quite a fatty joint.

3. **Shank, hough, hock or knuckle:** doesn't have very much meat on it and is best boiled or braised for stews and casseroles.

4. **Loin:** the best pork joint for roasting, either on the bone or boned and stuffed. Can be divided into small loin roasts with the kidney left in, or chops. The tenderloin also comes from the loin, though it is usually sold separately. This is the tenderest cut – ideal for grilling or frying, kebabs or quickly cooked dishes.

5. **Belly, streaky pork:** is thickly layered fat and meat, and mainly for adding flavour to other meats in stews or pot roasts.

6. **Chump:** this is mainly cut into chops for frying and grilling. Also good for casseroling.

7. **Fillet or middle cut:** slices of very tender meat cut from the end of the leg, best for grilling or frying. Ideal to use in place of veal escalopes.

8. **Shank, gigot or knuckle:** larger than the fore-end shank but used in the same way.

Tripe

Tripe is usually sold prepared and ready for cooking. It usually requires at least 1½–2 hours cooking. Often it is the colour that puts people off this very nutritious dish, but as it goes particularly well with tomatoes, bacon and rich brown sauces it can be cleverly masked.

Trotters and Heads

The best part of trotters and heads, especially from pigs, is the rich jelly stock they produce. It can be used to flavour cold jellied dishes, such as brawn or to enrich casseroles. There is a considerable amount of meat on both of these cuts, especially large pig's feet, and they can make extremely good stews. Both should be soaked in salted water, then cleaned – and trotters should be blanched – before cooking in flavoured liquid.

Cooking Meat

For slow, moist cooking stewing, braising, pot-roasting, or boiling – the principles are the same for all types of meat. Roasting, frying, grilling or barbecuing – the quicker and dryer cooking methods – vary slightly according to the fat content and tenderness of the cut.

Stewing ideal for the cheapest and toughest cuts. The meat is browned, then cooked with flavoursome vegetables, herbs and liquid for 2–3 hours or more until tender. The gravy can be thickened after cooking. A stew can be cooked in the oven or over direct heat.

Braising suitable for the cheaper cuts and some of the better quality joints. The browned meat should cook on top of the vegetables with a little stock in the steam the stock gives off – not in the liquid as in a stew. It should be in an airtight pan or casserole to keep in all the steam and flavour.

Boiling best for salted and cured meats and very tough cuts, but not good for very small joints. Don't use too much water and don't boil too fast – this toughens the meat – keep it simmering gently. Use the liquid for sauces or soups.

Pot-roasting this is best for all the cheaper joints, of any size. Brown the meat and vegetables in fat in the same pan first, then cook very slowly, covered tightly, either in the oven or on the top of the cooker. As in braising, the meat is cooked in the steam, not in liquid, so be sure you use a heavy pan. Allow at least 45 minutes per 0.5 kg/1 lb.

Frying only suitable for tender cuts of meat. Cook the meat quickly on both sides in heated fat. The leaner cuts, such as steaks and escalopes, require more fat and plenty of basting to keep them moist. Pork, bacon and gammon should not be fiercely cooked or they will toughen up. These cuts take longer to cook through. Chops take 10–15 minutes, depending on thickness. Kidney and liver take only 8–10 minutes. For steaks see notes on page 59.

Deep-frying meat should be protected with a coating of batter as the fat is hotter than that for shallow-frying. Heat the fat until it begins to haze, or a cube of bread turns golden in 1 minute (190°C/375°F). If the fat is not hot enough, the coating will not seal in the meat, but will absorb more fat and produce a greasy result. Drain well on absorbent kitchen paper. Do not mix different meat fats and be sure to clarify the fat immediately before putting aside for future frying. Do use a special, very solid pan for deep-frying.

Grilling suitable for all tender thin cuts of meat. Preheat the grill and lightly grease the tray and the meat on both sides. Cook fast to seal as for frying, then reduce the heat. Turn the meat once or twice, with tongs, not a fork as this pierces the flesh and lets the juices run out.

Roasting place the joint fat side uppermost in a roasting tin that is not much larger than the joint. Unless the meat is generously covered in fat, like some pork and lamb joints, add extra fat – preferably dripping or lard. Cover with foil or greased greaseproof paper, or a lid, to keep the joint moist and prevent the outside browning too quickly. Cook in a hot oven (220°C, 425°F, Gas Mark 7) for the first 15 minutes to seal the outsides, then reduce to moderate (180°C, 350°F, Gas Mark 4) for the remaining cooking time according to the meat.

Beef roast as above allowing 15 minutes per

0.5 kg/1 lb for rare; 20 minutes per 0.5 kg/1 lb for medium; and 25 minutes per 0.5 kg/1 lb for well done. (Illustrated on pages 46–7.)

Lamb roast as above allowing 20 minutes per 0.5 kg/1 lb for pink, and for well done 30 minutes per 0.5 kg/1 lb.

Pork and Veal roast in a moderate oven (180°C, 350°F, Gas Mark 4) for 35 minutes per 0.5 kg/1 lb, increasing to hot (220°C, 425°F, Gas Mark 7) for the last 20 minutes. If you like really crisp crackling, rub it well with oil and salt before cooking. To carve a loin of pork see below.

Bacon after boiling (allowing 20 minutes per 0.5 kg/1 lb), drain and cool slightly. Remove the rind if you wish and coat with crumbs or sugar. Roast in a hot oven (220°C, 425°F, Gas Mark 7) for 20 minutes only.

Very cheap or tough cuts should be very slowly roasted in a cool oven (150°C, 300°F, Gas Mark 2) for 40–45 minutes per 0.5 kg/1 lb. These can still be browned for 10 minutes or more at the end of cooking in a hot oven (220°C, 425°F, Gas Mark 7). It is worth remembering that the larger the joint, the less will be lost in shrinkage during cooking. Meat on the bone cooks more quickly than that off the bone. Weigh joints after stuffing to calculate the cooking time.

Fatless cooking when roasting, put joints on a trivet or rack to let the fat drain out. Slit the fat (not the meat) slightly to help it melt and drain off more quickly.

When frying, use a non-stick pan with no fat at all, or if using other pans, brush the meat very lightly with heated fat or oil. Don't cook too fast or the meat will burn and stick. Turn over frequently. Grilled meats need only be lightly brushed with fat. Wipe off all excess fat with absorbent kitchen paper before serving.

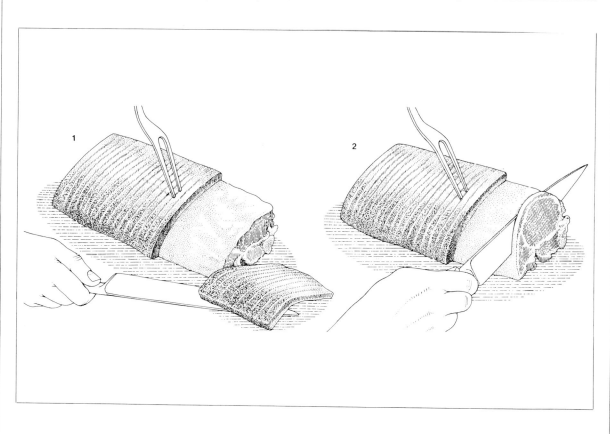

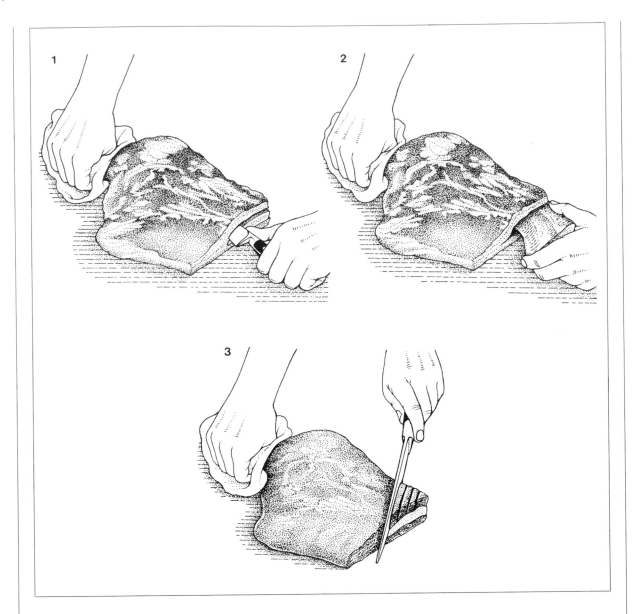

Beef Stroganoff

75 g/3 oz butter
3 onions, chopped
1.5 kg/3 lb braising steak, cut in strips
150 ml/$\frac{1}{4}$ pint dry white wine
300 ml/$\frac{1}{2}$ pint beef stock
salt and pepper
450 g/1 lb mushrooms, sliced
2 (142-ml/5-fl oz) cartons soured cream
675 g/1$\frac{1}{2}$ lb noodles or rice, cooked to serve

Melt the butter and fry the onion until tender. Add the braising steak and cook until browned all over. Stir in the wine, stock and seasoning. Cook in a moderate oven (160°C, 325°F, Gas Mark 3) for 2–3 hours. After 2$\frac{1}{2}$ hours add the mushrooms and then complete the cooking time. Add the soured cream just before serving. Serve with rice or noodles.

Noisettes of lamb in spinach (see page 65)

Boiled Silverside with Dumplings

1.75 kg/4 lb silverside, boned and rolled
1 onion, halved
1 carrot, halved
water or stock to cover
8 button onions
675 g/1½ lb carrots, sliced (optional)
1 bunch fresh herbs and few sticks celery,
tied together
salt and pepper
dumplings:
175 g/6 oz self-raising flour
50 g/2 oz shredded suet

Put the meat, onion, carrot and water into a pan. Bring to the boil, cover and simmer for 1¾ hours. Then add the whole button onions, carrots, herbs, celery and seasoning. Meanwhile cook for a further 25 minutes. Meanwhile, mix the flour, suet, seasoning and enough water to make a soft dough; form into small balls with floured hands. Add to the pan, cover and cook for a further 20 minutes. Serve the meat surrounded by the vegetables and dumplings. If liked, strain the liquor, and thicken to serve as gravy. **Serves 8–10**

Herbed Brisket in Ale

1–1.25 kg/2–2½ lb brisket or topside of beef
salt and pepper
pinch dry mustard
1 teaspoon flour
50 g/2 oz fat
6–8 old potatoes, coarsely chopped
6–8 medium onions, quartered
450 g/1 lb turnips or carrots, coarsely chopped
300 ml/½ pint beer (or 150 ml/¼ pint water and
150 ml/¼ pint beer)
1 tablespoon chopped parsley
¼ teaspoon chopped sage
¼ teaspoon chopped thyme
2 teaspoons chopped chives

Wash the meat and pat dry. Mix together the seasoning, mustard and flour and use to coat the meat. Heat the fat in a large saucepan and brown the meat all over. Lift out of the pan and toss the potato and onion in any remaining fat. Pour away any surplus fat. Add the turnips or carrots with the beer or beer and water. Season well and add half the parsley, sage, thyme and chives. Place the meat on the bed of vegetables and cover the pan. Simmer the liquid allowing about 30 minutes per 0.5 kg/1 lb of meat. Transfer to a hot dish and top with the remaining herbs. Serve the liquid as it is or thicken to make gravy. **Serves 6–8**

Timing Your Steaks

The timing for grilling or frying steak is crucial if you're not going to overcook it and ruin an expensive piece of meat. Use a little fat, to keep the steak moist, or use a lightly greased non-stick pan or grill pan.

However you prefer your steak, it is best to cook fast for 1 minute on each side first to seal in the juices and give a crisp outside. Reduce the heat and cook according to taste. Baste occasionally and turn once or twice to cook evenly. Never prick with a fork or pierce to see if it is done, or the steak will loose its moistness.

Rare: this is very pink in the middle. Cook fast for 1 minute on each side, then cook more slowly for 3 minutes on each side.

Medium: the steak is just loosing its pinkness in the middle but is still very moist. After 1 minute fast cooking on each side, cook gently for 5–6 minutes on each side.

Well done: the meat is evenly cooked through. This will need 9 minutes cooking on each side after the initial 1 minute for sealing.

Tournedos Marseillais

(Illustrated on page 168)

Tournedos are cut from the best part of the beef fillet and are usually cut thicker than steaks. Cook them as steaks according to taste. Serve on parsleyed croûtons with a little red wine sauce. Top with a few whole cloves of garlic, boiled in a little milk and quickly fried with the steaks.

Stuffed duck with port sauce and grapes (see page 90)

Steak in Port

50 g/2 oz dripping
50 g/2 oz bacon, diced
1 small onion, finely chopped
1 small carrot, finely diced
2 tablespoons flour
450 ml/¾ pint of stock
100 g/4 oz mushroom stalks and peelings
2 teaspoons tomato purée
4 tablespoons port
1 tablespoon oil
25 g/1 oz butter
4 sirloin steaks
salt and pepper

Heat the dripping in a large saucepan and fry the bacon. Remove the bacon and set aside. Add the onion and carrot. Cook very gently until golden brown (don't hurry this or the vegetables will burn). Stir in the flour and continue cooking very gently until it browns – about 10 minutes. Stir in the stock and add the bacon and mushroom stalks and peelings. Simmer for 30 minutes. Stir in the tomato purée and port and cook for a further 15 minutes. Strain. Heat the oil and butter and fry the steaks until nearly cooked to the desired degree. Drain away any excess juice from the pan, pour in the sauce, season to taste and heat through for 2–3 minutes with the steaks. Serve immediately. **Serves 4**

Meat Marinades

Marinades can help to make cheaper cuts more tender, add extra special flavour to any meat, act as a preservative in keeping meat a day or two longer and, if ever you are in doubt about the freshness of meat, you can wash it well and leave it in a wine marinade for 1–2 hours – any off smells and flavours will disappear.

There is no hard and fast rule about using a red wine marinade with red meat, or a white one with white. The best coq au vin, for instance, is made with red wine.

Classic marinades are based on wine, but you can also use cider vinegar. As this type of marinade has a quick tenderising action, some varieties of meat need very little time to soak (1–2 hours for chicken or good quality steak).

Cheaper cuts may need longer (4–6 hours).

Fruit juices also have sufficient acidity to tenderise food, at the same time adding a delicious flavour. Lemon and grapefruit are the best, but orange, tomato, apple and other juices can be used in their place, or can be mixed with wine in the classic recipe below, which is sufficient for 1–1.5 kg/2–3 lb of meat.

Wine Marinade

1 medium carrot, sliced
1 medium onion, chopped
1 stick celery, diced
1 clove garlic, sliced (optional)
few cloves
few black peppercorns
1 sprig parsley, chopped
1 sprig thyme, chopped
salt and pepper
450 ml/¾ pint red or white wine
150 ml/¼ pint salad oil

Mix the carrot, onion, celery, garlic, cloves, peppercorns, parsley and thyme together. Lay half in the base of a deep dish with the chosen meat on top. Season and cover with the remaining vegetables and herbs. Pour on the wine and oil, cover and leave until required.

Beef in Red Wine

900-g/2-lb piece flank or braising steak
Red wine marinade (see above)
25 g/1 oz dripping or lard
20 g/¾ oz flour
300 ml/½ pint beef stock
salt and pepper

Trim any gristle, but not fat, from the meat. Marinate the meat for about 4 hours. Pour off the marinade and reserve. Heat the fat and fry the meat until golden all over, then transfer to a large ovenproof dish with a lid. Stir the flour into the remaining fat, season and mix well. Cook until golden brown.

Stir in half the marinade liquid and the stock. Cook for a further 1–2 minutes until smooth, add the marinade vegetables and pour the mixture over the meat. Cook, covered, in a moderately hot oven (190°C, 375°F, Gas Mark 5) for about 1½ hours or until tender. Purée the sauce if you wish. **Serves 4–6**

Rich Beef Stew

25 g/1 oz dripping or lard or 2 tablespoons oil
225 g/8 oz button onions
675 g/1½ lb stewing steak, cut in cubes
3 tablespoons flour
900 ml/1½ pints beef stock
salt and pepper
1 clove garlic, crushed (optional)
225 g/8 oz ripe tomatoes, peeled and quartered
12 black olives, stoned

Heat the fat or oil in a large saucepan and fry the onions until light brown; remove with a draining spoon. Fry the meat, a few pieces at a time, in the fat left in the pan, until brown all over. Remove the meat and put to one side. Stir the flour into the remaining juices and cook gently, stirring, until a rich brown colour. Remove the pan from the heat and gradually stir in the stock, then the seasoning and garlic, if you're using it. Bring the liquid to the boil, then add the onions and meat. Cover and simmer gently for about 1½ hours. Add the tomatoes and olives, and continue to cook for a further 15 minutes. **Serves 4**

Ham and Beef Olives

12 thin slices braising steak or shoulder
12 thin slices ham
2 tablespoons chopped parsley
pared rind of ½ lemon, chopped
salt and pepper
25 g/1 oz lard or dripping
150 ml/¼ pint red wine
300 ml/½ pint stock
1 onion, sliced
2 teaspoons cornflour

Trim the fat from the meat and flatten each slice slightly with a rolling pin or meat mallet. Lay a slice of ham on each slice of beef and sprinkle with parsley. Add a few pieces of lemon rind and seasoning. Roll up and tie with thin string or thick cotton. Heat the fat in a frying pan and quickly fry the olives to seal and brown. Arrange the olives in an ovenproof dish and add the wine, stock and onion. Cover and cook in a moderate oven (180°C, 350°F, Gas Mark 4) for about 1¼ hours until just tender.

Mix the cornflour with 1 tablespoon water. Drain most of the liquid into a pan and stir in the cornflour. Cook, stirring, until thickened, then simmer until the sauce has reduced to a pouring consistency. Check the seasoning, remove the string from the meat and lightly coat the olives in the sauce before serving. **Serves 4**

Wiener Schnitzel
(Breaded Escalopes)

4 veal escalopes or 4 (5-mm/¼-inch) slices flank
of beef
seasoned flour
1 egg
75 g/3 oz fine white breadcrumbs
75 g/3 oz butter
4 tablespoons oil
wedges of lemon to garnish

Flatten out the veal or beef with a rolling pin or
meat mallet until really thin. Then dip into
seasoned flour to coat and shake off the excess.
Beat the egg with 2 tablespoons water and dip
the meat in this. Coat thoroughly in the
breadcrumbs and refrigerate for 30 minutes–1
hour. Heat the butter and oil until just bubbling and fry the meat, two pieces at a time, for
3–8 minutes on each side (depending on size)
until golden brown. Serve with lemon wedges
and, if you wish, one of the flavoured butters
on page 184. **Serves 4**

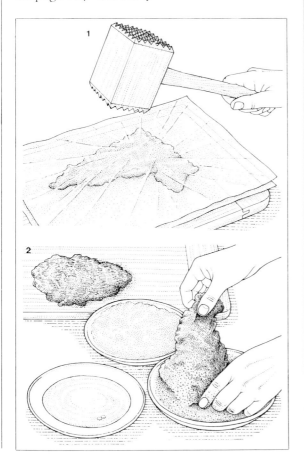

Veal Provençale

2 tablespoons oil
4 small veal chops
225 g/8 oz tomatoes, peeled and roughly chopped
1 onion, sliced
1 teaspoon paprika
1 (376-g/13¼-oz) can red wine sauce
salt and pepper

Heat the oil and fry the chops until golden,
turning once. Add the remaining ingredients,
stir well and cover tightly. Simmer for 15
minutes or until the meat is tender. **Serves 4**

Party Meat Roll

50 g/2 oz fresh breadcrumbs
3 tablespoons milk
pinch dried thyme
salt and pepper
350 g/12 oz minced beef
100 g/4 oz minced pork or bacon
1 egg
1 tablespoon chopped parsley
40 g/1½ oz margarine
2 medium onions, chopped
450 g/1 lb carrots, grated
glaze:
3–4 tablespoons tomato ketchup
1 tablespoon brown sugar
pinch dry mustard

Mix the breadcrumbs, milk, thyme and seasoning together thoroughly. Mix in the minced
meats, egg and parsley. Melt the margarine in a
small frying pan and fry the onion until tender.
Mix into the meat and spread this evenly in an
oblong on a sheet of damp greaseproof paper,
leaving a 2.5-cm/1-inch space at the edges.
Spread the grated carrots on top. Carefully roll
up from the narrow end, using the paper as a
support. Remove the paper and place the roll
on a sheet of foil on a baking tray. Chill. Heat
the glaze ingredients together until well mixed.
Brush the glaze liberally over the meat, close
the foil around the meat roll and bake in a
moderately hot oven (190°C, 375°F, Gas Mark
5) for about 45 minutes. Uncover the meat for
the last 10 minutes and brush with the glaze
again. Serve hot with green beans and buttered
button onions **Serves 4 5**

Plank Hamburger

25 g/1 oz butter, softened
1 teaspoon chopped parsley
pinch garlic salt or dry mustard
225 g/8 oz good quality braising or stewing steak
salt and pepper
1–2 tablespoons oil

Mix the butter, parsley and garlic or mustard together. Flatten between pieces of greaseproof paper and chill. For a really good hamburger, only mince or chop the meat coarsely. Season the meat and mould into an oval shape.

Make an incision through the middle and insert the piece of butter. Seal the edges together again. Heat the oil and fry the hamburger for 1 minute on each side to brown and seal. Then continue to cook on each side until cooked through as you like it. Serve immediately. **Serves 1**

Meat Balls with Rich Tomato Sauce

meat balls:
450 g/1 lb minced beef
1 clove garlic, crushed
25 g/1 oz fresh breadcrumbs
salt and pepper
½ teaspoon dried basil
1 egg, beaten
2 tablespoons flour
3 tablespoons oil
sauce:
1 onion, chopped
100 g/4 oz mushrooms, sliced
½ teaspoon dried basil
2 tablespoons flour
150 ml/¼ pint beef stock
2 tablespoons tomato purée
1 (227-g/8-oz) can tomatoes
4 tablespoons brandy or sweet sherry
pasta:
275 g/10 oz tagliatelle
50 g/2 oz butter

Mix the beef, garlic, breadcrumbs, seasoning and basil together, binding with enough beaten egg to give a firm mixture. Form into walnut-sized balls and dust with a little flour. Heat the oil in a frying pan and fry the meat balls until light brown all over. Remove from the pan.

Add the onion, mushrooms and basil to the pan and fry for a few minutes until soft. Stir in the flour and cook gently until light brown. Gradually stir in the stock, tomato purée, tomatoes and brandy or sherry. Adjust the seasoning and add the meat balls. Cover and simmer for 15 minutes until the sauce is thick. Meanwhile, cook the pasta in boiling salted water for 8–10 minutes until just tender, drain well and add the butter. Arrange the pasta on a serving dish and top with the meat balls and sauce. As a variation, skewer the meatballs, adding pieces of tomato, courgette, onion and bay leaves. Grill, turning occasionally for about 10 minutes. Serve with the tomato sauce and a salad. Illustrated on page 88. **Serves 4–6**

Lamb en Croûte

(Illustrated on page 177)

1 leg of lamb, about 1.75 kg/4 lb
675 g/1½ lb Shortcrust pastry (See page 136)
1 egg, beaten
stuffing:
100 g/4 oz cooked rice
100 g/4 oz mushrooms, finely chopped
1 tablespoon finely chopped mint
1 small red pepper, seeds removed and finely chopped
1 egg, beaten
salt and pepper

Ask your butcher to remove the bone from the lamb. Mix all the stuffing ingredients together and push into the cavity. Place the lamb in a roasting tin and roast in a moderate oven (160°C, 325°F, Gas Mark 3) for 1½ hours. Roll out the pastry to a large square, brush the edges with a little egg, and when the meat is cooked, place it upside down on the pastry. Fold the pastry over the meat and seal the edges with egg. Decorate with any remaining pastry trimmings and glaze with beaten egg. Cook in a moderately hot oven (190°C, 375°F, Gas Mark 5) for a further 20–25 minutes until the pastry is golden. **Serves 8**

Boiled Leg of Mutton

1 leg of mutton about 2.75–3.25 kg/6–7 lb
2 sticks celery, chopped
1 medium onion, chopped
3 carrots, chopped
$\frac{1}{2}$ turnip, chopped
salt and pepper
75 g/3 oz butter
3 tablespoons fresh rosemary, finely chopped
few sprigs rosemary

Put the mutton, celery, onion, carrot, turnip and seasoning into a pan with enough water to cover. Bring to the boil then lower the heat, cover and simmer very gently for about 35 minutes per 0.5 kg/1 lb and 35 minutes over. Lift the meat from the pan. Mix the butter and chopped rosemary together and spread over the meat. Cook in a moderately hot oven (190°C, 375°F, Gas Mark 5) for 1 hour, until the leg is well glazed and browned. Garnish with the fresh rosemary. **Serves 8**

Honeyed Ribs of Lamb

2 breasts of lamb, unboned
4 tablespoons honey
1 tablespoon vinegar
1–2 tablespoons sesame seeds
sauce:
2 tablespoons oil
1 onion, finely chopped
1 (227-g/8-oz) can crushed pineapple
1 tablespoon tomato purée
2 tablespoons brown sugar
juice of 1 lemon
1 green pepper, seeds removed and finely chopped

Cut between the bones to give separate ribs (rather like spare ribs). Warm the honey and vinegar together. Dip each rib into the mixture then coat with sesame seeds. Place on a baking tray and cook in a moderately hot oven (200°C, 400°F, Gas Mark 6) for 1 hour, until nicely golden brown. For the sauce, heat the oil and fry the onion until soft. Add the remaining ingredients and simmer for 30 minutes. Serve with the cooked ribs. **Serves 4–6**

Redcurrant Glazed Lamb

1 leg of lamb, about 1.5 kg/3 lb
6 tablespoons redcurrant jelly
1 teaspoon dried sage

Place the lamb in a roasting tin. Melt the redcurrant jelly, then stir in the sage. Brush this mixture generously over the lamb. Fast-roast according to weight (see page 55). Baste frequently with the juices during cooking. **Serves 6**

Fruity Lamb

1 large or 2 small breasts of lamb, boned (for special occasions use a best end or loin of lamb, boned)
watercress to garnish
stuffing:
1 (425-g/15-oz) can apricot halves
25 g/1 oz butter
1 small onion, finely chopped
1 tablespoon dried mixed herbs
50 g/2 oz fresh breadcrumbs
salt and pepper

First make the stuffing. Drain the apricots, chop the fruit and reserve the juice. Melt the butter and fry the onion until soft but not brown. Mix with the apricots, herbs, breadcrumbs and seasoning. Bind with a little of the apricot juice. Spread the stuffing over the lamb, roll up firmly and tie with string. Weigh the stuffed joint, place in a roasting tin and slow-roast in the centre of the oven according to weight (see page 55). Add the remaining juice to the tin 25 minutes before the end of the cooking time. Carve the lamb into slices and garnish with watercress. When making the gravy, use the skimmed juices and sediment from the roasting tin. **Serves 4**

Lamb Steaks Paprika

2 lamb steaks, from top end of leg
1 tablespoon paprika
1 teaspoon cumin seeds
salt and pepper
25 g/1 oz butter
1 tablespoon oil
150 ml/¼ pint natural yogurt
2 teaspoons cornflour

If necessary, trim any excess fat from the steaks. Mix together the paprika, cumin and seasoning and use to coat the steaks. Melt the butter with the oil and fry the steaks at a high temperature for 1 minute on each side, then reduce the heat and fry for a further 7 minutes on each side, or more if you like lamb well-cooked. Place on a heated serving dish. Mix the yogurt with the cornflour and stir into the frying pan. Boil for 1 minute then pour over the steaks. **Serves 2**

Barbecue Lamb Chops

4 loin chops
finely grated rind and juice of 1 lemon
pinch paprika
6 tablespoons salad oil
salt and freshly ground black pepper
1 tablespoon chopped parsley
4 sprigs rosemary

Dip each chop in lemon juice. Place in a shallow dish and cover with the lemon rind, a good sprinkling of paprika and the oil. Cover and leave to marinate for 3–4 hours, turning occasionally. Drain off the marinade and re-serve it. Lightly season each chop, sprinkle with parsley and top with a sprig of rosemary. Grill or barbecue quickly, for about 10 minutes, basting with the marinade. Turn once and sprinkle with more seasoning and parsley. **Serves 4**

Noisettes of Lamb in Spinach

(Illustrated on page 57)

1 best end of neck, boned and rolled
75 g/3 oz chicken liver pâté
225 g/8 oz spinach leaves (or cabbage or lettuce)
1 thin pancake, cut in strips
50 g/2 oz cheese, grated
1 teaspoon dried mixed herbs
½ teaspoon dry mustard
150 ml/¼ pint dry white wine
150 ml/¼ pint lamb or chicken stock
salt and pepper
2 teaspoons cornflour

Cut the lamb into six noisettes. Heat the oil and fry or grill the noisettes quickly until cooked to taste. Top each noisette with a little pâté. Blanch the spinach, cabbage or lettuce leaves for just 30 seconds, then drain. Wrap each noisette in a leaf and tie lightly with strips of pancake. Top with a little cheese.

Gently grill the wrapped noisettes until the cheese melts. Meanwhile simmer the herbs, mustard, wine, stock and seasoning with any left-over lamb fat. Mix the cornflour with a little of this liquid and return to the pan. Bring to the boil, stirring, and simmer until clear and slightly thickened. Pour over the noisettes and serve immediately. **Serves 6**

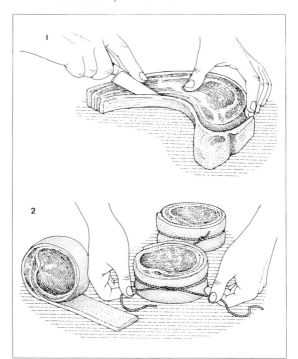

Lamb Italienne

2 tablespoons oil
8 best end of neck lamb cutlets
2 medium onions, sliced
150 ml/$\frac{1}{4}$ pint chicken stock
150 ml/$\frac{1}{4}$ pint dry white wine
2 tablespoons tomato purée
25 g/1 oz flaked almonds
25 g/1 oz plain chocolate, diced (optional)

Heat the oil in a large frying pan and fry the cutlets and onions until golden. Add the stock, wine, tomato purée, almonds and chocolate. Simmer for 10–15 minutes. Transfer the cutlets to a heated serving dish and pour the sauce over. Serve with rice or spaghetti. **Serves 4**

Brochettes of Lamb

1 small cauliflower
2 green peppers, seeds removed
salt and pepper
350 g/12 oz fillet or leg of lamb, trimmed
100 g/4 oz green grapes
50 g/2 oz walnuts
4 small sprigs rosemary
75 g/3 oz butter, melted

Trim the cauliflower and cut into bite-sized florets. Cut the green pepper into similar-sized pieces and blanch for 3 minutes in boiling salted water. Add the cauliflower and blanch for another 3 minutes. Plunge into cold water to prevent overcooking. Cut the lamb into 2.5–3.5-cm/1–1$\frac{1}{2}$-inch cubes and arrange on four large skewers or kebab sticks with the remaining ingredients. Brush with butter, season and grill for 10–15 minutes, turning and basting the kebabs as they brown. **Serves 4**

Lancashire Hot Pot

2–3 tablespoons oil
900 g/2 lb neck of lamb chops
225 g/8 oz onions, sliced
225 g/8 oz carrots, sliced
salt and pepper
2 tablespoons chopped parsley
900 g/2 lb potatoes, sliced
25 g/1 oz butter

Heat the oil and fry the chops until browned, then remove. Fry the onions and carrots quickly to brown and arrange in layers in an ovenproof dish with the chops, sprinkling each layer with seasoning and parsley. Add 300 ml/$\frac{1}{2}$ pint water to the frying pan, bring to the boil, stirring to remove the sediment, and pour over the meat and vegetables. Arrange the potatoes overlapping on top to cover the dish completely. Dot with butter, sprinkle with seasoning, cover and cook, in a moderately hot oven (190°C, 375°F, Gas Mark 5) for about 1$\frac{1}{2}$ hours. Remove the lid 15 minutes before serving to brown the potatoes. **Serves 4**

Spring Lamb Casserole

2–3 tablespoons oil
1 large onion, sliced
900 g/2 lb scrag or neck lamb chops
3 carrots, cut in matchsticks
3 sticks celery, cut in matchsticks
2 small apples, peeled, cored and diced
225 g/8 oz courgettes, sliced
225 g/8 oz spring cabbage, coarsely shredded
300 ml/$\frac{1}{2}$ pint lamb or chicken stock
salt and pepper
150 ml/$\frac{1}{4}$ pint apple juice
2–3 tablespoons double cream

Heat the oil in a large pan. Brown the onion and chops quickly. Add the carrot, celery, apple, courgette, cabbage, stock, seasoning and apple juice. Simmer gently for about 1$\frac{1}{2}$ hours or until the meat is tender. Stir in the cream just before serving. **Serves 6**

Lamb Tagine

1 leg of lamb, about 1.5 kg/3 lb, boned and cut in cubes
1–2 tablespoons oil
pinch ground ginger
salt and freshly ground black pepper
$\frac{1}{4}$ teaspoon ground coriander
$\frac{1}{2}$ teaspoon ground cinnamon
1 onion, chopped
1 (212-g/7$\frac{1}{2}$-oz) can mandarins, drained or 2 tangerines, peeled and segmented
2 tablespoons honey or to taste

Put the meat in a large saucepan and cover with water. Add the oil, ginger, seasoning coriander, cinnamon and onion. Bring to the boil, then cover and simmer very gently until the meat is tender, about 2 hours. Check the water occasionally and top up only if the pan is likely to become dry. After about 2 hours, you should have a rich sauce. Add the mandarins or tangerines and honey to the sauce and mix well. Cook for a further 15 minutes. Serve with rice, noodles or baked potatoes and a green vegetable. **Serves 6**

Moussaka

Traditionally, minced lamb rather than beef is used in Middle Eastern recipes. However your butcher may not be prepared to mince lamb, especially if your are only ordering a small quantity. Mince it yourself or use beef instead.

3 aubergines
salt and pepper
6 tablespoons olive oil
1 medium onion, chopped
2 cloves garlic, crushed
900 g/2 lb minced lamb or beef
2 large tomatoes, peeled and chopped
1 teaspoon dried oregano
1 tablespoon chopped parsley
$\frac{1}{4}$ teaspoon grated nutmeg
salt and pepper
6 tablespoons red wine
600 ml/1 pint Béchamel sauce (see page 185)
50–75 g/2–3 oz grated Parmesan cheese
2 eggs

Wash and slice the aubergines. Sprinkle generously with salt and leave for about 20 minutes. Heat half the oil and fry the onion and garlic until golden. Add the meat and tomato and cook for 10 minutes. Meanwhile rinse and drain the aubergines thoroughly and fry in the remaining oil in a separate pan until browned. Drain again. Add the oregano, parsley, nutmeg, seasoning and wine to the mince and simmer for about 25 minutes. Then stir 2–3 tablespoons Béchamel sauce into the meat mixture.

Layer the aubergines and mince alternately in a well-greased ovenproof dish, sprinkling each layer with cheese. Finish with an aubergine layer. Beat the eggs into the sauce and pour over the aubergines. Top with the remaining cheese and bake in a moderately hot oven (190°C, 375°F, Gas Mark 5) for 45 minutes, until golden. **Serves 6**

Roast Herbed Hand and Spring of Pork

1.5 kg/3$\frac{1}{2}$ lb hand and spring of pork
2 tablespoons oil
salt and pepper
2 tablespoons fresh breadcrumbs
2 tablespoons chopped parsley
2 teaspoons dried mixed herbs

Rub the meat all over with the oil and season. Roast the meat in a moderately hot oven (200°C, 400°F, Gas Mark 6) for 1 hour. Sprinkle the surface with the breadcrumbs, parsley and herbs. Return to the oven for 1 hour. The top crust should be crisp and the meat tender when tested. If it needs further cooking, cover with foil and reduce the oven heat to moderate (180°C, 350°F, Gas Mark 4) until the meat is tender. **Serves 6**

Pork in Milk

1.5 kg/3 lb boned and rolled blade of pork
1 tablespoon oil
salt and pepper
1 clove garlic, sliced
2 onions, chopped
2 slices ham or bacon, cut in strips
750 ml/1¼ pints milk

Rub the joint all over with a little oil and seasoning. Then make small incisions in the skin and stud with tiny slivers of garlic. Heat a little fat cut from the joint in a heavy-based casserole dish, and brown the joint quickly all over until golden. Remove the meat then fry the onion and ham. When golden return the joint to the pan. Bring the milk to the boil and pour over the meat.

Cover the joint and cook in a moderate oven (160°C, 325°F, Gas Mark 3) for about 2½ hours. Thicken the sauce by brisk boiling and reducing, or else add vegetables to cook through in the liquor just before serving. **Serves 6**

Bacon and Beer with Mustard Dumplings

1 bacon hock
300 ml/½ pint stock
300 ml/½ pint pale ale
1 small cabbage, quartered
6 small onions
dumplings:
225 g/8 oz self-raising flour
salt and pepper
3 teaspoons dry mustard

Soak the joint in water for 3–4 hours, or overnight if necessary. Drain. Place in a large saucepan and add the stock and pale ale with enough water to cover. Bring to the boil, cover and simmer for 1½ hours, adding extra liquid if necessary during the cooking time. To make the dumplings, mix the flour, seasoning and mustard with enough water to bind. Form into small balls and add to the cooking liquid with the cabbage and onions. Cook for 15 minutes, or until the dumplings have doubled in size. **Serves 4–6**

Glazed Roast Bacon with Peaches

1 large knuckle of bacon or gammon
few black peppercorns, crushed
1 tablespoon ground cinnamon
3 tablespoons soft brown sugar
1 tablespoon golden syrup
2–3 tablespoons chutney
few sprigs rosemary
1 (425-g/15-oz) can peach halves

Soak the joint in plenty of water for several hours or overnight. Drain and place in a large pan with fresh water to cover. Add the peppercorns and cinnamon. Bring to the boil and simmer until cooked, allowing 20 minutes per 0.5 kg/1 lb and 20 minutes over. Drain and cool slightly then cut away the skin with a sharp knife. Score the fat neatly. Mix together the sugar, syrup and chutney and rub over the joint. Roast with the rosemary and drained peaches in a moderately hot oven (200°C, 400°F, Gas Mark 6) for 20 minutes to crisp up the outside. Arrange on a heated serving dish surrounded by the peaches. Serve any juices separately. **Serves 6–8**

Pork Korma

(Illustrated on page 165)

50 g/2 oz butter
2 teaspoons ground ginger
1 clove garlic, crushed
2 medium onions, chopped
½ teaspoon chilli seasoning
2 tablespoons ground coriander
3 pork fillets (about 575 g/1¼ lb)
1 teaspoon salt
300 ml/½ pint natural yogurt
50 g/2 oz ground almonds
150 ml/¼ pint double cream
150 ml/¼ pint milk
½ teaspoon ground cinnamon
½ teaspoon ground cardamom
¼ teaspoon ground mace
1 teaspoon ground turmeric
1 tablespoon oil
100 g/4 oz mushrooms, halved
basil or mint leaves to garnish

Melt the butter in a large frying pan and add the ginger, garlic and onions. Cook for 1–2 minutes, then stir in the chilli and coriander. Trim the pork fillets of most of their stringy coating and then cut into thin slices at a sharp angle. Add to the pan and fry quickly until golden. Remove and keep hot.

Stir in the salt and a little of the yogurt. Stir and cook gently until the yogurt evaporates. Continue cooking, gradually adding the remaining yogurt, until there is very little liquid left in the pan. Remove from the heat and stir in the remaining ingredients. Bring to the boil and simmer for 5–10 minutes. Meanwhile, heat the oil and fry the mushrooms lightly. Serve the sauce with the pork fillet and mushrooms. Garnish with basil or mint leaves and serve on a bed of boiled rice. **Serves 4**

Stir-fried Chinese Leaves and Pork

1 pork fillet or 225 g/8 oz lean bacon or ham
2 tablespoons oil
1 small onion, coarsely chopped
1 clove garlic, crushed
½ small cauliflower, cut in florets
2 carrots, cut in matchsticks
½ bunch spring onions, cut into 2.5-cm/1-inch lengths
½ head Chinese leaves, cut into 2.5-cm/1-inch strips
1 teaspoon ground ginger
1 (198-g/10½-oz) can bamboo shoots, drained and sliced
4 tablespoons dry sherry
2 tablespoons brown sugar
1 teaspoon soy sauce
4 tablespoons chicken stock

Flatten the fillet, bacon or ham and cut into narrow strips. Heat the oil in a frying pan and fry the meat quickly to seal and brown. Remove with draining spoon and set aside. Put the onion, garlic, cauliflower and carrot in the pan, cover with a lid or foil and cook gently, shaking from time to time to prevent sticking, for 5 minutes. Stir in the remaining ingredients and the pork, cover and cook for a further 5 minutes. Serve with boiled rice. **Serves 4**

Swiss Roast Pork Loin

1 loin of pork, boned and rolled but not scored
salt
oil for brushing
10 small slices smoked ham
10 small thin slices of Emmenthal or Gruyère cheese

If the joint is tied, ensure that the string is evenly spaced. Make eight or ten slits in the rind, but not into the meat. Rub all over with salt and brush with oil. Wrap in foil and roast in a moderate oven (180°C, 350°F, Gas Mark 4) for 2 hours. Increase the oven to hot (220°C, 425°F, Gas Mark 7) for the last 30 minutes and turn back the foil to brown the outside. About 10 minutes before serving, make deeper cuts into the meat and insert the ham and cheese. Return to the oven to melt the cheese then serve immediately. **Serves 8–10**

Pork with Piquant Mushroom Sauce

6 loin pork chops
2–4 tablespoons oil or lard
225 g/8 oz button mushrooms
150 ml/¼ pint tomato juice
2 teaspoons cornflour
150 ml/¼ pint natural yogurt
few drops Worcestershire sauce
pinch cayenne pepper
wedges of lemon to garnish

Snip the outer fat of the chops to prevent curling. Heat the oil and fry the chops gently for 15–20 minutes on each side. Remove to a heated ovenproof dish or plate and keep hot. Fry the mushrooms in the remaining fat. Mix the tomato juice with the cornflour and stir into the pan with the yogurt, Worcestershire sauce and cayenne. Bring to the boil and simmer gently for 5 minutes. Pour over the chops and garnish with lemon wedges. **Serves 6**

Pork and Bean Bourguignon

2 large onions, sliced
450 g/1 lb pork chops, American spareribs or
shoulder
300 ml/½ pint red wine
150 ml/¼ pint oil
salt and pepper
1 sprig parsley
300 ml/½ pint beef or chicken stock
225 g/8 oz red kidney beans, soaked
2 apples, cored and sliced
100 g/4 oz button mushrooms
2 teaspoons cornflour
2 tablespoons water

Place the onions, pork (cut into pieces if necessary), wine, oil, seasoning, parsley, stock and beans in a large shallow dish. Cover and leave overnight to marinate. Then place in a flameproof dish, cover with a lid or foil and cook in a moderately hot oven (180°C, 350°F, Gas Mark 4) for about 45 minutes. Stir occasionally and make sure there is sufficient liquid – if necessary, add up to 300 ml/½ pint water.

When the meat and beans are tender, add the apple and mushrooms. Mix the cornflour with the water, stir into the casserole and cook over a gentle heat until thickened and smooth. Boil for 2–3 minutes until the mushrooms and apples are just tender. **Serves 4**

Devilled Bones

900 ml/2 lb spareribs
sauce:
50 g/2 oz butter
1 tablespoon plain flour
1 teaspoon dry mustard
300 ml/½ pint gravy or stock
1 teaspoon French mustard
1 tablespoon chutney
1 tablespoon Worcestershire sauce

Mix the sauce ingredients together and spread over the spareribs. Grill or roast in a moderately hot oven (200°C, 400°F, Gas Mark 6) until crisp and tender. **Serves 4**

Sweet and Sour Spareribs

2 tablespoons soy sauce
2 tablespoons oil
2 teaspoons sherry
juice of 1 lemon
salt and pepper
1 teaspoon dried mixed herbs
675 g/1½ lb pork spareribs
25 g/1 oz butter
1 green pepper, seeds removed and chopped
2 onions, sliced
100 g/4 oz button mushrooms, chopped
1 (425-g/15-oz) can sliced peaches
2 teaspoons cornflour
toasted nuts (optional)

Mix together the soy sauce, 1 tablespoon of the oil, the sherry, lemon juice, seasoning and herbs for the marinade. Put the spareribs into a shallow dish with the marinade. Cover and chill for 1–2 hours. Remove the spareribs from the marinade and place in roasting tin. Brush with a little oil. Cook in a hot oven (220°C, 425°F, Gas Mark 7) for 35–40 minutes. Meanwhile heat the butter and remaining oil and fry the pepper and onion for 5 minutes. Add the mushrooms and cook for a further 5 minutes. Drain the juice from the peaches. Measure off 300 ml/½ pint of the juice and mix with the marinade. Mix a little of this with the cornflour then stir in all the marinade. Add to the fried vegetable mixture and bring to the boil, stirring, until thickened. Add the sliced peaches and heat through. Arrange the spareribs on a heated serving dish. Spoon the sauce over the top and sprinkle with the nuts if used. **Serves 6**

Pork and Prune Hotpot

675 g/1½ lb boned blade of pork
seasoned flour
3 tablespoons oil
2 onions, sliced
600 ml/1 pint stock
2 tablespoons redcurrant jelly
100 g/4 oz prunes, soaked

Cut the meat into cubes and coat in seasoned flour. Heat the oil and fry the onions for 3 minutes. Add the meat and cook until brown all over. Stir in the stock and jelly and heat to thicken. Turn into a casserole and add the prunes. Cook in a moderate oven (160°C, 325°F, Gas Mark 3) for 1¾ hours. Serve with boiled potatoes. **Serves 4–6**

Bacon and Parsley Mould

25 g/1 oz parsley, chopped
8 teaspoons aspic powder or 5 teaspoons powdered gelatine made up to 900 ml/1½ pints
350 g/12 oz bacon, coarsely minced
garnish:
few slices cucumber
little mustard and cress

Add the parsley to 150 ml/¼ pint of the aspic. Coat the base of a 15-cm/6-inch square mould with 2–3 tablespoons clear jelly, and the sides with the parsley jelly, resting each coated side on a bed of ice until firm before coating the next side. Add the bacon to the remaining aspic jelly and pour into the prepared mould. Leave to set in a cool place. To turn out, loosen the sides and, if necessary, dip the mould into hot water for a few seconds. Turn out on to a plate and garnish with cucumber and cress before serving. **Serves 4–6**

Tripe with Bacon

450 g/1 lb dressed tripe
600 ml/1 pint milk
2 onions, sliced
2 tablespoons chopped parsley
grated rind of ½ lemon
salt and pepper
100 g/4 oz bacon rashers
15 g/½ oz butter
25 g/1 oz flour
extra milk or water if necessary

Wash the tripe well. Put into cold water and bring to the boil. Drain and cut into small pieces. Return the tripe to the saucepan with the milk and simmer for 1 hour. Then add the onion, half the parsley, the lemon rind and seasoning. Cook for a further 30 minutes. Drain the tripe, reserving the cooking liquid and keep warm. Remove the rind from the bacon and fry the rashers until crisp. Add the bacon to the tripe. Add the butter to the pan which was used for the bacon, stir in the flour, then the cooking liquid and bring to the boil, whisking. Add extra liquid if necessary, stir in the onions and adjust the seasoning. Pour the thickened sauce over the tripe and bacon, sprinkle with the remaining parsley and serve. **Serves 4**

Kidneys in Cream

450 g/1 lb lambs' kidneys
25 g/1 oz butter
2 teaspoons oil
1 onion, finely chopped
150 ml/¼ pint double cream
1–2 teaspoons French mustard
2 teaspoons tomato purée
salt and pepper

Skin, core and halve the kidneys. Heat the butter and oil in a frying pan and fry the onion gently until softened. Add the kidneys and continue cooking, stirring occasionally, for about 5 minutes. Stir in the cream, mustard, tomato purée and seasoning. Simmer until the kidneys are tender and the sauce thickened, about 5–10 minutes. **Serves 4**

Liver Espagnole

4 large thin slices lamb's liver
50 g/2 oz fat
4 large tomatoes, peeled and sliced
2 onions, finely chopped
100 g/4 oz mushrooms, sliced
salt and pepper
little paprika
25 g/1 oz flour
450 ml/¾ pint brown stock
1 tablespoon sherry
1 tablespoon chopped parsley

Wash the liver and dry on absorbent kitchen paper. Heat half the fat in a frying pan and fry the tomato, onion and mushrooms until soft. Season lightly. Spread half the vegetables over the liver slices. Roll and secure each slice of liver with a wooden cocktail stick, or tie with fine string. Coat with the paprika and flour. Heat the remaining fat in a frying pan and cook the rolls for 2–3 minutes, turning several times. Add the stock, the remaining cooked vegetables, sherry and parsley. Cook in the open pan for 10 minutes, turning once or twice until just cooked through. Serve with boiled rice or noodles. **Serves 4**

Old English Faggots

225 g/8 oz pig's liver, chopped or minced
225 g/8 oz minced beef
2 onions, chopped
100 g/4 oz fresh breadcrumbs
1 egg
1 teaspoon dried sage
2 teaspoons dried mixed herbs
salt and pepper

Mix all the ingredients together until well combined. Divide into about 12 balls and shape neatly. The traditional way of cooking them is to wrap each tightly in muslin and then cook in boiling, seasoned water for about 10 minutes until cooked through. As the muslin part is time-consuming, you could place in the fridge for 2–3 hours to chill before frying gently. If you prefer, they can be cooked in the oven. Pack the faggots tightly in a roasting tin and dot with a little lard or fat. Bake in a moderate oven (180°C, 350°F, Gas Mark 4) for 45 minutes. Make a well-flavoured gravy with the juices from the roasting tin or with the cooking water. Serve hot or cold. **Serves 4**

Brawn

1 pig's head, split (by the butcher)
salt and pepper
2 pig's trotters
6 peppercorns
2 bay leaves
1 blade mace
3 cloves
1 bouquet garni
shells and whites of 3 eggs

Remove the brains and any chips of bone, then brush the teeth and nostrils well with salt, to clean. Rinse, then soak for 3–5 hours in brine (50 g/2 oz salt to each 600 ml/1 pint water). Rinse again, wash the trotters and put the head and trotters in a large saucepan. Tie the peppercorns, bay leaf, mace and cloves in muslin and add to the pan with the bouquet garni. Cover with water and season well. Simmer for 4 hours; remove the head and trotters and allow to cool. Remove the tongue and slice; remove all the other meat and dice. Return the bones to the stock and simmer for 1 hour. Strain the stock and reduce to 600 ml/1 pint by brisk boiling. Add the crushed egg shells and whites. Whisk well and bring almost to the boil. Remove from the heat just before it reaches boiling point and allow the foam to subside. Repeat this boiling and subsiding twice more. Then strain the foam and stock through absorbent kitchen paper or muslin. Put the chopped meat into a damp 1.25-litre/2-pint mould, cover with the strained stock and chill to set. Turn out on to a serving dish and slice. **Makes 1.5 kg/3 lb**

Marrow Toasts

1 large marrow bone
salt
4 slices hot buttered toast

Ask your butcher to cut the bone into 5-cm/2-inch pieces. Simmer these in salted water for 15–20 minutes until the marrow is clear and soft. Serve hot – scoop out the marrow from the bones and spread it on the buttered toast. **Serves 4**

Oxtail Stew

(Illustrated on page 48)

50 g/2 oz fat
1 large onion, sliced
1 oxtail, cut in pieces
5 tablespoons flour
1.15 litres/2 pints stock or stock and red wine, mixed
225 g/8 oz button onions
4 sticks celery, sliced
225 g/8 oz carrots, sliced
1 bouquet garni
salt and pepper
1 teaspoon lemon juice

Heat the fat in a large pan and fry the onion. Remove the onion from pan, then brown the oxtail in the same fat. Return the onion to the pan and stir in the flour. Cook very slowly, stirring, until brown. Remove from the heat and gradually stir in the stock. Bring to the boil then add the onions, celery, carrot, bouquet garni and seasoning. Simmer gently, covered, for about 3 hours, or until the meat falls away from the bones easily. Leave to stand for several hours until the fat rises to the surface. Skim off the fat. When ready to serve, add the lemon juice and reheat. **Serves 4**

Nottinghamshire Haslet

450 g/1 lb belly of pork
900 g/2 lb pig's liver
1 pig's heart
1 teaspoon salt
2 teaspoons pepper
1 teaspoon dried sage or 1 tablespoon chopped sage
6 tablespoons water
1 egg
100 g/4 oz fresh breadcrumbs
veil from pig's stomach (order from your butcher) for cooking in

Finely mince the pork, liver and heart together. Then mix in all the remaining ingredients except the veil until the mixture is fairly stiff. If you cannot get hold of a veil you could use foil or put the mixture into a mould. Pack the mixture in the veil, tucking under the loose ends and shaping it neatly. Place on a baking tray and cook in a moderately hot oven (190°C, 375°F, Gas Mark 5) for 20–30 minutes until brown and succulent. Leave on the tray to cool for a while and to let it reabsorb some of the liquid which helps to keep it moist. Haslet provides excellent dripping. It should be quite peppery and not too bread-like. It is traditionally served cold. **Serves 6**

Poultry and Game

Chicken has become a regular weekly meal for many of us and turkey is no longer just a Christmas treat. Now that they are mass-produced and frozen there is always a constant and economical supply. But this is slowly beginning to happen with game too. Some game birds and venison are farmed for gaming purposes and are frequently frozen and rabbit is imported frozen in vast quantities. Soon, regardless of the seasons, specialist shops will often have supplies of game available for us all to taste.

If you think the characteristic flavour of game is not for you, try guinea fowl or rabbit which have the mildest of flavours. If you appreciate the flavour of game, but do not like game too high, you don't have to wait three weeks for pheasant and grouse to 'hang' – eat them fresher so you can really enjoy them.

Poultry

Chicken is sold under different names according to age and most are now available frozen.

Poussins are the very youngest (7–12 weeks) weighing 450–900 g/1–2 lb each. They are best roasted or cut in half and grilled and will serve one or two people.

Roasting chickens usually weigh from 1.5 kg/3 lb upwards though some 1.25-kg/2½-lb chickens are available. These can be roasted whole, or may be portioned and grilled, fried or quickly casseroled.

Capons are very large male birds specially fattened up, weighing 3.25–5.5 kg/7–12 lb. They are very good value for money, having a larger amount of meat on the carcass than large chickens or small turkeys.

Boiling fowl are the much older birds used for breeding. They usually sell at premium prices, although unfortunately they are less and less available nowadays. Because of their age they have a very good flavour, but can be tough, hence they are ideal for boiling, stewing and braising and for soups.

Turkeys range in size from 3.25 kg/7 lb to 9 kg/20 lb. Regardless of size they are all good for roasting; grilling or frying in portions, or casseroling.

Buying Poultry

When buying fresh poultry be sure the bird has no strong smell whatsoever. Choose a bird with a plump breast for best meat value. The wings and breastbone should be pliable and the feet soft and slightly moist if the bird is really fresh. Hen turkeys are usually more tender and plump. Keep fresh poultry for no more than 2 days, and cook the giblets immediately.

Frozen poultry can be bought in almost any convenient form to suit your needs, freezer or pocket, from bulk packs of your favourite portion to small packs of giblets or just livers. Buying four individual portions for a meal for four is the most extravagant purchase though – for you could buy one small chicken and portion it yourself.

Never cook chicken from frozen. It must always be completely thawed out first to make sure it cooks right through to the centre. Leave it covered and on a tray to catch the drips in a cool place or in the refrigerator. Allow 8–10 hours for an average chicken at room temperature, and up to 24 hours in the refrigerator. Allow 2 hours for small portions at room temperature or 4–5 hours in the refrigerator. Allow 24 hours for a 4.5–5.5 kg/10–12 lb turkey at room temperature or 48 hours in the refrigerator.

To speed up the process, remove the giblets and any ice crystals as soon as possible, and if necessary, cut into portions when manageable.

Potato fry-up (see page 111); Potato and vegetable hot pot (see page 111); Mashed potato (see page 109); Nut potatoes (see page 110); Piquant potato scones (see page 112); Fried potatoes (see page 109); Colcannon (see page 100); Filled baked potatoes (see page 111) and Pommes Anna (see page 110)

Roasting Poultry

Never over-cook poultry or it will become dry and tasteless. You may prefer even to wrap it in foil, or cook it in a covered roaster or cooking brick to keep the moisture in. For plain roasting, season inside and out first, and for extra flavour, put half an onion or lemon or a bunch of herbs inside.

Poultry can be fast or slow roasted.

Roasting Times		
	Oven Temperature	Timing
Chicken up to 1.25 kg/ 2½ lb	*Fast roast* 220°C, 425°F, Gas Mark 7	15 minutes per 0.5 kg/1 lb + 15 minutes over
Chicken up to 2 kg/ 4½ lb	*Fast roast* 220°C, 425°F, Gas Mark 7	15 minutes per 0.5 kg/1 lb + 15 minutes over
	Slow roast 190°C, 375°F, Gas Mark 5	20 minutes per 0.5 kg/1 lb + 20 minutes over
Turkey up to 5.5 kg/ 12 lb	*Fast roast* 230°C, 450°F, Gas Mark 8	18 minutes per 0.5 kg/1 lb + 20 minutes over
	Slow roast 160°C, 325°F, Gas Mark 3	25 minutes per 0.5 kg/1 lb + 25 minutes over
up to 9 kg/ 20 lb	*Fast roast* 220°C, 425°F, Gas Mark 7	12 minutes per 0.5 kg/1 lb + 15 minutes over
	Slow roast 160°C, 325°F, Gas Mark 3	18 minutes per 0.5 kg/1 lb + 18 minutes over

NOTE If the bird is stuffed, allow extra time, according to the weight inclusive of the stuffing.

Sweet spinach salad (see page 113); Fruity fennel salad (see page 104); Cucumber salad (see page 103); Potato and mussel salad (see page 112); Creamed beetroot salad (see page 99); Garlic swede salad (see page 113); Sprouts Provençale (see page 100); Cabbage salad (see page 100); Sweet red cabbage salad (see page 101); Nutty root vegetables (see page 108) and Chinese green salad (see page 101)

To Truss a Chicken

Before roasting or boiling, and after stuffing the bird it is advisable to tie it into a good shape. (If you intend to wrap it tightly in foil there is no need to do this.) With a piece of string about 45 cm/18 inches long, draw the legs together, the string high up on the breast but under the parson's nose. Cross the loose ends of string underneath the bird, wrap them around the wing tips so the bird is sitting on its wings, and tie the string underneath.

To Joint a Chicken

With a small sharp knife, cut around the top of the leg bone, where it joins the body. Pull it away from the main carcass until you can cut through the tendons at the joint. This can be cut again into two portions, the drumstick and the thigh. Starting from the top of the breast, carefully scrape away the breast from the rib cage until you reach the wingbone. Again twist the bone from the carcass until you can cut through the tendons. Cut this portion into two if you wish, to give the breast fillet and the wing.

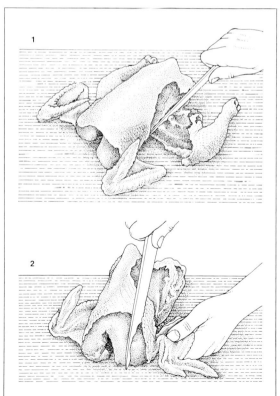

Boning a Chicken

It won't take long to transform your plump fresh chicken into a succulent boned roast for cold- or hot-weather entertaining. And if you pack it with a delicious stuffing (see opposite for recipes), as well as serving twice as many people as usual, there will be no waste and no carving problems.

Have all your equipment around you before you start – a small, very sharp knife or a boning knife; a board; a clean cloth; the prepared filling; a trussing needle and string; and foil for cooking the chicken.

You can do the same with a turkey but it will take longer. If you ask your butcher in good time he may well do it for you.

I. Wash and dry the chicken. Lay it upside down (on the pointed breast bone) on a board, with the drumsticks away from you. Slit the skin straight down the middle of the back. Keeping the knife as near to the carcass as possible, scrape away all the skin and flesh but be careful not to pierce the skin. Continue until one side comes free and is joined only by the leg and wing bones. Cut through the sinews at the joints to release the bones. Don't forget the juicy 'oyster' pieces of flesh. These and any other bits of meat can be packed into the corners later.

2. Beginning at the body-end of the leg bone, scrape the flesh down the bone to the foot-end, turning the flesh inside out as you go. Release all the sinews at the middle joint so you can twist and pull out the two bones.

3. Leave the wing bones attached by the skin but with the bones released. They have too little flesh on them to bone but they do help to give a good shape to the cooked chicken.

4. With one side completely released, repeat the process for the other side. You will then be left with the carcass, attached to the flesh by only a thin layer of skin along the top of the breast bone. Make sure you cut this very carefully so you do not pierce the skin.

5. Lay the bird out flat on the board. Mix together all the filling ingredients and season well. Spread the filling evenly over the chicken, pushing it into the legs as well. Starting with the legs, sew the skin together in neat, overlapping stitches until the centre is sewn up. Thin string or strong cotton will do. Then pull over the neck end flap and sew down to give a completely sealed parcel.

6. Turn the chicken over and gently mould it back into its original shape. Tuck the wings under for support and secure the legs in place with skewers. Sprinkle with extra seasoning. Wrap very tightly in foil to keep it in shape and cook in a moderately hot oven (190°C, 375°F, Gas Mark 5) for 1½–2 hours. At this stage you could undo the foil to brown off the top if you wish. Make the juices into gravy in the normal way and serve hot.

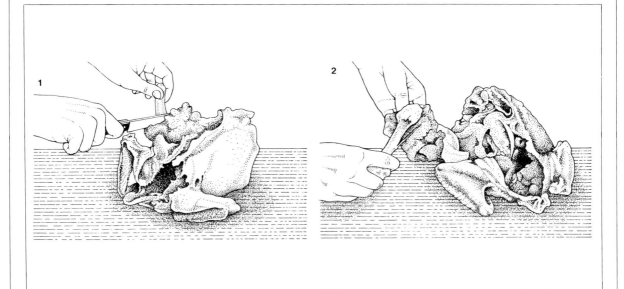

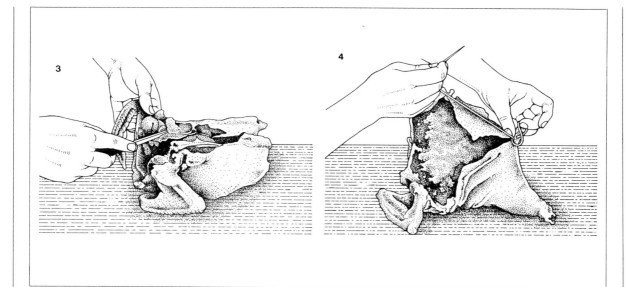

Stuffings

All poultry and game can be stuffed, whether they are boned or not, and it does help to keep them moist.

Use the following quantities to stuff a 1.5-kg/3-lb boned chicken or a 1.75-kg/4-lb chicken on the bone:

Orange, Rice and Walnut Stuffing Mix together 350 g/12 oz cooked long-grain rice; 4 oranges, peeled and chopped; 100 g/4 oz dates, chopped; 50 g/2 oz walnuts, chopped; and seasoning to taste.

Pâté and Herb Stuffing Mix together 225 g/8 oz minced pork; 2 small onions, grated or minced; 100 g/4 oz chicken or lamb's liver, finely chopped; salt and freshly ground black pepper; the rind and juice of 1 small lemon and 1 tablespoon each of chopped parsley, tarragon and thyme.

Bacon and Apricot Stuffing Mix 225 g/8 oz bacon, chopped with 225 g/8 oz sausagemeat, 1 teaspoon dried tarragon, 1 small onion, chopped, 1 (396-g/14-oz) can apricots, drained and chopped; 50 g/2 oz chopped blanched almonds and seasoning.

Chestnut Stuffing This quantity will fill a medium turkey. Pierce the skin of 900 g/2 lb chestnuts (this prevents them exploding when they cook) and cook in boiling water for 10–15 minutes. Drain and peel off the shells – if you have time, leave the chestnuts in a warm oven to crisp up the skins before you peel them, as this is much easier. Mash the chestnuts and mix in the chopped turkey liver, 2 rashers bacon, chopped; 50 g/2 oz butter and seasoning.

Sage and Onion (Ideal for goose, as well as chicken, turkey or duck). This quantity is sufficient for one goose or two ducks. Simmer 4 medium onions, chopped, in 300 ml/$\frac{1}{2}$ pint chicken stock until tender, adding the giblets or liver if you have them. Then remove the giblets and mix in 2 teaspoons chopped dried sage or 1 tablespoon chopped fresh sage, 100 g/4 oz fresh white breadcrumbs, 25 g/1 oz butter and seasoning. Beat in a little egg to bind and mix thoroughly.

Crispy Herb Chicken

(Illustrated on the jacket)

1 (1.5-kg/3-lb) chicken
salt and pepper
1 large onion, halved
100 g/4 oz butter, softened
3 tablespoons chopped mixed herbs – parsley,
thyme, tarragon, sage (or 1 tablespoon dried
mixed herbs)
1 tablespoon lemon juice

Wash and dry the chicken. Sprinkle the inside with seasoning. Put the onion inside the chicken (use it later for the sauce, or add it to the vegetables). Beat the butter until creamy then mix in the herbs, lemon juice and a little seasoning. Spread three-quarters of the butter over the outside of the chicken and the rest inside. Cover with foil and roast in a hot oven (220°C, 425°F, Gas Mark 7) for about 50 minutes. Remove the foil, baste and continue to cook for 5–10 minutes until golden. Transfer the chicken to a heated serving plate and boil the juices to reduce as much as possible. Thicken if you wish or just pour over the chicken when serving each portion. **Serves 6**

Celebration Roast

1.6-kg/3½-lb roasting chicken
salt and pepper
stuffing:
2 tablespoons oil
2 sticks celery, chopped
1 small onion, chopped
100 g/4 oz frozen sweetcorn, thawed
50 g/2 oz walnuts, chopped
100 g/4 oz pâté
25 g/1 oz fresh white breadcrumbs
salt and pepper
garnish:
apricots
cherries
sauce:
1 tablespoon brandy
200 ml/7 fl oz double cream

Sprinkle the chicken with seasoning. Heat the oil in a frying pan and fry the celery and onion lightly to soften. Drain and mix with the remaining stuffing ingredients and use to stuff the chicken. Truss and cook in a moderately hot oven (190°C, 375°F, Gas Mark 5) for about 1½ hours. Transfer the chicken to a heated serving platter and surround with the fruit. Drain off all the fat from the juices in the roasting tin. Add the brandy and cream to the juices and transfer to the top of the cooker. Boil briskly, stirring, until it reaches a coating consistency. Serve with the garnished chicken. **Serves 5–6**

Chicken Fricassee

Use a boiling fowl in this recipe for a delicious and inexpensive white stew.

1.75-kg/4-lb boiling fowl, jointed
2 onions, chopped
225 g/8 oz carrots, chopped
salt and pepper
1 teaspoon dried tarragon
50 g/2 oz butter
50 g/2 oz flour
150 ml/¼ pint milk

Put the chicken joints in a saucepan with the onion, carrot and sufficient cold water to cover. Add the seasoning and tarragon and bring to the boil. Simmer, covered, for 1½ hours or until the chicken is tender. Remove the chicken and strain the stock. Reserve the vegetables and measure 600 ml/1 pint of the stock. Pull the chicken meat from the bones and cut into pieces. Melt the butter in a large saucepan, stir in the flour and cook, stirring, for 1–2 minutes. Remove from the heat and gradually stir in the measured stock and the milk and bring to the boil. Simmer for 2–3 minutes, stirring. Add the chicken and vegetables and heat through for a few minutes before serving. **Serves 4–5**

Chicken Pepperata

1 (2.25-kg/5-lb) chicken, capon or ½ turkey
2–3 tablespoons oil
3 large onions, sliced
3 large green peppers, seeds removed and sliced
1 head celery, chopped
450 g/1 lb courgettes
1 (425-g/15-oz) can tomatoes
salt and pepper
2 tablespoons paprika
1 tablespoon Worcestershire sauce
3 tablespoons red wine
1 tablespoon cornflour (optional)

Divide the chicken into eight portions. Wash and dry the joints. Heat the oil in a large frying pan and fry the joints until golden. Transfer to a flameproof casserole. Fry the onion, pepper and celery in the oil left in the pan. Slice the courgettes and add to the pan for about 1 minute. Then stir in the tomatoes, seasoning and paprika. Mix well and add to the casserole with the chicken. Stir in the Worcestershire sauce and wine and cover. Bake in a moderately hot oven (190°C, 375°F, Gas Mark 5) for about 1¼ hours, until the chicken is tender. Transfer the chicken and vegetables to a large serving dish. Mix the cornflour with a little of the liquid and stir it into the casserole. Cook over a gentle heat, stirring until smooth. Pour over the chicken and mix well. **Serves 8**

Tandoori Chicken

Although the secret of a true Tandoori dish is the clay Tandoori oven in which the food is cooked, you can still get very good results at home in the oven, under the grill or over a barbecue. For speed and convenience you can now buy ready-mixed Tandoori seasoning. Replace 4–5 teaspoons of this mixture for all the spices and colouring given below.

1 medium onion, finely chopped
1–2 cloves garlic, crushed
1 teaspoon ground coriander
1 teaspoon ground cumin
½ teaspoon ground ginger
¼ teaspoon chilli powder
½ teaspoon ground fenugreek
1 teaspoon ground mixed spice
1 teaspoon paprika
150 ml/¼ pint natural yogurt
few drops red food colouring
1.5-kg/3-lb roasting chicken
2 lemons
1½ teaspoons salt
40–50 g/1½–2 oz butter, melted

Mix the onion, garlic, all seven spices and yogurt together. Add the colouring (this Tandoori marinade should be bright red before being cooked). Wipe and trim the chicken. Cut off and discard the wing tips. Gently pull off and discard the skin. Make three or four 1-cm/½-inch deep cuts into the breast and legs. Then joint the chicken and sprinkle with the juice of one lemon and salt – this helps the marinade to penetrate and tenderise the flesh. Coat the joints thoroughly with the marinade and leave for up to 24 hours in the refrigerator or in a cool place.

To cook, put the joints on a wire rack over a roasting tin. Cook in a moderate oven, (160°C, 325°F, Gas Mark 3) for 35–40 minutes or until tender. Once or twice during cooking brush the joints with the melted butter to keep them moist. Cut the remaining lemon in wedges. Serve hot with the lemon wedges. Rice is a good accompaniment. **Serves 4**

Chicken Kiev

4 chicken breast portions, with wing bone still
attached
100 g/4 oz butter, softened
2 tablespoons chopped parsley
1–2 cloves garlic, crushed
salt and pepper
½ lemon
1 egg, beaten
100 g/4 oz fresh white breadcrumbs
oil for deep-frying

Discard the wing tips and gently pull the skin from the chicken portions. Place the flesh between sheets of wetted greaseproof paper and flatten out until really thin by beating with a rolling pin or meat mallet. Mix the butter, parsley, garlic and seasoning together. Form into a long sausage, wrap in greaseproof paper and chill. When firm, cut into four and place the pieces lengthwise on each breast. Squeeze a little lemon juice on top of each. Fold the edges of the flesh tightly over the butter. Then coat very thoroughly with beaten egg and bread-crumbs. Chill for at least 1 hour to set into shape. Heat the oil to 190°C/375°F or until a cube of bread turns golden in 1 minute. Deep-fry the chicken, one or two pieces at a time, in the oil for 7–8 minutes. When crisp and golden, drain on absorbent paper and serve immediately. Put cutlet frills on the tiny wing bones for easy eating if you wish. **Serves 4**

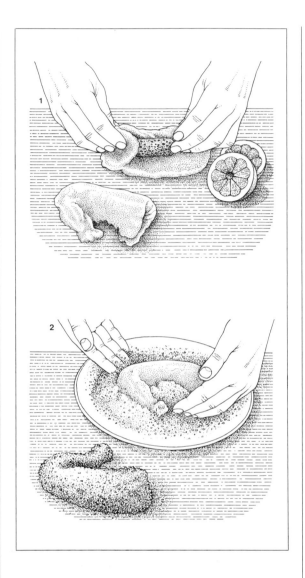

Barbecue Drumsticks

2 tablespoons soy sauce
2 tablespoons sugar
2 tablespoons dry sherry
2 tablespoons chopped spring onion
1 clove garlic, crushed
¼ teaspoon ground ginger
4 chicken or 2 turkey drumsticks

Thoroughly mix together all the ingredients except the chicken and coat the drumsticks thoroughly in this. Grill, turning occasionally and basting with the liquid until cooked through. The chicken will take 15–20 minutes. If you prefer, roast the joints in a moderately hot oven (190°C, 375°F, Gas Mark 5) for 30–40 minutes, basting frequently. Carve the turkey joints into two portions before serving. **Serves 4**

Escalopes in Marsala

The breast of chicken or turkey is exceptionally good for quick cooking, and makes an economical replacement for expensive veal escalopes.

4 small chicken breasts or pieces turkey breast
2 eggs, beaten
100–175 g/4–6 oz crisp breadcrumbs
3–4 tablespoons oil
sauce:
25 g/1 oz butter
25 g/1 oz flour
4 tablespoons Marsala (or a sweet white wine)
450 ml/$\frac{3}{4}$ pint stock
salt and pepper

Flatten the chicken breasts between sheets of wetted greaseproof paper using a rolling pin or meat mallet. Cut each breast in half. Dip each piece in egg then coat in breadcrumbs. Heat the oil in a frying pan and fry until cooked, about 3–5 minutes each side.

Melt the butter in a saucepan, stir in the flour then cook, stirring, for 1 minute. Gradually stir in the Marsala and stock. Season and bring to the boil, stirring gently. Serve with the escalopes. **Serves 4**

Tangy Chicken in a Spinach Case

This is the perfect entertaining dish for slimmers and the cholesterol-conscious.

450 g/1 lb spinach
675/1$\frac{1}{2}$ lb minced cooked chicken or turkey
salt and freshly ground black pepper
$\frac{1}{4}$ teaspoon grated nutmeg
2 tablespoons chopped chives or spring onion tops
100 g/4 oz cottage cheese
1 cucumber
3–4 tablespoons natural yogurt

Set aside about 12 large spinach leaves, then shred the rest and blanch them in boiling salted water for 1 minute. Drain well. Put the whole leaves into boiling water and take out immediately, just to soften them. Drain. Line an 18–20-cm/7–8-inch sandwich tin with the large leaves, with enough of each hanging over the edges to cover the top later. In a bowl, mix the chicken, shredded spinach, seasoning, nutmeg, chives and cheese; pack into the lined tin. Fold the spinach leaves over the top. Chill, with a weight on top for about 1 hour. Grate or liquidise the cucumber and mix with the yogurt and seasoning to taste. Chill. Turn out and serve with the sauce. **Serves 6–8**

Chicken Satay with Peanut Sauce

Satays (satee) are a typical starter or snack in countries like Malaysia, Indonesia or Thailand. Beef or lamb can be used instead, but all are usually served with this spicy peanut sauce.

2 large chicken breasts
3 tablespoons soy sauce
1 tablespoon treacle
1 tablespoon brown sugar
2 cloves garlic, crushed
2 tablespoons water
1 tablespoon lemon juice
grated carrot for serving
sauce:
2 tablespoons oil
1 medium onion, very finely chopped
100 g/4 oz peanuts, ground
2 cloves garlic, crushed
2 tablespoons coconut
300 ml/$\frac{1}{2}$ pint milk
1 tablespoon soy sauce
1 teaspoon brown sugar
salt and pepper
1 teaspoon ground ginger
1 teaspoon ground coriander

Cut the chicken into very small strips and thread on to 12 cocktail sticks or small metal skewers. (The true satay sticks are very, very thin, about 20–25 cm/8–10 inches long and are occasionally available from butchers or speciality shops.) Mix the soy sauce, treacle, sugar, garlic, water and lemon juice and marinate the chicken sticks in this for 3–6 hours.

To make the sauce, heat the oil and fry the onion until golden. Then stir in the peanuts and cook for 2–3 minutes, stirring. Add the remaining ingredients, mix well and leave to cook for about 5 minutes until the sauce thickens. Remove the chicken from the marinade and grill quickly for 2–3 minutes on each side until cooked. Serve on a bed of grated carrot with the hot peanut sauce. **Serves 4**

Chicken Parcels

225 g/8 oz chicken or turkey flesh
1 onion, chopped
4 tablespoons sage and onion
stuffing mix
1 clove garlic, crushed
225 g/8 oz sausagemeat
2 tablespoons tomato purée
salt and pepper
225 g/8 oz Shortcrust pastry (see page 136)
milk to glaze

Mince the chicken or turkey with the onion. Make up the stuffing according to the instructions on the packet and mix with the chicken, garlic, sausagemeat, tomato purée and seasoning. Roll out the pastry on a lightly floured surface and cut into eight rectangles measuring 15 × 10 cm/6 × 4 inches.

Divide the chicken mixture into eight and put a portion in the centre of each pastry rectangle. Moisten the edges with water and fold the pastry over the filling, sealing the edges well. Put on a baking tray and brush with milk to glaze. Bake in a moderately hot oven (200°C, 400°F, Gas Mark 6) for 15 minutes, then reduce to moderate (180°C, 350°F, Gas Mark 4) for 30–40 minutes. Serve hot or cold. **Serves 4**

Creamed Turkey Gratinée

100 g/4 oz left-over cooked turkey or chicken
100 g/4 oz cooked potato
2 spring onions, chopped
3 tablespoons top of the milk
salt and pepper
2 sticks celery, chopped
7.5-cm/3-inch piece cucumber, chopped
150 ml/¼ pint thin White wine sauce (see page 185)
50 g/2 oz fresh white breadcrumbs
50 g/2 oz cheese, grated

Mash the turkey, potato, onion, milk and seasoning together and spoon into an oven-proof dish. Mix the celery and cucumber with the white sauce and spoon over the chicken. Sprinkle with the breadcrumbs and cheese and cook in a moderate oven (180°C, 350°F, Gas Mark 4) for about 40 minutes. Brown the top quickly under the grill. **Serves 4**

Chinese Stir-fry

1 tablespoon soy sauce
2 tablespoons dry sherry
2 tablespoons orange marmalade
2 teaspoons cornflour
2.5-cm/1-inch piece root ginger, peeled and
grated
¼ teaspoon Tabasco sauce
175–225 g/6–8 oz raw chicken or turkey, diced
50 g/2 oz blanched almonds, fried
225 g/8 oz mange tout or young French beans
2 tablespoons oil
slices of orange to garnish

Mix together the soy sauce, sherry, marmalade, cornflour, ginger and Tabasco sauce, and mix with the chicken and nuts. Cook the mange tout or beans in boiling salted water until just tender. Drain and keep hot. Heat the oil and fry the chicken mixture, stirring rapidly until cooked and slightly thickened. Serve with the mange tout or beans and garnish with slices of orange. **Serves 2–3**

Giblets

The term giblet includes all the extras from a chicken or turkey – its liver, heart, gizzard, head, neck, pinions, feet and comb. However, in this country, only the liver, heart, gizzard and neck are usually sold with a trussed bird, and giblets bought separately do not normally include the neck. Many frozen birds are sold without giblets, so check before you buy.

You can make full use of almost every part of a chicken, for although there is little meat on some parts, they do add extra flavour to stocks or casseroles – do remember to take them out!

Chicken livers can be bought separately (normally frozen) in tubs. They are a very cheap and nutritious buy and make delicious pâtés and pastes as well as many other dishes. Duck

Right: Pasta alla carbonara (see page 120)

Cream cheese pâté (see page 225); Chillied fish stew
(see page 26); Rice and orange pudding (variation, see
page 164); Rice fritters (see page 121); Banana rice cake
(see page 160); Vegetable rice (see page 121) and Curried
onion soup (variation, see page 13)

and goose livers are highly prized for use in pâtés so are seldom sold in a prepared bird.

For use in recipes, one chicken will, on average, give 100 g/4 oz giblets. Always be sure they are well thawed and then well washed. If cleaning a bird yourself, discard the greenish-looking part as this is very bitter.

Chicken Liver Puddings

65 g/2½ oz plain flour
salt and pepper
1 egg
150 ml/¼ pint milk
225 g/8 oz chicken livers
2 tablespoons oil
1 small onion, chopped
300 ml/½ pint stock
1 tablespoon tomato purée
few drops Worcestershire sauce

Beat 50 g/2 oz of the flour with the seasoning, egg and milk to make a smooth batter. Stand for 30 minutes. Meanwhile grease well and heat about 12 tartlet or patty tins in a hot oven (220°C, 425°F, Gas Mark 7) for 5 minutes. Pour in the batter and cook for 7–8 minutes until puffed up and crisp. Wash and quarter the livers. Toss in remaining flour. Heat the oil in a saucepan and fry the onion until golden. Add the livers and fry until browned. Stir in the stock, mix well and simmer, stirring occasionally until thickened and the livers are cooked. Add the tomato purée and Worcestershire sauce – check the seasoning, then spoon into the hot patty cases. **Serves 6–8**

Giblet Dumplings

100 g/4 oz giblets
salt and pepper
50 g/2 oz margarine
50 g/2 oz flour
1 tablespoon chopped parsley
1 egg
2 slices bread

Meatball kebabs (variation, see page 63)

Clean the giblets and simmer in 1.15 litres/2 pints seasoned water until really soft. Cool slightly and then drain, reserving the liquid, and chop up all the meat very finely. Mix the giblets with the margarine, flour, parsley, seasoning and egg. Soak the bread in enough of the stock to become soft and then bind with the giblet mixture until pliable. Form into small balls and chill for 1 hour if possible. Add to a soup or casserole (the remaining stock can be used up here), and poach for about 10–15 minutes just before serving. **Serves 4**

Giblet Stew

350 g/12 oz giblets
3 tablespoons oil
100 g/4 oz streaky bacon, diced
2 large onions, chopped
4 carrots, sliced
4 sticks celery, chopped
25 g/1 oz flour
150 ml/¼ pint dry cider
150 ml/¼ pint stock
salt and pepper
1 bouquet garni

Wash and clean the giblets carefully and chop into 2.5-cm/1-inch cubes. Heat the oil and quickly toss the giblets to seal. Transfer to an ovenproof casserole. Fry the bacon, onion, carrot and celery in the oil left in the pan; stir in the flour and cook for 1 minute. Add the cider, stock, seasoning and bouquet garni and stir until smooth. Pour this sauce over the giblets and cook in a moderate oven (160°C, 325°F, Gas Mark 3) for 1½ hours. **Serves 4**

Duck

Duck can weigh up to 3.25 kg/7 lb but at this size it can be a bit tough. Those more often sold, especially frozen, are duckling up to 1.75 kg/4 lb in weight which will only just provide enough meat for four portions. Ducks are very fatty, so it is best to prick the skin in several places before roasting on a trivet or wire rack in the roasting tin. Wild duck is occasionally available from August to January.

Duck à l'Orange

1 (1.75–2.25-kg/4–5-lb) duck
salt and pepper
2 tablespoons oil
2 small oranges
2 tablespoons sugar
2 tablespoons white wine vinegar
juice of 1 small lemon
1–2 tablespoons Grand Marnier or brandy
300 ml/½ pint chicken stock
25 g/1 oz beurre manié (see page 186)
1 tablespoon double cream

Divide the duck into four portions and sprinkle all over with seasoning. Heat a little oil in a frying pan and fry the duck gently, turning frequently, until cooked through and the skin is crisp and golden. This will take about 20–30 minutes. Meanwhile, carefully remove the rind of 1 orange, without any white pith, and cut into long, very thin julienne strips. Put the rind into boiling water and boil for 1 minute. Drain and rinse the rind quickly under cold water. Put the sugar and vinegar in a small pan, dissolve the sugar and cook rapidly until thickening and turning golden, but do not burn. Squeeze the juice from both oranges and add to the pan with the lemon juice, liqueur and stock. Leave to simmer gently. Place the duck portions on a heated serving dish and keep warm. Strain the fat from the frying pan and add any meat juices to the sauce. Then add the beurre manié mixture, a very little at a time, to the simmering sauce, whisking all the time, until just thickened to the consistency you require. Add the orange rind and cream and check the seasoning. Pour a little over the duck pieces and serve the rest separately. As this is a very rich dish, serve with simple vegetables such as boiled potatoes, young green beans or carrots. **Serves 4**

Goose

Goose under two years old can simply be roasted; the larger ones should be stuffed with a sage and onion mixture. Like duck, they are fatty and you should pierce the skin before cooking. A good-sized goose, 3.25–3.5 kg/ 7–8 lb will usually serve eight people. Wild goose is not easily available even when it is in season from August to March.

Stuffed Duck with Port Sauce and Grapes

(Illustrated on page 58)

1 tablespoon oil
1 large onion, chopped
1 (1.75–2.25-kg/4–5-lb) duck, with giblets
100 g/4 oz fresh white breadcrumbs
25 g/1 oz butter, melted
1 egg, beaten
4 sticks celery, chopped
1 large cooking apple, chopped
salt and pepper
1½ teaspoons arrowroot
150 ml/¼ pint port or red wine
150 ml/¼ pint stock
1–2 teaspoons lemon juice
450 g/1 lb green grapes
watercress to garnish

Heat the oil in a frying pan and fry the onion and duck liver for 2–3 minutes. Mix the breadcrumbs, butter, egg, celery and apple together. Add the onion, liver and seasoning and use to stuff the duck. Truss the duck and rub the skin with salt and pepper. Prick the skin several times. Stand on a trivet in a roasting tin and cook in a moderately hot oven (200°C, 400°F, Gas Mark 6) for 1½–1¾ hours.

To make the sauce, mix the arrowroot, wine and stock and bring slowly to the boil, stirring all the time. Cook for a further 2–3 minutes then add the lemon juice, seasoning and any meat juices (not fat) from the roasting tin. Add the grapes, in small bunches, and cook for 1 minute. Transfer the cooked, crisp duck to a heated serving dish and glaze with a little sauce. Garnish with the grapes and watercress and serve the remaining sauce separately **Serves 4**

Hare and Rabbit

Hare is at its best up to one year old. It can be eaten very fresh or hung for up to one week. It is only available from August to February. It should always be very thoroughly cooked. Rabbits should be very young and eaten very fresh. They are available frozen all year. Rabbit and hare have whitish-coloured flesh and are not unlike chicken in flavour, but are much more bony. Hare and rabbit can be cooked in the same ways; portioned and slow-roasted or casseroled. However they can become dry, so it is best to cover or baste them during roasting. One rabbit will usually serve four people easily and a hare six to eight. To portion a rabbit or hare, cut away the back legs from the end of the backbone (saddle) to give two portions. Cut away the front legs but keep them attached to the rib cage to give two more portions. Cut the saddle across the bone into two or three portions more.

Poacher's Casserole

salt and pepper
1 (1–1.5-kg/2–3-lb) rabbit, jointed
50 g/2 oz butter
2 onions, sliced
300 ml/$\frac{1}{2}$ pint brown stock
150 ml/$\frac{1}{4}$ pint red wine
1 (227-g/8-oz) can tomatoes
1 tablespoon treacle
1 tablespoon cornflour
$\frac{1}{2}$ red cabbage, shredded

Season the rabbit pieces well. Melt the butter in a saucepan and brown the joints all over. Add the onion, stock, wine and tomatoes and simmer for 45 minutes. Remove the meat and onions and keep warm. Add the treacle to the liquid. Mix the flour with 2 tablespoons water and add to the liquid, stirring until thickened. Blanch the cabbage in the boiling sauce for 3 minutes then return the meat and onions. Heat through thoroughly. Serve with boiled potatoes. **Serves 6**

Jugged Hare

Don't be put off by the idea of cooking hare in its own blood – the result is rich and quite delicious. However, some people do not like the very gamey flavour, so be careful who you serve it to. Be sure to tell your butcher how you are going to cook the hare, so he can keep the blood for you.

1 large hare with its blood
50 g/2 oz flour
25 g/1 oz dripping or lard
2 onions, sliced
1 clove garlic, crushed
25 g/1 oz bacon fat, rind or belly pork
2 carrots, chopped
2 sticks celery, chopped
few cloves
1 bay leaf
1 sprig parsley
1 sprig thyme
150 ml/$\frac{1}{4}$ pint red wine
300 ml/$\frac{1}{2}$ pint stock
1–2 tablespoons redcurrant jelly
salt and pepper
to garnish:
croûtons
1 tablespoon chopped parsley

Divide the hare into portions and coat lightly in the flour. (If you get the liver with the hare, cook this in the stock for 30 minutes.) Heat the dripping or lard and fry the onion, garlic and bacon fat slowly until the bacon fat runs and the onion is just golden. Transfer the onion to an ovenproof casserole. Quickly fry the hare portions until golden on all sides and add these to the casserole. Add the carrot and celery. Tie the bacon fat, cloves, bay leaf, parsley and thyme in a muslin bag and add to the casserole. Add the remaining flour to the juices in the frying pan and cook for 1 minute. Gradually stir in the blood, wine, stock and redcurrant jelly. (Sieve the liver if used, and add to the pan.) Then bring to the boil slowly, stirring frequently, and cook for 2 minutes. Sieve the sauce into the casserole dish and cook, covered, in a cool oven (150°C, 300°F, Gas Mark 2) for about 2$\frac{1}{2}$ hours or until the meat is tender. Remove the muslin bag and check the seasoning. Serve topped with croûtons and chopped parsley. **Serves 6–8**

Vegetables and Salads

Vegetables are a vital part of our diet, not just nutritionally, but also in the variety and interest they can provide. So learn to make the most of them and enjoy cooking with them. Your family, your purse and your own interest in cooking will all benefit.

We are very lucky to have a vast choice of fresh vegetables all year round, but buying vegetables according to their true season is still wise shopping. They are always a better price, often richer in flavour, and provide the interested cook with an ever-changing selection of ingredients. Good quality fresh vegetables should always look 'fresh' – crisp, crunchy, brightly coloured. Vegetables that have been around for too long will always be disappointing, however hard you try to cheer them up with extra flavours.

Vegetables provide our main source of vitamins A and C. For this reason we all need one or two portions of fresh vegetables every day, in particular potatoes and a green vegetable. But unless they are carefully cooked, much of this goodness, and also delicious flavour, will be lost.

All vegetables should be eaten as soon as possible after purchase. Light, warmth and water destroy many vitamins, so only store in a cool, dark place. Whenever possible, leave the skins on, simply wash them well, as this outer layer contains much of the nutritional value and flavour. For extra goodness, add washed peelings and outer leaves to stocks or cooking liquid. Prepare vegetables just before cooking and try not to soak them for too long. Vitamin C in particular is water-soluble, so if you leave vegetables such as potatoes and cabbage to soak, cook them in this soaking liquid. Use as little water as possible to cook in. Leafy vegetables need only a little water, root vegetables need only just enough to cover. Always put vegetables into gently boiling, not cold, water. This seals in the vitamins and flavour immediately. Cook for as little time as possible; in fact you will find that slightly undercooked or only just cooked vegetables taste better and have a better texture.

Keeping vegetables hot, or reheating them is best done in a colander over a pan of boiling water. If it is more convenient, put the well-drained, slightly undercooked vegetable in a buttered dish in the oven for a short time. Never reheat in a pan of water or you will destroy all that you have tried to preserve!

Artichokes (*Globe*)

These are like large green thistles. Available fresh during most of the year.

Artichoke hearts (the best part) can be bought canned in brine. These are ideal for salads and cold starters or for puréeing for soups and sauces.

To prepare artichokes, allow a whole artichoke per person. Cut off the stalk, the points of the leaves and any brown outer leaves. Drop into boiling salted water with lemon juice added, and boil for 40–45 minutes until the base is soft. Serve hot with melted butter or cold with vinaigrette dressing. Pull out the leaves one at a time and eat just the softened base of the leaves dipped in butter or dressing. After all the leaves have been removed, scrape away the hairy fronds in the middle and eat the soft heart with a knife and fork.

Artichokes (*Jerusalem*)

A root vegetable, smaller and more knobbly than potatoes. Available only in the winter months. Treat as potatoes but cook with lemon juice to prevent discoloration. They can be served as a vegetable or used for sauces, soups and many other dishes.

Artichoke Cottage Pie

675 g/1¼ lb Jerusalem artichokes
salt and pepper
2 teaspoons lemon juice
50 g/2 oz butter
5 tomatoes
2 onions, chopped
350 g/12 oz minced beef
1 green pepper, seeds removed and diced
1 teaspoon chopped parsley
50 g/2 oz cheese, grated

Cook the artichokes in boiling salted water with the lemon juice until tender. Drain and reserve 300 ml/½ pint of the cooking liquor. Keep 3–4 artichokes whole and mash the remainder with half the butter. Peel 3 tomatoes and chop the flesh. Heat the remaining butter and fry the onion and tomato. Add the beef and the reserved cooking liquor. Bring the mixture to the boil, add the pepper, parsley and seasoning. Simmer steadily for about 35 minutes then remove the lid. Stir the mixture and simmer, uncovered, for a further 10 minutes to thicken. Dice the reserved artichokes and add to the mixture. Spoon into an ovenproof dish. Slice the remaining tomatoes and top the pie with the mashed artichokes, tomato and cheese. Brown under the grill. **Serves 2–3**

Artichokes with Blue Cheese Dressing

225 g/8 oz Jerusalem artichokes, cooked
5–6 spring onions, chopped
½ cauliflower, cut in florets
75 g/3 oz blue cheese
150 ml/¼ pint single cream
salt and pepper

Chop the artichokes and mix with the spring onion and raw (or crisply-cooked) cauliflower. Mash the cheese into the cream, season to taste and toss into the vegetables. Chill. **Serves 4**

Asparagus

Long, thin green and white stalks with a very delicate unusual flavour. Available either home-grown or imported through most of the year. Cut off and discard the very thick, hard white end of the stalks. Wash well, tie in a bundle and stand upright in a large pan of boiling salted water, tips upwards. Cook until tender; this could take anything from 20 to 40 minutes, depending upon thickness. Drain and serve with melted butter or Hollandaise sauce, or serve cold with a salad dressing.

Avocado Pear

This fruit became known as a 'pear' because of its shape. The flesh is golden yellow with a smooth creamy texture when ripe. Depending on the time of year and where the fruit has come from, the skin varies from smooth light green, to a very rough dark purple colour. Ask your greengrocer to choose the correct 'ripeness' for your needs, either to eat that day or several days later. When ready to eat, the flesh should just give if gently pressed – but to avoid ruining the fruit for other people, don't touch them yourself.

To serve halved with a vinaigrette dressing, cut them just before serving and brush with lemon juice. To purée for dips, soups or sauces, blend with 1–2 tablespoons lemon juice immediately. Avocados can be sliced for attractive salads or starters, or can be quickly warmed with a cheese and cream or crab filling, but be sure to cover all the flesh with filling, cream or foil.

Avocado and Crab Gratin

4 avocados
juice of ½ lemon
1 medium onion, finely chopped
salt and pepper
225 g/8 oz fresh, frozen or canned crabmeat, flaked
4 tablespoons whipped cream
100 g/4 oz Gruyère cheese, grated
watercress to garnish

Halve the avocados and remove the stones. Brush all the cut surfaces with lemon juice. Mix the remaining lemon juice with the onion, seasoning and crab and fold into the whipped cream. Spoon on to the avocado halves and sprinkle with cheese. Prepare these no more than 1½ hours in advance and, when required, pop under a hot grill for about 5 minutes until the top is golden. Garnish with watercress. **Serves 8**

Aubergines

Also known as eggplant. They have a smooth, shiny purple skin. Buy when firm and glossy, and store in the refrigerator. There's no need to skin aubergines but to remove the excess moisture, slice thickly and sprinkle well with salt. Leave for 1 hour and then rinse and dry well. Fry in butter, or coat in batter and fry. Use in cooked dishes or stuff and bake.

Lamb Stuffed Aubergines

2 large aubergines
100 g/4 oz cold cooked lamb, diced
1 tablespoon chopped parsley
1 tomato, peeled and chopped
50 g/2 oz fresh breadcrumbs
$\frac{1}{2}$ onion, grated
salt and pepper
100 g/4 oz Cheddar cheese, grated
$\frac{1}{2}$–1 teaspoon lime or lemon juice
50 g/2 oz butter, melted

Remove the stalk ends from the aubergines. Halve lengthwise and scoop out the flesh, leaving about 5 mm/$\frac{1}{4}$ inch in the shell. Chop the flesh and mix with the remaining ingredients, but reserve half of the cheese. Pile the mixture back into the aubergines and sprinkle with the reserved cheese.

Put in an ovenproof dish, cover and cook in a moderately hot oven (200°C, 400°F, Gas Mark 6) for about 20 minutes. Remove the cover for the last 10 minutes to brown. **Serves 4**

Beans (*Dried*)

Aduki, black, black-eye, borlotti, broad, butter, haricot, kidney, mung, pinto, soya and canellini. These are just some of the dried beans now available in this country. Several are only available in health food shops, but others are available ready-cooked and canned. They vary in size enormously, and in colour or shape, as their names indicate. However, they are mostly treated in the same way and are interchangeable in many recipes. Depending on size and skin thickness, they need soaking in cold water for 1 to 4 hours. To speed up this process, add 2 teaspoons bicarbonate of soda to the soaking water or soak in warm water. Then 1 hour is sufficient soaking time. Aduki and mung beans need no soaking and only take about 40 minutes to cook. Other beans take up to 1$\frac{1}{2}$ hours, soya beans requiring longer. They can be cooked in water, stock or other flavoured liquids and are ideally suited to pressure cooking.

Beans (*Fresh*)

Broad, runner, French, bobbi beans, and two more recent additions from France and Israel, red and yellow beans. The young broad beans can be cooked as two vegetables, the fresh bean boiled and served in white or parsley sauce, or the green shell sliced and cooked as other fresh beans. Fresh beans should only be lightly cooked (5–10 minutes) in a little boiling salted water to keep their crisp texture. Top and tail, but only slice the beans if they are very thick or tough.

French Beans Hungarian-style

450 g/1 lb French beans, trimmed and washed
$\frac{1}{2}$ teaspoon salt
pinch dried thyme
4 tablespoons oil
2 medium onions, sliced
1 clove garlic, crushed
1 (142-ml/5-fl oz) carton soured cream
1 teaspoon paprika

Place the beans in about 5 cm/2 inches of boiling water with a little salt and the thyme. Cook until the beans are tender. Drain. Heat the oil in a large pan and cook the onion and garlic until soft and translucent but not browned. Remove from the heat and stir in the cream and paprika, mixing thoroughly. Return the pan to a low heat and add the beans, stirring until well coated. **Serves 4**

Raised salmon and prawn pie (see page 144)

Salad Niçoise

225 g/8 oz cooked green beans
4 tomatoes, peeled and chopped
2 hard-boiled eggs, chopped
75 g/3 oz green olives
Vinaigrette dressing flavoured with garlic (see page 183)

Arrange all the vegetables and egg attractively on a platter. Sprinkle with chilled dressing just before serving. **Serves 4**

Beansprouts

These are the crisp, juicy tiny stems of dry beans when freshly germinated. You can grow them at home from mung beans or soya beans in 5–8 days, or buy them fresh from some supermarkets. They are also available canned in brine. Beansprouts can be eaten raw in salads, or hot, cooked very lightly and quickly in oil or stock for only a couple of minutes.

Stir-fried Vegetables

1 tablespoon soy sauce
1 tablespoon sherry
1 teaspoon cornflour
2–3 tablespoons olive oil
1 clove garlic, crushed (optional)
1 small onion, thinly sliced
2 carrots, grated
450 g/1 lb beansprouts
salt and pepper

Mix the soy sauce, sherry and cornflour together. Heat the oil in a wok, or large shallow, light-weight frying pan. Add the garlic, onion and carrot and fry quickly, stirring and tossing all the time, until turning golden. Add the beansprouts and toss for about 30 seconds. Stir in the cornflour mixture and cook until thickened and smooth. Season to taste. Serve immediately. **Serves 4**

Beetroot

Usually sold ready-cooked and often peeled. To cook, boil with their skins on until soft for about 1 hour. Allow to cool and then peel. Serve on their own in a dressing, or in a salad. If liked serve hot – peel while still hot and serve with a parsley, béchamel or other lightly-flavoured sauce.

Creamed Beetroot Salad

(Illustrated on page 76)

225 g/8 oz beetroot, cooked and peeled
4 tablespoons soured cream
1 tablespoon orange juice
salt and pepper
1 (141-g/5-oz) can butter beans, drained

Grate or roughly mash the beetroot, then mix with the remaining ingredients and serve chilled. **Serves 4**

Broccoli

Just like a deep purple version of cauliflower but on individual stalks. Calabrese is the one with green florets. Cut off and chop the thick part of the stalk and discard the outer leaves. Cook as for cauliflower. Serve buttered or with a Hollandaise sauce.

Brussels Sprouts

Trim the base and outer leaves of the sprouts. Wash well and then cut a cross in the base of each one to ensure they cook evenly. Drop into very little boiling salted water and cook until just tender, 8–10 minutes. Drain immediately. If you need to keep them hot, in the oven or on top, be sure to undercook them slightly.

Pigeon pudding (see page 92)

Sprouts Provençale

(Illustrated on page 76)

1 tablespoon oil or lard
1 onion, chopped
4 tomatoes, peeled and chopped
225 g/8 oz Brussels sprouts, cooked and halved
1 teaspoon dried rosemary
100 g/4 oz button mushrooms, halved
salt and pepper
150 ml/¼ pint tomato juice or stock and tomato
purée blended together

Heat the oil and fry the onion until browned. Add the tomatoes, sprouts, rosemary and mushrooms. When just golden add the remaining ingredients and mix well. Serve hot or chilled. **Serves 4**

Cabbage

Primo, Savoy, red, Chinese are types of cabbage available at different times of the year. They can all be treated in exactly the same way. When choosing, make sure the colour is deep and they are firm and heavy. Trim off the stalk, and any ruined outer leaves (never discard the trimmed greenery, it can always be washed and added to stocks or soups to give flavour). Then shred the cabbage, or cut in larger pieces as required and wash quickly. Put into very little boiling salted water and cook for as little time as possible, or braise. Like all green vegetables, cabbage contains vitamin C which is water-soluble, so overcooking destroys the vitamin. Drain immediately.

Red cabbage can be treated in exactly the same way, but don't cook it with other foods as the water turns blue. It is more often braised with wine or vinegar and apples or sultanas.

Chinese cabbage, although good cooked, is especially good in salads as it has a sweeter, more succulent flavour when raw. It is often used stir-fried in Chinese dishes.

For an unusual coleslaw, mix shredded cabbage with sliced onion and mandarin segments (illustrated on page 76).

Orik Orak

Indonesian-style cabbage

900 g/2 lb cabbage
3 tablespoons oil
1 onion, sliced
2 eggs
½ teaspoon grated nutmeg
salt and pepper
25 g/1 oz butter

Shred the inner part of the cabbage, keeping the outer leaves to use in other recipes. Heat the oil in a large pan and stir-fry the cabbage and onion for about 10 minutes. Whisk the eggs, nutmeg and seasoning together and lightly scramble with the butter. Place the cabbage mixture on a heated serving dish and top with scrambled egg. Serve with baked chicken drumsticks. **Serves 4–6**

Colcannon

(Illustrated on page 75)

This Irish dish is served with a luscious pool of melted butter in the middle.

2 leeks, sliced
300 ml/½ pint milk
450 g/1 lb cabbage, shredded and cooked
450 g/1 lb potatoes, cooked and mashed
salt and pepper
75 g/3 oz butter, melted

Simmer the leeks in the milk until really soft. Stir in the cabbage and potato to make a smooth mixture. Season to taste. Pile into a serving dish and make a well in the centre. Pour the butter into the well and serve. **Serves 4–6**

Braised Red Cabbage with Chestnuts

1 small red cabbage, shredded
25 g/1 oz butter
1 large onion, sliced
1 large cooking apple, peeled, cored and sliced
2 tablespoons wine vinegar
1 tablespoon soft brown sugar
salt and pepper
2 tablespoons water
100 g/4 oz chestnuts, peeled
25 g/1 oz butter
25 g/1 oz flour

Blanch the cabbage in boiling water for 2 minutes and drain well. Melt the butter in a frying pan over a low heat and cook the onion and apple until soft. Mix the vinegar, sugar, seasoning and water together. Place a layer of cabbage in the bottom of a greased casserole and sprinkle with a little of the vinegar mixture. Cover with some apple and onion and a few chestnuts. Repeat the layers, finishing off with cabbage. Cover the dish with buttered greaseproof paper and a lid and cook in a moderate oven (180°C, 350°F, Gas Mark 4) for 1 hour. Knead the butter and flour together to make a beurre manié and add to the mixture, stirring well. Leave for a further 10 minutes before serving with hot or cold roast meats. **Serves 4**

Chinese Green Salad

(Illustrated on page 76)

100 g/4 oz leeks, thinly sliced
225 g/8 oz Chinese cabbage, shredded
1 (425-g/15-oz) can red kidney beans
150 ml/¼ pint Vinaigrette dressing (see page 183)
1 teaspoon soy sauce

Mix the leeks, cabbage and drained beans together. Mix the dressing with the soy sauce, then mix well into the vegetables. Serve well chilled. **Serves 4–6**

Sweet Red Cabbage Salad

(Illustrated on page 76)

175 g/6 oz red cabbage, shredded
2 red-skinned apples, cored and sliced
3–4 tablespoons Vinaigrette dressing (see page 183)
salt and pepper

Mix all the ingredients together and toss well. Serve immediately. **Serves 4**

Carrots

Carrots are available throughout the year but new tiny carrots are only around in early summer. They need only topping and tailing and very little cooking – about 7 to 10 minutes if sliced. Older carrots will need about 20 minutes if thinly sliced. When buying, be sure they are not still green at the top as these are too young, or very wrinkled and soft – these are old and will be tough and tasteless. Besides being a delicious vegetable, carrots are a traditional ingredient for flavouring many casseroles, sauces and soups. In most cases only one or two carrots are necessary, so always have some at hand.

Carrots are best slightly undercooked, so they are still just crisp in the centre. Just flavour lightly before serving. When nearly cooked, drain off the liquid and return to the pan with a knob of butter and some chopped herbs, or butter and brown sugar, or double cream and black pepper. Then finish cooking very gently so they are lightly coated in a glaze when served.

Cauliflower

This should always be creamy white with a firm, tightly-packed head of florets when really fresh. Try to persuade your greengrocer not to trim the leaves down, they can provide a good green vegetable when cooked by themselves. Either cook the cauliflower whole, or break carefully into small florets for quicker cooking. Although usually boiled, cauliflower is also very good raw and crisp in salads.

Cauliflower with Peppered Cheese Sauce

1 large cauliflower
300 ml/½ pint thick White sauce (see page 185)
1 (227-g/8-oz) can tomatoes
50–75 g/2–3 oz cheese, grated
1 teaspoon chilli powder
salt and pepper

Trim and wash the cauliflower. Cook it whole, stalk end down, in gently boiling salted water for about 12 minutes. When cooked, drain and transfer to an ovenproof serving dish. Mix the white sauce with the tomatoes, two-thirds of the cheese, the chilli and seasoning. Pour the sauce over the cauliflower, top with remaining cheese and brown under the grill. **Serves 4**

Celeriac

This is the edible root of a variety of celery. Although a somewhat ugly-looking vegetable, it has a deliciously mild celery flavour and can be used in all celery recipes. Peel thoroughly, then slice and quarter, or chop before cooking in salted water with lemon juice or vinegar added to prevent discoloration. Simmer for about 20 minutes or more and serve with butter or a cream sauce or make into a purée.

Celery

Although available all the year, it is at its best during the winter. Choose the firmest, palest heads, for the darker it is the more stringy the stalks will be. These can be removed however when trimming the stalks. The best part is the heart, which is yellowish and has short stalks. This can be braised whole or cut in half lengthways. The larger outer stalks give an excellent flavour to stews, soups and sauces.

Braised Celery à la Français

25 g/1 oz butter
1 clove garlic, crushed
1 onion, chopped
4 rashers bacon, chopped
4 small heads celery
salt and pepper
300 ml/½ pint chicken stock
150 ml/¼ pint medium sherry or sweet white wine

Melt the butter in a frying pan and fry the garlic, onion and bacon together until golden. Wash the celery, trim off the base and the outer thick stalks and tie lightly with cotton if the hearts are falling apart. Spread the bacon, onion and garlic over the base of an ovenproof dish. Arrange the celery on top and season. Add the stock and sherry or wine and sufficient water to cover the vegetables completely. Cover the dish and bake in a moderately hot oven (190°C, 375°F, Gas Mark 5) for about 1 hour or until the celery is just tender. Remember to remove the cotton if used and serve with the cooking liquid which can be thickened or reduced if you wish. **Serves 4**

Chicory

This is only available in the winter months. Choose thick, firm heads with no discoloration. Use as soon as possible or store in a cool, dark place, as it turns brown. Chicory is very good raw in salads but can be braised (as in the celery recipe) or stewed in butter. Remember to add lemon juice or vinegar to prevent discoloration and avoid cutting the stalks with steel knives.

Chillies

These are very small finger-shaped hot peppers. Don't expect red chillies to be the hottest, they are often milder than the green ones. Do be careful how you handle chillies – they are very strong. If possible wear rubber gloves, or wash your hands immediately after touching them. Never touch your eyes or face until you have done so. Remove the stalk, cut in half lengthways and scrape out the seeds – these are the hottest part! Then chop or shred, or leave whole to add to casseroles or vegetable dishes. One chilli is usually enough to give a good flavour to most dishes.

Corn on the Cob

Only available fresh for a short time at the end of the summer. Choose ones with a green outer husk and very small kernels at the tip. Remove the base, husk and hair-like strands. Cook whole, or scrape the kernels off the stalk before cooking in salted water for 5 to 20 minutes. Serve with butter and seasoning.

Courgettes

Courgettes are also known as zucchini. The courgette belongs to the marrow family but is not as pulpy. Courgettes are usually available all the year, but are at their best in the summer, when only about 13–15 cm/5–6 inches long and bright green in colour. Wash and trim off the ends but don't peel. They can be boiled, baked or fried or coated in batter and deep-fried.

Courgettes with Lettuce and Sorrel Sauce

25 g/1 oz butter
½ round lettuce, cut in strips
½ small onion, chopped
2 tablespoons chopped fresh sorrel or spinach
150–300 ml/¼–½ pint chicken stock
150 ml/¼ pint double cream
1 egg yolk
salt and pepper
8 courgettes, quartered lengthways and cooked

Melt the butter in a saucepan. Add the lettuce, onion and sorrel or spinach and cook, stirring gently, for 2–3 minutes. Stir in the stock and simmer, covered for about 15 minutes. Liquidise the mixture or pass through a sieve. Return to the pan, mix the cream with the egg yolk and add to the sauce. Heat, stirring, until thickened, but don't let it boil. Season and serve over the cooked courgettes. **Serves 3–4**

Cucumber

When buying, always be sure they are firm and dark green. Although most often served raw, they are excellent boiled, baked, braised or sautéed. They should be peeled for cooking. The small 'ridge' cucumber, often home grown, is the best for pickling. Mix cucumber chunks with walnut halves, black olives and vinaigrette dressing for an interesting salad (illustrated on page 76).

Endive

This looks like spiky, curly lettuce and is used in just the same ways. However, it has a bitter-sweet taste which makes an interesting addition to salads.

Fennel

This is a bulb-shaped vegetable with a texture and stringiness similar to celery. However, it has a mild aniseed flavour which is very refreshing. Serve raw in salads, or cook like celery, quartered or trimmed and cut in horizontal slices. Choose white, firm bulbs to buy. The heads often have feathery green fronds on the top which serve as a good replacement for dill. Particularly good with fish.

Fruity Fennel Salad

(Illustrated on page 76)

2 grapefruit
1 onion, sliced
1 head fennel, sliced
2 heads chicory, broken into leaves
150 ml/¼ pint natural yogurt
pinch dry mustard
salt and pepper

Pare the yellow rind from 1 grapefruit, leaving the pith, and shred finely. Put aside for the dressing. Peel and segment both grapefruit, removing the membrane from each segment, and mix with the onion, fennel and chicory. Mix the yogurt, mustard, seasoning and grapefruit rind and toss the vegetables well in this. Chill. **Serves 4**

Crunchy Blue Cheese Salad

450 g/1 lb chicory, broken into leaves
1 large head fennel, cut in rings
1 carton mustard and cress
50 g/2 oz white grapes, halved
50 g/2 oz walnuts, chopped
4 tablespoons Vinaigrette dressing (see page 183)
4 tablespoons cream
50 g/2 oz blue cheese
salt and pepper

Mix the chicory and fennel with the mustard and cress, grapes and walnuts. Chill. Mix the dressing, cream and cheese in a liquidiser or beat well until smooth. Season to taste, pour a little over the salad and serve the rest separately. **Serves 6**

Kale

This belongs to the cabbage family and is often sold as 'winter' or 'spring' greens. The individual curly leaves have a stronger flavour than cabbage and are best lightly boiled and served with butter.

Greens Salad

225 g/8 oz spring greens
1 avocado
1 tablespoon lemon juice
50 g/2 oz peeled prawns or shrimps
2 tablespoons thick mayonnaise
2 teaspoons tomato purée
2 tablespoons Vinaigrette dressing (see page 183)
few drops Worcestershire sauce

Wash and shred the greens. Cook for only 1 minute in boiling, salted water, then drain thoroughly and chill. Peel and chop the avocado, dipping the flesh in lemon juice immediately. Mix the avocado, greens and prawns together. Mix the remaining ingredients together and toss into the salad. Chill. **Serves 4**

Kohlrabi

A firm, bulbous, pale green-white vegetable often sold with the leaves still on. The base tastes a little like cabbage but should be prepared like a root vegetable. If the leaves are fresh and crisp they can be cooked like kale.

Leeks

A long, thick, white to dark green cylindrical vegetable, like a larger spring onion. They have a mild, sweetish onion flavour, and are very good used in casseroles as well as served on their own. To cook, trim off the base and coarse dark green part. Slice and wash thoroughly, or split lengthways and wash. Cook whole.

Sage and Leek Tart

200 g/8 oz Shortcrust pastry (see page 136)
25 g/1 oz butter
3 large leeks, sliced and washed
150 ml/¼ pint cream or milk
1 egg, beaten
1 tablespoon chopped sage
1 teaspoon chopped parsley
100 g/4 oz bacon, chopped
salt and pepper

Make up the pastry and use to line a 20-cm/8-inch flan ring. Melt the butter in a saucepan and fry the leeks until beginning to soften. Add the cream or milk, egg, sage, parsley, bacon and seasoning and pour into the flan. Bake for 30–35 minutes in a moderately hot oven (190°C, 375°F, Gas Mark 5). **Serves 4**

Lettuce

Batavia, Cos, Iceberg, round and Webb's Wonderful are names of the different types of lettuce available in this country. They can all be used for salads, or may be cooked very briefly, like beansprouts, to add to vegetable dishes, or to serve on their own with a delicate sauce. Lettuce is also good in soups or puréed sauces. The crisper lettuces, Webb's, Cos and Iceberg are particularly good cooked and served like spinach.

Marrow

Marrow is only available from July to October and is at its sweetest early in the season when it is small. Peel, chop and boil lightly to serve with butter or a cheese sauce, or for larger marrow, halve or slice and scoop out the seeds and fill the centre with a savoury stuffing. Bake slowly to make a juicy, tasty dish.

Cheesy Stuffed Marrow

1 marrow, about 20 cm/8 inches long
2–3 tablespoons oil
450 g/1 lb minced beef
1 large onion, chopped
salt and pepper
1 teaspoon dried mixed herbs
2 tablespoons tomato purée
100 g/4 oz cheese, grated
3–4 tablespoons double cream

Wash the marrow and cut off a thick slice lengthways to form a lid. With a spoon, scoop out the centre seeds and discard. Heat the oil in a saucepan and fry the beef and onion quickly until well browned. Then add the seasoning, herbs, tomato purée and 2–3 tablespoons of water. Cook quickly for 5 minutes. Then stir in half the cheese and spoon the mixture into the marrow shell. Put the lid on and place in an ovenproof dish. Mix the remaining cheese and cream, pour over the marrow and cook in a moderately hot oven (200°C, 400°F, Gas Mark 6) for 45 minutes or until the marrow is tender. **Serves 6**

Mushrooms

Mushrooms are now available fresh all the year round, and can easily be grown at home too. (Only pick wild mushrooms if you really know which ones are safe to eat.) Of the types usually in the shops, button mushrooms are the best for serving raw in salads, as they have a very crisp texture and delicate flavour. Cup or flat mushrooms are good for casseroling as they have a stronger flavour. The large flat ones are delicious stuffed and baked. There should be no need to peel mushrooms, as the skin has the best flavour, so just wash thoroughly and chop off the base of the stems. If you prefer to peel them, keep the skin to add flavour to stocks and soups.

Mushrooms and Leeks à la Grecque

450 g/1 lb firm, white mushrooms
50 g/2 oz butter
2 tablespoons oil
2 leeks, sliced and washed
2 tablespoons lemon juice
2 teaspoons dried mixed herbs
2 bay leaves
1 teaspoon sugar
sea salt
freshly ground black pepper
2 small cloves garlic, crushed
1 medium glass dry white wine
chopped parsley to garnish

Wash and thoroughly dry the mushrooms, then slice thinly. Melt the butter with the oil in a frying pan. Drain the leeks and add to the pan. Cook gently for 5 minutes without browning. Add the mushrooms, lemon juice, herbs, bay leaves, sugar, salt and pepper. Cook gently until the liquid is reduced to just butter and oil – about 15 minutes. Add the garlic and wine, bring back to the boil gradually and remove from the heat. Season to taste. Garnish with the parsley. Serve hot or cold. **Serves 4**

Mushroom and Bean Casserole

1 tablespoon oil
1 clove garlic, crushed
2 onions, sliced
225 g/8 oz courgettes, chopped
300 ml/½ pint tomato juice
1 tablespoon chopped parsley
100 g/4 oz haricot beans, soaked, cooked and drained
175 g/6 oz mushrooms, sliced
salt and pepper
15 g/½ oz butter

Heat the oil and fry the garlic and onion until browned. Add the courgettes and brown quickly. Stir in the tomato juice and parsley and simmer gently for about 10 minutes until the courgettes are tender. Stir in the beans and half the mushrooms, season and simmer for 30 minutes. Melt the butter and toss the remaining mushrooms. Pour into a heated dish and garnish with the mushrooms. **Serves 4**

Crispy Fried Mushrooms

100 g/4 oz sausages or sausagemeat
2 tablespoons tomato purée
2 tablespoons chopped parsley
salt and pepper
1 clove garlic, crushed (optional)
1 onion, finely chopped
25 g/1 oz peanuts, coarsely chopped
8 large, flat mushrooms
25 g/1 oz flour
25 g/1 oz fresh breadcrumbs
1 egg
3–4 tablespoons water
oil for deep-frying

Mix the sausagemeat with the tomato purée, parsley, seasoning, garlic, onion and peanuts. Finely chop the mushroom stalks and add to the mixture. Divide the mixture between the mushrooms, shaping the mixture on to each of the flat caps. Mix the flour, breadcrumbs, egg and water to make a thick batter. Heat the oil to 190°C/375°F, or until a cube of bread turns golden in 1 minute. Dip the mushrooms in the batter and fry for 5–7 minutes, turning once. Drain on absorbent kitchen paper and serve immediately. **Serves 4**

Okra

These are also known as ladies fingers. They are becoming more widely available but are only to be found fresh in the shops during the spring and summer. The little pods should be bright green and unblemished. Inside are small, edible seeds. The flavour is refreshingly warm and the vegetable is used mostly in Creole and Caribbean dishes. Young okra needs only washing and then topping and tailing before being boiled or braised. However, they can be sliced and fried and served with butter or a creamy sauce, or even eaten raw. The older vegetables get a thick stubbly coating and need longer cooking.

Onions

Spanish, red and yellow onions are the ones we use most regularly. They vary a great deal in pungency, from the mild sweet red onion, to the very strong yellow onions. However, in most cooked dishes the flavour mellows during cooking. When using onion raw, you should take more notice of its strength. You could drop quickly into boiling water, and then chill, to lessen the strength of the flavour and also the indigestibility. Shallots and small pickling onions are less frequently available. Shallots have a mild, sweeter flavour with a hint of garlic, ideal for subtly flavoured dishes. If you find these difficult to peel, dip into boiling water first. Spring onions have a strong flavour when used raw; use the whole spring onion, white and green parts, either in salads or for a mild flavour in many cooked dishes. If liked, reserve the green part to add to soups or use finely chopped as a garnish. When peeling any type of onion, hold them under running water to reduce the effect on your eyes.

Baked Stuffed Onions

6 large onions
1 tablespoon oil or lard
100 g/4 oz minced beef
175 g/6 oz cottage cheese
½ teaspoon Worcestershire sauce
salt and pepper
25 g/1 oz cheese, grated

Peel the outer skin from the onions and cut a thin slice off the top and a thicker slice from the bottom. Remove as much of the centre of the onions as possible and cook the remaining shells in boiling salted water for 10 minutes. Drain. Reserve the rest of the onions for other use. Heat the oil or lard and fry the beef until golden. Stir in the cottage cheese and Worcestershire sauce and season to taste. Pack into the onion shells. Place in an ovenproof dish, sprinkle with the cheese and bake in a moderately hot oven (190°C, 375°F, Gas Mark 5) for about 30 minutes. **Serves 4**

Beetroot and Onion Salad

225 g/8 oz cooked beetroot
4 spring onions
1 tablespoon orange juice
2 tablespoons oil
salt and pepper
pinch each sugar and dry mustard

Roughly chop the beetroot and spring onion bulbs (keep the green stems in the refrigerator and use for a garnish for another recipe). Mix the remaining ingredients together to make a dressing and stir into the beetroot and onion. Serve, well chilled, with cold meats and potatoes baked in their jackets. **Serves 4**

Parsnips

This long, pointed vegetable with its creamy coloured skin has a delicate, almost nutty flavour. They are best when small and young, in late autumn after the frosts have improved their flavour. Choose crisp, clean-looking parsnips, avoiding split or dried up roots. The older vegetables tend to have tough centres. Peel thinly and either quarter lengthways or slice. They can be boiled to serve with butter or a sauce, or can be quickly fried or roasted after parboiling. As with all root vegetables, parsnips can be puréed to serve as an unusual vegetable, a soup base, or an alternative to potato.

can be stored in sacks in a cold place for much longer. Avoid potatoes with too many cracks, cuts, eyes, or soft patches. Cut away the green parts as these can be bitter tasting and will take longer to cook. Don't prepare potatoes and leave them soaking in water for too long, leave the skins on wherever possible and don't cook in too much water – just enough to cover.

Crisps Peel the potatoes, then peel thin slices from them using a mandolin or potato peeler. Soak in cold water for 10–15 minutes. Pat dry with absorbent kitchen paper. Heat a deep pan of oil to 190°C/375°F, or until a cube of bread turns golden in 1 minute. Deep-fry for 1–2 minutes, then toss in salt or sea salt or vary the flavouring with curry, onion salt or celery salt.

Chiplets Cut into small 'sticks', slightly larger than matches. Soak, drain, dry and fry as for crisps. These can be stored in an airtight tin for up to 1 week before eating.

Potato Puffballs Sieve or rice (using a special potato ricer to force the potato through the fine holes) 225 g/8 oz boiled potato; season well and fold in the stiffly beaten whites of 2 eggs. Heat a deep pan of oil to 190°C/375°F, or until a cube of bread turns golden in 1 minute. Drop teaspoonfuls into the oil and deep-fry, turning once, until crisp and golden. Drain on absorbent kitchen paper and sprinkle with salt. Add 25 g/1 oz finely grated strong Cheddar to the mixture for extra flavour.

Nut Potatoes (*Illustrated on page 75*) Boil and mash the potatoes (as above), then form into small balls. Brush all over with egg white and roll in slivered or nibbed almonds. Deep-fry as above until golden. Drain and salt as above.

Potato Fritters Boil potatoes until just cooked and slice. Dip in batter (see page 153) and deep-fry as for crisps, until golden.

Latkes Grate 450 g/1 lb potatoes and 1 onion. Soak in cold water for 10 minutes, then drain. Squeeze dry. Mix with 25 g/1 oz self-raising flour, seasoning to taste and 1 egg yolk. Shallow-fry spoonfuls until golden all over.

Potato Croquettes Boil 450 g/1 lb potatoes until tender, drain and dry over a moderate heat. Mash well. Beat in 1 egg yolk, 25 g/1 oz butter and 1 tablespoon hot milk. With floured hands, form the potato into 10 sausage shapes, each of them with a cube of cheese in the middle. Brush with egg white, then roll in fresh white breadcrumbs. Fry in shallow or deep oil until golden all over.

Pommes Parisiennes The true way to make these is to cut balls of potato with a melon baller from raw potatoes and then deep-fry in hot fat (as for crisps) until golden. An easier way is to make up instant potato to a fairly firm mixture or use mashed potato, well seasoned. Mix with enough egg and flour to give a firm mixture and form it into tiny balls. Deep-fry, as for crisps, for 1–2 minutes. Sprinkle with chopped parsley.

Pommes Anna (*Illustrated on page 75*). Peel 675 g/1½ lb potatoes and slice very thinly. Well butter an ovenproof dish and arrange the potatoes in neat overlapping layers with butter and seasoning between each layer. Cover with greased greaseproof paper and a tightly fitting lid then cook in a moderately hot oven (190°C, 375°F, Gas Mark 5) for about 35 minutes. When ready, the potatoes can be turned out on to a heated serving dish.

Chips Peel the largest potatoes available, then slice into even-shaped chips. Dry them quickly on absorbent kitchen paper. Meanwhile, heat a pan one-third full of fresh oil to 190°C/375°F, or until a cube of bread turns golden in 1 minute. Heat the frying basket in the fat, then put the chips into the basket and lower into the

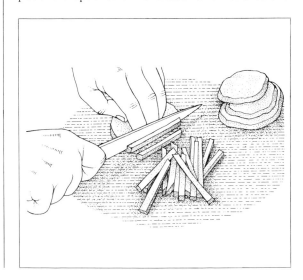

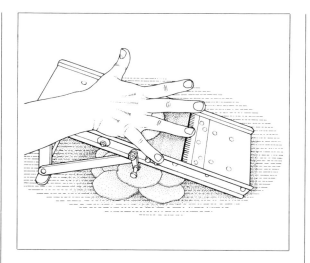

fat. Cook steadily for 5–7 minutes until the chips are cooked and golden brown. Remove and drain on absorbent kitchen paper. Serve immediately. To prepare in advance cook only for 4 minutes or until the potatoes are cooked but not browned. Then pop into hot fat to brown for 1–2 minutes immediately before serving.

Baked Potatoes Scrub unblemished potatoes well then rub in oil and lightly coat with salt or sea salt. Place in a moderately hot oven (190°C, 375°F, Gas Mark 5) for about 1 hour, depending on size. They can be successfully reheated, if not kept for longer than 1 day after cooking – wrap them in foil and reheat in a hot oven (220°C, 425°F, Gas Mark 7) for about 15 minutes.

Toppings for Single Baked Potatoes (*Illustrated on page 75*).
1 Mash the cooked flesh with 25 g/1 oz grated cheese, 50 g/2 oz chopped ham, 1 tablespoon cream or top of the milk and seasoning to taste. Return the mixture to the potato shell, sprinkle with 25 g/1 oz grated cheese and bake in a hot oven (220°C, 425°F, Gas Mark 7) for 5–10 minutes.
2 Mix together 1 tablespoon tomato purée, 3 tablespoons thick mayonnaise, a pinch of cayenne pepper and 50 g/2 oz peeled prawns. Pour over the split potato.
3 Slice a small onion and fry in a little oil until brown. Mix with 50 g/2 oz diced garlic sausage and spoon into the split potato. Top with pepper or sweetcorn relish.
4 Mash the cooked potato flesh with 15 g/½ oz

butter, 2 tablespoons whipped double cream, 1 very small egg yolk, salt and freshly ground black pepper. Fold in 1 whisked egg white and pile back into the shell. Bake in a moderately hot oven (200°C, 400°F, Gas Mark 6) for about 15 minutes until well-risen and golden.

Potato and Vegetable Hot Pot

(Illustrated on page 75)

450 g/1 lb potatoes, thinly sliced
1 large onion, sliced
225 g/8 oz cabbage, spinach or greens, shredded
2–3 sticks celery, chopped
1–2 teaspoons Italian seasoning
50 g/2 oz butter
300 ml/½ pint milk
300 ml/½ pint chicken stock
50 g/2 oz cheese, grated

Layer the sliced and chopped potato, onion, green vegetable and celery in an ovenproof dish, sprinkling each layer generously with Italian seasoning and adding a little butter. End with a potato layer. Pour on the milk and stock, sprinkle with the grated cheese and cook in a moderately hot oven (190°C, 375°F, Gas Mark 5) for 45–55 minutes until the potatoes are tender and the top is golden. **Serves 4**

Potato Fry-up

(Illustrated on page 75)

2 carrots, grated
1 small onion, finely chopped
25 g/1 oz butter
1 tablespoon oil
350 g/12 oz cold boiled potatoes, roughly chopped
1 teaspoon dried basil
75 g/3 oz salami or sausage, diced

Soak the carrots in water then drain and squeeze dry in absorbent kitchen paper. Melt the butter and oil and fry the carrot and onion for 1–2 minutes. Add the potato to the pan with the basil and cook, turning, until the potato begins to brown. Add the salami and continue cooking until the potato is a rich brown colour. **Serves 4**

Piquant Potato Scones

(Illustrated on page 75)

The perfect way to use up left-over mashed potatoes for any time of day, from breakfast to supper. In fact, it's worth cooking more potatoes, just for these.

225 g/8 oz mashed potato
50 g/2 oz flour
2 tablespoons horseradish sauce
butter for serving

Mix the first three ingredients together and form into a round shape. Divide into eight sections and transfer with palette knife to a greased griddle or frying pan. Cook, a few at a time if necessary, until golden brown, turning once. Serve topped with butter, with any cooked meat or fish. **Serves 4**

Spiced Hot Potato Salad

225 g/8 oz potatoes, peeled and diced
225 g/8 oz turnips, peeled and diced
1 small onion, grated
$\frac{1}{4}$ teaspoon ground coriander
pinch ground ginger
salt and freshly ground black pepper
50 g/2 oz butter, melted
2 tablespoons cream

Cook the potatoes and turnips in boiling salted water and drain. Mix in the remaining ingredients and serve hot or cold. **Serves 4**

Potato and Mussel Salad

(Illustrated on page 76)

225 g/8 oz potatoes, cooked and diced
175 g/6 oz mussels, canned or freshly cooked and shelled
$\frac{1}{2}$ red pepper, seeds removed and finely diced
2 tablespoons chopped parsley
6 tablespoons Vinaigrette dressing (see page 183)

Mix all the ingredients together and chill well. **Serves 4**

Pumpkin

Pumpkins are a winter 'squash' from the marrow family. Usually large and round or oval in shape, they are coarse textured. The British use them more to make Hallowe'en lanterns while the Americans make many delicious dishes from them. Peel the pumpkin, remove the seeds, then chop and cook. Serve as a vegetable, simply tossed in seasoning and butter, or make into a purée for a soup or pumpkin pie filling.

Pumpkin Pie

175–200 g/6–8 oz Shortcrust pastry (see page 136)
450 g/1 lb pumpkin flesh, puréed, or canned purée
$\frac{1}{2}$ teaspoon salt
1 teaspoon ground cinnamon
1 teaspoon ground ginger
$\frac{1}{2}$ teaspoon grated nutmeg
75 g/3 oz brown sugar
3 eggs, beaten
150 ml/$\frac{1}{4}$ pint milk
2 tablespoons sherry

Roll out the pastry thinly and use to line a 20-cm/8-inch pie dish, keeping a little for decoration. Bake the pastry blind in a moderately hot oven (190°C, 375°F, Gas Mark 5) for 15–20 minutes until crisp. Meanwhile, mix the purée with the salt, cinnamon, ginger and nutmeg, then beat in the sugar, eggs, milk and sherry. Pour into the pastry case. Cut out a piece of the remaining pastry in the shape of a pumpkin and place it in the middle of the pie. Bake in a moderately hot oven (190°C, 375°F, Gas Mark 5) for about 45 minutes. Serve hot with cream, or cold with cheese. **Serves 4–6**

Radishes

There are several varieties of radish – long, round, pink, white and black, although we really only see one or two types in the shops. Although mainly used in salads or as a garnish, radishes can be lightly boiled to make interesting sauces or soup. Slice raw in quiches and savoury dishes. Black radish needs to be soaked for 30 minutes after peeling and before cooking.

Salsify

Salsify and black-skinned salsify (scorzonera) are only available between October and February. They are very long thin wrinkled vegetables which need to be cooked but are then generally used in salads, as the French frequently do, or as a vegetable. The flavour is very delicate and not quite as sweet as that of parsnips or turnips. Wash and scrape or peel. Cook in boiling salted water with a little lemon juice for about 30 minutes. Serve hot with butter or herb sauces. Lightly fry cooked salsify or chill it and use in salads.

Sorrel

Not an easily available vegetable, but delicious when you can find it. It looks a little bit like spinach but has smaller, more delicate leaves. Its delicate sharp flavour is good with fish, chicken, egg and veal dishes. To cook, wash well and trim off any thick stalks. Cook quickly in butter or blanch the larger leaves in boiling water first. Serve like spinach, or purée and use for a sauce or soup. If liked add a very little to other sauce or casserole ingredients.

Spinach

Spinach is a very good source of iron and other minerals, like many of our dark green vegetables, but these are water soluble – so preferably serve young small spinach leaves, quickly washed, in salads. Its tangy flavour makes a very good salad base and goes well with most fish, eggs and light meats. To cook, wash, trim off the stalk and shred or chop, as liked. Don't use any water, just a knob of butter, and cook for only a couple of minutes. Drain and toss in more butter. Ideal for quiche or flan fillings, soup bases or for purée sauces.

Sweet Spinach Salad

(Illustrated on page 76)

225 g/8 oz spinach
100 g/4 oz dried apricots, soaked overnight
6 tablespoons clear honey

Wash the spinach, shake dry and tear (don't cut) into shreds. Put the apricots in a pan with the honey and bring to the boil. Allow to cool and chill. Toss with the spinach before serving. **Serves 4**

Swede

This is a reddish-skinned root vegetable with pale yellowy orange flesh. It has a slightly sweet flavour. Peel and chop the swede then boil in a little salted water until tender, about 12 to 15 minutes. Drain well and mash or chop. Serve buttered, or with cream or mixed with other root vegetables.

Garlic Swede Salad

(Illustrated on page 76)

450 g/1 lb swede, chopped
150 ml/¼ pint thick mayonnaise
2 cloves garlic, crushed
salt and pepper

Cook the swede in boiling salted water for 10–12 minutes until just tender. Drain and then mix immediately with the mayonnaise, garlic and seasoning. Allow time to chill and for the flavours to mingle before serving. **Serves 4**

Sweet Potato

These are nothing like potatoes, for they have pinkish orange coloured flesh, pink skin and a very sweet flavour, not unlike that of artichokes. They are available only through the winter and can be cooked in just the same way as potatoes. They are usually served as a savoury dish, mashed with butter and seasoning. They can be baked in their skins, or candied.

Swiss Chard (*Seakale, Beetroot Spinach*)

This is a member of the spinach family. It has thick white stalks and very curly green leaves. In fact it can be used as two vegetables. Cut out the firm white stalks and treat like celery or fennel. Pull off their thin outer coating first, chop and then boil or braise and serve with a butter sauce. The green leaf part should be cooked and served like spinach. If liked use for flavouring or in stuffings.

Tomato

A vegetable/fruit once known as 'love-apples'. Home-grown varieties are really only available between March and November. Tomatoes should be firm to the touch, but the shape only indicates where they come from and not their flavour. In fact the oddly-shaped Mediterranean tomatoes have often a much more exciting flavour. Yellow tomatoes are ones which have not quite ripened but will do so on a window-ledge or in a warm place. Many recipes call for peeled tomatoes; to do this easily, hold the tomato on a fork or skewer over a gas flame until the skin bursts in enough places to peel it off, or dip pricked tomatoes into boiling water for 30 seconds, then peel.

Turnips

These can be totally white-skinned or whitish pink in colouring. They can also be round, or long and cigar-shaped. The younger they are, the better the flavour and texture. Top, tail and peel, then chop before cooking like swedes. If they are very young and round, cook them whole and serve gratinéed or with a cream sauce.

Victorian Mashed Turnips

900 g/2 lb turnips
50 g/2 oz butter
2 tablespoons single cream
salt and pepper
the yolks of 2 hard-boiled eggs, sieved
25 g/1 oz fried breadcrumbs

Slice and cook the turnips in boiling salted water until tender. Reserve a few slices and mash the rest with butter, cream and seasoning. Spoon on to a heated serving dish and shape into a cone with a fork. Garnish with the reserved turnip slices, sieved yolks and the fried breadcrumbs. **Serves 4**

Black Forest gâteau (see page 159)

Everyday family meals need not become a bore or a slog if you make the most of the many easy-to-cook and economical foods available. Pasta and rice, for instance, cook quickly and can be deliciously flavoured – cheaply. Eggs and cheese are perfect for quick protein meals and are infinitely flexible. Foods such as canned beans, sausages or minced meats will all make meals in minutes that will please both family and friends. In this chapter is a selection of recipes including all these ideas and how to cook many of these foods.

Pasta and Rice

Pasta and rice can provide us with many nutritious and economical dishes which are quick to make and very tasty. In fact, little more than bacon, oil, garlic, herbs and seasoning can turn rice or spaghetti into a delicious meal to cope with any appetite.

Pasta

Pasta is made from flour and water, enriched with egg. Pasta verde has spinach added and wholewheat pasta is made with wholewheat flour. There are four groups of pasta; the many different shapes like shells, spirals, bows and spaghetti which are cooked on their own and served with a sauce; very small shapes, stars and alphabet letters for instance, which can be used to enrich soups, and the filled pasta shapes, ravioli and tortellini, which are usually cooked and served in a broth or with a meat or tomato sauce.

The larger pieces of pasta, lasagne or cannelloni, are cooked lightly first and then layered or filled with a meat or tomato sauce. The dish is often topped with a tomato or cheese sauce and then baked.

How to Cook Pasta

Use a large pan with plenty of boiling salted water – about 2.25 litres/4 pints and 1 tablespoon salt to every 225 g/8 oz pasta. (As a general guide, allow 50 g/2 oz uncooked pasta per portion; pasta at least doubles its size and weight during cooking.) Add the pasta a little at a time, so that the temperature of the water doesn't fall below boiling point, then reduce the heat to a rolling boil, stirring occasionally. Do not cover.

The cooking time required depends on the shape and thickness of the pasta; spaghetti takes 8–10 minutes, tagliatelle 10–12 minutes and small pasta, such as bows, take about 5 minutes. Never overcook. (Packed pasta carries a recommended cooking time.) Cooked pasta should still have a 'bite' to it (it's called *al dente* in Italian) and should never be soft and mushy.

When cooked, drain the pasta in a sieve or colander and return to the pan with a knob of butter or a little olive oil. Toss well before serving or using in a recipe.

An unorthodox but convenient way to cook pasta – especially if you're entertaining – is to add it to boiling water as we've said, and boil for only 2–3 minutes. Remove it from the heat, cover with the pan lid and leave for 3–5 minutes longer than the cooking time prescribed for that type of pasta.

Scones (see page 152)

How to Make Pasta

It is much easier than you might think to make your own pasta and the result is much tastier than packet pasta. Pasta machines are available to cut or shape the dough for you.

100 g/4 oz strong plain flour
100 g/4 oz fine semolina
1 teaspoon salt
1 egg
1 tablespoon olive oil
4 tablespoons hot water

Sift the flour, semolina and salt into a bowl and make a well in the centre. Break the egg into the well and add the oil and hot water (start off with 4 tablespoons; add 1 more if too dry). Work to a dough with the fingertips. Divide the dough into two equal pieces. Cover a working surface with a clean cloth or tea towel and dust heavily with flour. Put one piece of dough on the floured cloth and roll out as thinly as possible, stretching the dough gently until the pattern of the cloth shows through. Cut the dough into the shapes you want – long thin strips for tagliatelle, wide bands for lasagne. Repeat using the second piece of dough. Cover the rolled out and shaped dough with a clean cloth and leave for 30 minutes – 1 hour to dry. If the dough is not to be cooked that day, store in an airtight container for up to three days. Home-made pasta need not be cooked for as long as the bought variety. **Makes about 450 g/1 lb**

Rice

There are more types of rice to confuse us than just Patna and pudding rice. Patna is a long-grain rice used for savoury dishes. Basmati is a less known long-grain rice of Indian origin which is used in most Indian recipes and many other savoury dishes. Brown rice is white rice with its outer husk retained, so it is higher in vitamin B, has more flavour and a firmer texture but takes longer to cook. Wild rice is not rice at all, but the seed of a wild grass. It is rather expensive but very tasty – it takes longer to cook than common rice. Short-grain rice is also known as Carolina rice, pudding rice or round rice. It softens more than other types on cooking so it is ideally suited to sweet dishes. Medium-grain rice again becomes a little softer than long-grain rice. It comes from Italy and produces just the right consistency for risottos and stuffings. Par-boiled rice is not quicker to cook but has been heated to remove the starch and prevent sticking when cooked.

How to Cook Rice

There are two ways to cook rice; both are given here.

Free boiling: Bring a large pan of salted water to the boil (at least 1.15 litres/2 pints to 100 g/4 oz rice). Pour in the rice slowly and bring back to the boil. Stir to separate the grains. Reduce the heat to a rolling boil and cook for 8–10 minutes for Patna and medium-grain rice; 20 minutes for Basmati and 40–45 minutes for brown or wild rice. Correctly cooked rice should be 'al dente' just like pasta. Strain and quickly pour over a little boiling water to separate the grains. Toss in a little oil or butter before serving. Rice almost triples in size and weight during cooking, 25 g/1 oz raw rice becomes 80 g/3¼ oz cooked, 100 g/4 oz cooked weight is 40 g/1½ oz raw rice.

Dry Boiling: This method uses a specified quantity of liquid, water or stock, so after the recommended cooking time no draining is required and the grains are fluffy and separate. Each type of rice requires different quantities of liquid and cooking time. For every 100 g/4 oz rice (enough for two portions) allow:-

Patna and medium grain rice: 250 ml/8 fl oz liquid; cook for 15 minutes.

Basmati rice: 325 ml/11 fl oz liquid; cook for 25 minutes.

Brown or wild rice: 350 ml/12 fl oz liquid; cook for 40–45 minutes.
Put the rice and salt in a small pan with the liquid. Bring to the boil, stir once, then cover and simmer slowly for the required time.

Flavoured Rice

Different flavours can be added to rice during cooking, either in the form of liquid or other dry ingredients. Use chicken or beef stock instead of water; use half water and half tomato juice; add a little fried onion and curry powder; or add a squeeze of lemon juice and 1–2 tablespoons of chopped fresh herbs.

Keeping Pasta and Rice Warm

Once cooked, place the drained rice or pasta in a colander or sieve over a pan of simmering water. Cover and allow the water to simmer gently until required. This is also a good way to reheat pasta and rice but make sure you don't overcook it in the first place.

Salads with Pasta and Rice

Both pasta and rice are excellent in salads. They blend with so many other flavours and give a good texture and colour contrast. However, be sure to undercook slightly so they don't break up on mixing or tossing. You will get the best results by mixing rice or pasta in a thin mayonnaise or Vinaigrette dressing immediately after draining. Then cool and mix in other ingredients – in this way more flavour is absorbed by the cereal.

Beef Risotto

2–3 tablespoons oil
1 small onion, chopped
225–275 g/8–10 oz medium-grain Italian rice or Patna rice
salt and pepper
225–275 g/8–10 oz cold beef, chopped
600–900 ml/1–1½ pints beef stock
1 tablespoon Worcestershire sauce
350 g/12 oz cooked mixed vegetables, chopped
100 g/4 oz sultanas or dried apricots (soaked for 2 hours) or other fruit with liquid

Heat the oil and fry the onion until translucent. Add the rice and toss for 2–3 minutes until lightly coloured. Add the seasoning, beef, 600 ml/1 pint of the stock and the Worcester-

shire sauce. Cover and simmer, stirring occasionally, for about 15 minutes. Top up with extra stock if necessary, but remember you should not need to drain this dish at the end of the cooking time. Add the vegetables and fruit, cook for a further 3–4 minutes, check the seasoning and serve. **Serves 4**

Rice and Ham Balls with Mustard Sauce

225 g/8 oz uncooked ham
225 g/8 oz long-grain rice, cooked
1 tablespoon finely chopped parsley
grated rind of ½ lemon
salt and pepper
1 egg, beaten
1 bay leaf
few parsley stalks
sauce:
4 tablespoons mayonnaise
1 tablespoon French mustard
1 tablespoon single cream

Mince the ham finely and mix with the rice, parsley, lemon rind and seasoning. Add the beaten egg to bind all the ingredients and form into walnut-sized balls. Bring a shallow pan of water to the boil with the bay leaf and parsley stalks. When boiling, carefully place the rice balls in the water. Turn once or twice during cooking time (about 15 minutes), then remove with a slotted spoon. Serve hot or cold with a sauce made by mixing all the sauce ingredients together. **Serves 4**

Egg Curry with Brown Rice and Raisins

225 g/8 oz brown rice
50 g/2 oz raisins
salt
2 tablespoons oil
1 medium onion, thinly sliced
100 g/4 oz almonds, blanched
2 teaspoons curry paste
300 ml/½ pint chicken stock
1 tablespoon cornflour
1 tablespoon chutney
100 g/4 oz frozen mixed vegetables
4 hard-boiled eggs, halved
3 green chillies, chopped (optional)

Boil the rice and raisins in salted water for 40–45 minutes. Meanwhile, heat the oil and lightly fry the onion and almonds. When the rice is cooked, mix with the onion and almonds and keep warm. Mix the curry paste with a little stock; stir in the cornflour and chutney and add the remaining stock. Bring to the boil, stirring all the time; add the frozen vegetables and simmer for 10 minutes. Arrange the eggs on a heated serving dish and pour over the sauce. Garnish with chillies and serve with the rice and raisins. **Serves 4**

Baked Onion Rice

675 g/1½ lb long-grain rice
2–3 tablespoons oil
1 large onion, finely chopped
salt and pepper
750 ml/1¼ pints chicken stock

Rinse the rice, heat the oil then toss the rice until golden. Transfer to an ovenproof dish. Fry the onion in the remaining oil and add to the rice with the seasoning and stock. Cover and bake in a moderate oven (180°C, 350°F, Gas Mark 4) for about 45 minutes until tender. **Serves 8**

Pasta alla Carbonara

(Illustrated on page 85)

350 g/12 oz short-cut pasta
(bows, shells or macaroni)
salt
6 rashers bacon, rind removed, chopped and fried
3 eggs, beaten
25 g/1 oz butter
1 tablespoon Parmesan cheese
freshly ground black pepper

Cook the pasta in boiling salted water for about 15 minutes. Drain, return to the pan and add the bacon. Stir in the eggs and butter and cook gently until the eggs have just scrambled. Serve topped with Parmesan and lots of pepper. **Serves 4**

Spaghetti Pescatori

350 g/12 oz spaghetti
225 g/8 oz peeled prawns
225 g/8 oz squid, cleaned and cut in rings
450 ml/¾ pint milk
1 bay leaf
25 g/1 oz butter
25 g/1 oz flour
2 tablespoons tomato purée
salt and pepper
½ teaspoon anchovy essence
unpeeled prawns to garnish

Cook the spaghetti in boiling salted water until tender. Hold it upright in the water for the first few seconds until it begins to soften, then you can twist it round inside the pan. Meanwhile, cook the prawns and squid in the milk with the bay leaf for 5–10 minutes. Drain, reserving the liquid. Make the liquid back up to 450 ml/¾ pint with more milk if necessary. Discard the bay leaf. Melt the butter in a saucepan, stir in the flour and cook, stirring, for 1 minute. Gradually stir in the reserved liquor and bring to the boil. Add the prawns, squid, tomato purée, seasoning and anchovy essence. Simmer, stirring, for 1–2 minutes. Serve the fish sauce on a bed of drained spaghetti. Garnish with the unpeeled prawns and serve with a green salad. **Serves 4**

Tagliatelle alla Panna Fresca con Cipolla

(Pasta in a creamy cheese sauce)

350 g/12 oz tagliatelle
50 g/2 oz butter
1 small onion, chopped
1 clove garlic, crushed
pinch dried mixed herbs
300 ml/½ pint double cream
salt and pepper
50 g/2 oz Mozzarella cheese, finely grated

Cook the pasta in boiling salted water. Meanwhile, melt the butter and cook the onion, garlic and herbs until the onion is soft. Stir in the cream. Bring to the boil and simmer for 1–2 minutes. Season to taste and stir in the cheese. Drain the pasta, mix with the sauce and serve immediately with a salad. **Serves 4**

Vegetable Rice

(Illustrated on pages 86–7)

225 g/8 oz cooked long-grain rice
100 g/4 oz mushrooms, sliced
50 g/2 oz radishes, sliced
2 spring onions, chopped
2 sticks celery, sliced
½ lettuce
150 ml/¼ pint natural yogurt
1 teaspoon chopped herbs
salt and pepper

Mix the rice, mushrooms, radishes, onion and celery together. Line a bowl with the lettuce and turn the rice mixture into the bowl. Mix the yogurt, herbs and seasoning and pour over the salad just before serving. This could be served as a hot vegetable dish if you prefer. **Serves 6**

Rice Fritters

(Illustrated on pages 86–7)

2 eggs, lightly beaten
50 g/2 oz plain flour
salt and pepper
100 g/4 oz medium-grain rice, cooked and drained
4–5 tablespoons oil

Beat the eggs and flour together until smooth. Then add the seasoning and rice to make a firm mixture. Form the mixture into small flat fritters. Heat the oil and fry the fritters for 2–3 minutes each side until firm and golden. Serve with cold meats or just with a little fruit for a snack. **Serves 4**

Special Fried Rice

1–2 tablespoons oil
½ egg, lightly beaten
50 g/2 oz lean pork, cut in cubes and crisply fried
50 g/2 oz peeled prawns
225 g/8 oz cooked long-grain rice, drained
4 spring onions, chopped
salt and pepper
pinch monosodium glutamate
1 tablespoon chicken stock

Heat the oil in a wok or light-weight frying pan. Add the egg and stir-fry, or toss rapidly with a fork, until set (about 20 seconds). Add the pork, prawns, rice, onion, seasoning and monosodium glutamate. Toss over a high heat for 2–3 minutes. Add the stock to moisten and serve immediately. **Serves 2**

Eggs

Eggs are nature's own pre-packaged convenience food. Full of protein, minerals, vitamins and flavour, they are a very economical food and a good alternative to meat. Not only are they vital for baking, they are the basis of many extremely good, substantial and often very quick, main meals.

Buy eggs regularly in small quantities, so you always have some on hand as fresh as possible. Old eggs loose their flavour and colour, as well as their thickening and whipping qualities. Egg boxes should now be stamped with the number of the week of the year, so check this before buying, to see how old they are. (If eggs have gone bad they will usually float when put into water.) Store in a cool dark place. The refrigerator will naturally help them to keep better, but they tend to firm up and will not whip or beat up to full volume until brought back to room temperature. Most recipes use standard size 3 or 4 eggs unless otherwise specified.

Boiling Eggs

Use only very fresh eggs. To be sure they won't crack, they should be at room temperature and can be pricked at the pointed end with a pin, where the air sack is.

Either lower them carefully into gently boiling water, or put them in cold water and bring to the boil. Use only just enough water to cover. If they crack, add a little salt or vinegar immediately.

Once the water boils again, reduce the heat to a simmer and start timing, allowing 1–2 minutes less for eggs put into cold water. Soft-boiled take $3\frac{1}{2}$ minutes; for a firm white and soft yolk allow 5–6 minutes; and to hard-boil cook for 10–12 minutes.

When cooked to your taste, gently tap and crack the shell and serve, or, to keep hard-boiled eggs for later, put immediately into cold running water and crack the shells.

Coddled Eggs

Put the required number of eggs into boiling water, cover and remove from the heat. Leave for 4–7 minutes before serving.

Poaching Eggs

Either use a special poaching pan or a small frying pan. A poaching pan is the easiest but produces a very different result. Fill the base of the poacher with water, put the egg container on top and put a knob of butter in as many containers as necessary. When the water is boiling and butter is melted, carefully pour in the eggs, from a cup. Season and cover. Cook gently until as firm as you wish.

To use a frying pan, half fill it with water and add 1–2 tablespoons vinegar. Bring to a gentle boil. Crack the eggs, one at a time, into a cup. Then tip them gently, but quickly into the pan, keeping the whites together with a spatula. Cook gently for 2–3 minutes. Remove with a slotted spoon and drain. To help keep them in a better shape, tip the eggs into greased pastry cutters, in the frying pan, then cook as above.

Frying Eggs

Melt dripping or lard (or fry bacon first) in a small frying pan until just smoking. Slide the eggs in, one at a time, from a cup or saucer and reduce the heat slightly. Baste frequently with fat while cooking for 2–3 minutes. When cooked to your taste, carefully remove with a fish slice.

Scrambling Eggs

Melt a little butter or lard in a small saucepan. Lightly beat together the required number of eggs, plus 1 tablespoon milk or water per egg, a little salt, pepper, herbs or any other seasonings. Stir into the hot fat and then cook gently, stirring frequently with a wooden spoon, until the eggs are as cooked as you like. Flavour scrambled eggs with herbs or seasonings, grated cheese, onion, chopped ham, fish or vegetables. For sandwich fillings, scramble only very softly, remove from the heat and stir in a little mayonnaise. Cool before using.

Omelettes

The correct pan will help you make perfect omelettes easily. You can buy small omelette or pancake pans, or use a thick-based small frying pan which you should keep especially for omelettes and pancakes. A non-stick pan is the most foolproof, as long as you treat it properly and never scratch it. A cast iron pan will need 'seasoning' before and after use. Burn a thin layer of salt in the base, gently rub round with paper and then wipe clean. Never wash or scour an omelette pan.

Slowly heat the pan to get an even, moderate heat. Melt about 15 g/$\frac{1}{2}$ oz butter, dripping or lard in the pan. Beat together 2 eggs per person with seasoning and a little milk or water. Pour quickly into the pan and swirl round to give an even coating. While cooking, disturb gently with a wooden spoon, pulling the cooked egg from the edges into the centre and pushing the soft egg mixture to the edges to cook. When the base is set and the top is just setting, the omelette is ready – some people may however prefer their omelettes more firmly cooked. Tilt the pan and with a spatula, flip one half over the other and then quickly slide on to a warmed plate.

Filled and Flavoured Omelettes

Omelettes can be cooked with flavourings mixed into the egg or spooned on to the nearly cooked omelette just before serving. Try fresh herbs, grated cheese, chopped mushrooms, tomatoes, ham, fish, a mixture of chopped vegetables or a mixture of finely chopped left-over ingredients. Remember to season the filling as well as the egg mixture.

Soufflé Omelettes

Separate the eggs from the yolks. Beat the yolks with water and seasoning or sugar. Whisk the egg whites stiffly and fold carefully into the yolks. Cook as for a plain omelette until the base is golden. Then pop under a hot grill until golden and just firm on top. Serve immediately.

Soufflé omelettes are more often served sweet, filled with luxury jams, preserves, or fruit purées flavoured with a liqueur, then sprinkled with icing sugar. However, they can be just as good with any savoury filling.

Soufflés

Soufflés are surrounded by mystique and tend to worry many cooks, but they really are quite simple to make successfully. The most important thing is not to keep the soufflé waiting – you must wait for the soufflé and be ready to eat it immediately. Once it begins to fall you are bound to be disappointed.

Cheese Soufflé

25 g/1 oz butter
25 g/1 oz flour
salt and pepper
pinch dry mustard
150 ml/$\frac{1}{4}$ pint milk
100 g/4 oz strong Cheddar cheese, grated
4 eggs, separated
1 tablespoon grated Parmesan cheese

Melt the butter in a large saucepan, stir in the flour and cook for 1 minute. Add the seasoning and mustard and gradually stir in the milk until smooth. Cook gently, stirring all the time, for 1 minute until thickened and smooth. Remove from the heat and stir in the Cheddar cheese. Beat the egg yolks into the mixture. Stiffly whisk the whites and fold in carefully using a metal spoon, until evenly distributed, being careful not to break down the whisked eggs. Spoon into a greased 15–18-cm/6–7-inch soufflé dish. Sprinkle with Parmesan cheese and make a cut through the top with a spoon to give an interesting 'top hat' effect when cooked. Bake in a moderately hot oven (200°C, 400°F, Gas Mark 6) for 30–35 minutes. It should be well risen, golden on top and just firm to the touch, though slightly wobbly. Serve immediately. **Serves 4**

Alternative Soufflé Flavourings

Using the basic recipe:

Chicken make the sauce with half chicken stock and half milk. Add 100–150 g/4–5 oz minced cooked chicken in place of cheese.

Haddock add 100 g/4 oz flaked cooked haddock instead of cheese to the sauce with 2–3 tablespoons single cream.

Ham add 75–100 g/3–4 oz minced ham in place of cheese, 1 tablespoon chopped parsley and a little single cream. Don't be too generous with the salt.

Chocolate mix 1–1$\frac{1}{2}$ tablespoons cocoa or 2–3 tablespoons chocolate powder with the flour. Sweeten with castor sugar to taste and add a little cream, then fold in the egg whites.

Grand Marnier sweeten the sauce to taste with vanilla sugar, or add a few drops of vanilla essence with the sugar. Add 1 tablespoon ground almonds and 2–3 tablespoons Grand Marnier to the sauce.

Bacon and Egg Pudding

15 g/$\frac{1}{2}$ oz butter
8–10 slices white bread
225–275 g/8–10 oz bacon rashers or pieces cut in strips
225 g/8 oz mushrooms, sliced
3 large eggs
450 ml/$\frac{3}{4}$ pint milk
pinch grated nutmeg
salt and pepper
75 g/3 oz Cheddar cheese, grated
$\frac{1}{2}$–1 tablespoon oil
1 small onion, sliced

Butter a 1.25-litre/2-pint ovenproof dish and line its sides and base with the bread, cut to fit. Put alternative layers of bread, bacon and mushroom in the dish. Beat the eggs and milk together and season well with nutmeg, salt and pepper. Pour over the layers, sprinkle the cheese over the top and cook in a moderate oven (180°C, 350°F, Gas Mark 4) for 45–55 minutes until the mixture on top is set. Heat the oil and fry the onion until golden. Top the pudding with a layer of fried onion rings. **Serves 4**

Right: Pizza (see page 153)

Assorted ice cream flavours (see page 179) and Mint ice cream (see page 180)

Ham Scotch Eggs

175 g/6 oz cooked ham
25 g/1 oz butter or margarine
25 g/1 oz flour
150 ml/¼ pint milk
50 g/2 oz fresh breadcrumbs
1 tablespoon chopped parsley
salt and pepper
½–1 teaspoon prepared mustard
4 hard-boiled eggs
2 tablespoons seasoned flour
1 egg
1 tablespoon water
50 g/2 oz crisp breadcrumbs
oil for deep-frying

Mince the ham. Melt the butter or margarine in a saucepan, stir in the flour and cook for 1 minute, stirring. Gradually add the milk to make a thick sauce. Add the crumbs, parsley, ham, seasoning and mustard to the sauce. Leave to cool. Shell the eggs, coat them with the ham mixture and shape neatly. Roll first in the seasoned flour, then in beaten egg mixed with water and finally in the crisp breadcrumbs. Heat the oil to 190°C/375°F, or until a cube of bread turns golden in 1 minute. Fry the Scotch eggs until crisp and brown, drain on absorbent kitchen paper and serve hot or cold.

Variation Split the hard-boiled eggs, remove the yolks and mash with a little seasoning, then add 50–75 g/2–3 oz grated cheese and 25 g/1 oz butter. Spoon back into the whites; press the two halves together then continue to coat as above. **Serves 4**

Egg and Meat Pie

6 tablespoons oil
675 g/1½ lb aubergines, sliced
1 onion, chopped
1 clove garlic, crushed
350 g/12 oz minced lamb or beef
salt and pepper
½ teaspoon dried mixed herbs
1 (64-g/2¼-oz) can tomato purée
4 eggs
25 g/1 oz butter
25 g/1 oz flour
450 ml/¾ pint milk
50 g/2 oz Cheddar cheese, grated
2 tablespoons grated Parmesan cheese

Heat the oil in a frying pan and fry the aubergines until they are golden brown on both sides. Drain on absorbent kitchen paper. Fry the onion, garlic and meat for a few minutes in the oil remaining in the pan. Season, stir in the herbs and tomato purée and cook for 15 minutes. Turn into an ovenproof dish and top with the eggs, carefully cracked, and then the aubergines. Melt the butter in a saucepan, stir in the flour and cook for 1 minute, stirring. Gradually add the milk and stir until boiled and thickened. Stir in the Cheddar cheese. Pour the sauce over the pie, sprinkle with Parmesan cheese and cook in a moderately hot oven (190°C, 375°F, Gas Mark 5) for 1½ hours. **Serves 4**

Buttered oranges (see page 179)

Tunisian Briks

1 (370-g/13-oz) packet frozen flaky pastry,
thawed
1 small onion, chopped
225 g/8 oz minced lamb or beef
50 g/2 oz cheese, grated
2 teaspoons ground cumin
1 teaspoon chilli powder
salt and pepper
milk for brushing
4–5 small eggs
150 ml/¼ pint oil

Roll out the pastry on a floured surface as thinly as possible and cut into 8–10 (13-cm/5-inch) diameter circles. Fry the onion and mince together in the meat's own fat until browned, then cook gently for another 10 minutes. Drain off any excess fat. Stir in the cheese, cumin, chilli and seasoning.

Place a generous spoonful of meat on half the pastry circles, making a hollow in the centre. Brush the edges with milk and then place a raw egg in the centre of the meat. Quickly cover each with a pastry round and seal the edges well. Heat the oil in a frying pan and fry until the pastry is puffed and golden. Serve immediately. **Serves 4–5**

Cheese

Cheese is compressed milk – that is, milk which has had most of the water content removed, leaving the milk solids. It is high in fat and has up to twice as much protein as beef, weight for weight. It also supplies vitamin A, calcium and minerals.

Hard cheeses (Cheddar, Cheshire, Edam and so on) contain less fat than the soft creamy varieties (Port Salut, cream cheese) and have a higher percentage of protein.

Fresh cut cheese keeps its flavour better – don't buy more than 5–6 days in advance. Store in a cool, even temperature. Don't wrap too tightly in foil or polythene as this can make the cheese sweat. Overcooking will make cheese tough and indigestible so cook it slowly or very lightly; using grated cheese helps. Hard cheese is better for cooking; soft cheese is better for adding to creamed mixtures or fillings.

A–Z of Cheeses

There are hundreds of cheeses made all over the world. The ones we have covered here are those readily available in most supermarkets or delicatessens in Britain.

Bel Paese (*Italy*) A soft creamy cheese, with a mild flavour. It has a pale yellow rind and the cheese itself has very small holes. It is good for eating on its own, for pizzas and for some cooked dishes.

Bleu de Bresse (*France*) A rich, creamy blue cheese without the very strong flavour of some blue cheeses. Usually comes in small portions, packaged in foil.

Blue Dorset (*England*) This cheese is often called Blue Vinny. It is now rarely found. It is usually a hard, blue-veined cheese.

Brie (*France*) A soft, creamy cheese which has a mild flavour which develops rapidly during aging or storing to a strong, sharp taste. Buy Brie in small quantities to eat it at its best; serve at room temperature when the centre is just softening. Although mainly a cheeseboard cheese, it can be creamed to make delicious quiches. Many varieties of Brie are available in France. Available in portions ready-packaged, or cut from one large flat cheese.

Caboc (*Scotland*) A full fat cream cheese, made in a cylindrical shape and usually covered in oatmeal.

Caerphilly (*Wales*) It is now made mainly in the south of England. The flavour is mild and tangy and although it is a hard cheese, it flakes and crumbles easily. Caerphilly is good to eat on its own but also can be used in sauces and cooked dishes. Very good with fruit.

Camembert (*France*) A rich, soft cheese with very similar qualities to Brie. It is normally sold in small triangular packaged portions, half and whole packaged cheeses.

Cheddar (*England*) The best-known English cheese, which, like many others, is reproduced in most other cheese-making countries as well. It is a firm, smooth cheese with a close texture. Although mild when young, it rapidly develops a good mellow flavour. Really mature farmhouse Cheddar has a very special flavour. Good for cooking or eating on its own.

Cheshire (*England*) The oldest English cheese, which is still made mainly in Cheshire. It is a firm, flaky cheese with a distinctive, piquant flavour. Good to cook with or eat on its own.

Chevre (*France*) This name applies to a whole range of French goat's milk cheeses, their flavours varying from mildly tangy to strong. The popular kind is firm and yet creamy, with a chalky, crumbly centre. Not good for cooking.

Cottage Cheese This is made from skimmed milk which has been allowed to sour naturally. The curds (solids), after draining are slightly seasoned, but not pressed – as hard cheeses are – to extract much liquid. Now it is usually commercially made, although it can be made at home. Very low in calories, it can be used in sweet or savoury dishes for even the weight-conscious.

Cream Cheese This is made from creams of varying fat contents. The curds are seasoned and then creamed. It is high in calories but is very good for sweet or savoury cooking.

Danish Blue (*Denmark*) The best-known cheese from Denmark. It is a smooth, creamy, blue-veined cheese with a mellow flavour. As it is creamy it can be used in some cooked dishes and sauces.

Derby (*England*) A firm cheese, not unlike Cheddar, which improves with age. Sage Derby has now become very popular too. Crushed sage leaves are marbled through it to give a very pleasant flavour. Not often used in cooking.

Double Gloucester (*England*) A hard, yellow cheese with a mild but distinctive flavour. The younger cheese is good for cooking with, but well-matured Gloucester should be eaten on its own.

Dolcelatte (*Italy*) A recent addition to the cheeses of Italy, it is a blend of Gorgonzola and cream cheese. A very mild, especially soft, blue-veined cheese, it has quickly become popular in this country. However, it does not keep very long. It can be used in cooking too.

Dunlop (*Scotland*) A pale, moist but firm cheese, with a pleasant mild flavour. Used in Scotland a great deal to replace Cheddar.

Edam (*Holland*) A round cheese, about 1.75 kg/4 lb in weight, with a bright red protective wax rind. The deep yellow cheese is smooth, with a pleasant mild flavour. It is comparatively low in calories and very good to cook with.

Emmenthal (*Switzerland*) This is a hard cheese, very similar to the more famous Swiss cheese, Gruyère. It is a smooth cheese with large holes, often the size of cherries. It has a mild nutty flavour and is excellent for cooking with.

Esrom (*Denmark*) This is a full-cream cheese with a rich, sweet flavour that can become very pungent as the cheese is kept. The smooth yellow cheese has small holes.

Feta (*Greece*) Although originally made from goat's milk, modern manufacturers use a mixture of goat's, cow's or sheep's milk. It is a semi-hard, very white cheese which forms no rind. It is sold in rectangular blocks and has a salty, sourish taste. Very good for salads and vegetable dishes but not for cooking with.

Fontina (*Italy*) This is a large smooth cheese, with a high fat content. Occasionally it has tiny holes. It has a creamy, mild flavour and is very good for cooking with.

Gorgonzola (*Italy*) A rich, creamy blue-veined cheese, with a distinctive flavour. It is best eaten when just becoming soft and mature, on its own with fresh, crusty bread.

Gouda (*Holland*) A large round cheese with a bright yellow rind. It is a very yellow, firm cheese with a mild, slightly nutty flavour. It is very good for cooking with.

Gruyère (*Switzerland*) This is a firm, pale yellow cheese, which, when cooked, has an unusual, slightly granular texture. A smooth cheese with pea-sized holes, it has a characteristic sweet, nutty flavour which is used for the famous Swiss Fondue.

Havarti (*Denmark*) This semi-hard cheese is made in rounds or loaf shapes. It is creamy yellow with tiny holes and a fresh, slightly sour taste. Good for cooking or eating.

Lancashire (*England*) Tasty Lanky, as it is known west of the Pennines, is a pale, creamy white hard cheese which is usually very crumbly. This tangy cheese is good to use in many cooked dishes and with fruit or fruit pies.

Leicester (*England*) This red-orange coloured hard cheese, is often crumbly or flaky. It keeps well, has a good mellow flavour and is good for cooking.

Livarot (*France*) One of France's oldest cheeses, it is definitely an acquired taste. It is slightly elastic in texture, with an interesting smell and taste and an edible reddish-brown rind enjoyed by the connoisseur.

Mozzarella (*Italy*) A soft, moist, very white cheese with a mild buttermilk taste. We normally buy it lightly smoked with a pale yellow rind, but it is best bought fresh packed in polythene bags and kept moist in water. It is best known in Britain for its use in pizzas but it is good in other cooked dishes, or with salads and vegetables for a starter.

Neufchâtel (*France*) A cheese from Normandy, sold in squares, cylinders or attractive heart shapes. It is a soft, pale creamy cheese with a slightly salty taste.

Parmesan (*Italy*) There are very many varieties of Parmesan available in Italy. It is the hardest cheese of all and should have at least two years to mature to become pale grey-yellow and grainy. It is the perfect grating and flavouring cheese for many dishes as it has a strong flavour and therefore little is needed. Store tubs or sachets carefully to keep its dry, fresh qualities, or buy fresh in small pieces and store tightly wrapped in the refrigerator.

Petit Suisse (*France*) A fresh, very soft, creamy cheese made with a large percentage of fat. It has a mild, fresh, slightly nutty taste which is good on its own or with fruit and sugar for desserts. Demi-sel is very similar but lightly salted. Eat within 2–3 days.

Pont l'Evêque (*France*) A square cheese with a soft pliable texture and yellow-orange rind. It has a creamy, faintly nutty flavour which can rapidly become very pungent.

Port Salut (*France*) A classic French monastery cheese which is subtle and delicate in taste. It has an orange rind and the cheese is a pale, creamy yellow. Good for salads or on its own.

Reblochon (*France*) A semi-hard cheese, with a dark yellow rind. This rich, creamy cheese has a mild and characteristically fragrant flavour.

Red Windsor (*England*) A recent addition to English cheeses, it is Cheddar impregnated with red wine.

Ricotta (*Italy*) A very white, soft cream cheese, not unlike our cottage cheese but much creamier. It can be used in many sweet or savoury cooked dishes, or served with fruit.

Roquefort (*France*) Made from sheep's milk, this very famous French cheese is matured in the caves of Roquefort to produce its unique flavour. A semi-hard white cheese, delicately veined and marbled.

Saint Paulin (*France*) A very mild and creamy cheese similar to Port Salut.

Samso (*Denmark*) A large round, semi-hard cheese with Swiss origins. Made from the full-cream milk it is pale yellow and smooth with large holes. It has a sweet nutty flavour that develops as it ripens. Good for cooking and eating.

Smoked Cheese Many cheeses are smoked (lightly cooked) to give a firmer texture and longer lasting qualities. Some are blended with ham or herbs and have a stronger flavour which makes them good for cooking with – but do so carefully – as the cheese can become very rubbery.

Stilton (*England*) The king of cheeses and world famous. It is a semi-hard, double-cream, blue-veined cheese. Stilton is mild, velvety and creamy when young, or rich and full-flavoured when properly matured. It should be moist and when matured it becomes flaky or crumbly. To keep it well, wrap tightly and keep in a cool, dark place, but not in the refrigerator. Cut in small triangular wedges, not scoops, to expose less cut surface to the air, and keep lightly covered. Although best eaten accompanied by a good red wine or port, the habit of pouring port into the centre of the cheese should only be practised when the cheese is very dry – otherwise it will ruin the true Stilton flavour. There is a white Stilton, which is a young, quick ripening and tangy cheese.

Tomme de Savoie au Raisin (*France*) A soft, ivory white creamy cheese which has a fresh, slightly sourish taste. it is coated in black grape skins or pips.

Wensleydale (*England*) A rich, creamy soft cheese, delicately blue-veined and sweet. The ripe cheese has a greyish-white skin. There is also the better known White variety which is eaten younger. Use either for cooking.

Welsh Rarebit

25 g/1 oz butter
1 tablespoon flour
pinch salt
pinch cayenne
pinch dry mustard
150 ml/¼ pint beer or milk
few drops Worcestershire sauce
175–225 g/6–8 oz Leicester or Double Gloucester cheese
2 large or 4 small slices bread
butter for spreading

Heat the butter in a pan and stir in the flour, seasoning, and cayenne. Then stir in the beer and sauce carefully. Stir over a low heat until a coating consistency is reached, then add the cheese and leave to melt, but do not cook further. Meanwhile, toast and butter the bread. Top with the cheese mixture. Grill until golden and serve immediately. **Serves 2 as a light meal, 4 as a savoury**

Spinach and Cheese Pie

1 (370 g/13-oz) packet frozen puff pastry, thawed
450 g/1 lb spinach, cooked, well seasoned and puréed
225–275 g/8–10 oz Mozzarella cheese
2 tangerines, divided in segments
1 egg, beaten

Roll out the pastry on a floured surface to a large square and place on a greased baking tray. Press all the excess moisture from spinach. Dice the cheese and mix with the spinach and tangerines. Place this mixture in the centre of the pastry. Moisten the pastry edges with egg

and bring the four corners to centre; seal and flute the edges. Make a split in the top to release the steam. Brush all over with beaten egg and bake in a hot oven (230°C, 450°F, Gas Mark 8) for 15 minutes. Lower the heat to moderately hot (200°C, 400°F, Gas Mark 6) for 15–20 minutes until the pastry is crisp and golden. **Serves 4–6**

Cheesy Vegetable Casserole

2 tablespoons oil
2 medium onions, sliced
450 g/1 lb tomatoes, peeled and quartered
1 (425-g/15-oz) can butter beans, drained
1 (425-g/15-oz) can red kidney beans, drained
225 g/8 oz mushrooms, sliced
2 tablespoons tomato ketchup
1 teaspoon Worcestershire sauce
175 g/6 oz cream cheese or other cheese
3–4 tablespoons double cream

Heat the oil and fry the onion until golden. Stir in the tomatoes, butter and kidney beans, mushrooms, ketchup, Worcestershire sauce and seasoning and place in an ovenproof dish. Stir in 100 g/4 oz of the cheese, cut into small pieces. Cream or grate the rest, mix with the cream and pour over the vegetables. Cook in a moderately hot oven (190°C, 375°F, Gas Mark 5) for 25–30 minutes. **Serves 4–6**

Beef and Potato Layer

450 g/1 lb mashed potato
50 g/2 oz butter
1 tablespoon grated Parmesan cheese
450 g/1 lb minced beef
2–3 tablespoons chutney or ketchup
2 eggs
salt and pepper

Mix the mashed potatoes with half the butter. Season to taste and add the cheese. Mix the beef with the chutney, eggs and seasoning. Layer the potato and beef mixtures in a small, deep ovenproof dish, finishing with a potato layer. Top with the remaining butter and bake in a moderately hot oven (200°C, 400°F, Gas Mark 6) for 45 minutes until golden. **Serves 4–6**

Westmorland Pie

350 g/12 oz Shortcrust pastry (see page 136)
350 g/12 oz cooked meat
225 g/8 oz streaky bacon rashers or cooked ham
225 g/8 oz stuffing mix
50 g/2 oz sultanas
salt and pepper
little stock or stock and white wine mixed

Roll out three-quarters of the pastry thinly on a floured surface and use to line a 20-cm/8-inch cheesecake mould or loose-bottomed cake tin. Cut the meat into small pieces. Remove the rind from the bacon. Prepare the stuffing according to the instructions on the packet. Mash the stuffing and mix with the sultanas. Fill the pastry-lined mould with a thick layer of the stuffing mixture, then add the rashers of bacon, laid out flat and the meat. Sprinkle with seasoning and stock.

Roll out the remaining pastry for the top (which will form the base when turned out). Seal the edges with a little water and then flute evenly. Bake in a hot oven (220°C, 425°F, Gas Mark 7) for 20 minutes, then in a moderate oven (180°C, 350°F, Gas Mark 4) for 1¼ hours. Remove the mould, invert the pie on a tray and brush with egg. Return to a moderately hot oven (200°C, 400°F, Gas Mark 6) for 15–20 minutes until golden. Lift carefully on to a serving dish and serve hot or cold with hot redcurrant or cranberry sauce. **Serves 6–8**

Frankfurter Hot-pot

2 tablespoons oil
2 onions, coarsely chopped
2 carrots, cut in narrow strips
½ cabbage, thinly sliced
225 g/8 oz potatoes, coarsely chopped
100 g/4 oz button mushrooms
1 clove garlic, crushed (optional)
1 tablespoon tomato purée
1 teaspoon chilli sauce (optional)
600 ml/1 pint chicken stock
4 frankfurters
225 g/8 oz French sausage or salami, sliced

Heat the oil and fry the onion until lightly browned. Add all the other ingredients except the frankfurters and sausage or salami. Simmer for 30 minutes, then add the frankfurters and sausage. Heat through for a further 15 minutes, then serve. **Serves 4**

Corned Beef in a Crust

1 (340-g/12-oz) can corned beef
1 (425-g/15-oz) can whole carrots, drained and sliced
1 (227-g/8-oz) can baked beans
1 beef stock cube, crumbled
200 g/8 oz Flaky pastry (see page 145)
1 egg, beaten

Roughly dice the corned beef and mix with the carrots, baked beans and stock cube. Turn into a pie dish. Roll the pastry out thinly on a lightly floured surface and cut a strip for the rim of the dish. Moisten the rim and put the pastry strip on. Use the remaining pastry to cover the pie. Make any trimmings into a decoration for the top of the pie. Glaze all over with egg and bake in a hot oven (220°C, 425°F, Gas Mark 7) for 25–35 minutes until the pastry is well-risen and golden. **Serves 4–5**

Barbecued Sausages

450 g/1 lb pork sausages
2 tablespoons oil
1 small onion, sliced
2 tomatoes, peeled and seeds removed
1 teaspoon dried mixed herbs
3 tablespoons light soft brown sugar
salt and pepper

Prick the sausages and grill in the normal way until almost cooked. Heat the oil and fry the onion with the tomatoes, herbs, sugar and seasoning. When the tomatoes are tender and the sausages are cooked, add the sausages to the sauce and simmer for about 5 minutes. Serve immediately. **Serves 4**

Black-eyed Suzie

225 g/8 oz black-eyed beans, or other dried beans,
soaked
2 onions, sliced
1 teaspoon cumin seeds
600 ml/1 pint chicken stock
4 chicken wings
1 tablespoon oil
salt and pepper
225 g/8 oz spiced garlic sausage, coarsely chopped
225 g/8 oz green beans, sliced
100 g/4 oz tagliatelle
1 teaspoon dried thyme

Drain the beans and place in a large saucepan
with the onion, cumin and chicken stock.
Bring to the boil and simmer for about 45
minutes. Meanwhile brush the chicken wings
with a little oil and seasoning and grill or fry
until just golden. Add the chicken to the pan
of beans with the sausage.

After a further 20 minutes, add the green
beans, tagliatelle and thyme. Continue simmering until the beans and chicken wings are
tender. Serve with boiled cabbage. **Serves 4**

Ham Galantine

225 g/1 oz fat
2 small onions, finely chopped
350 g/12 oz boiled bacon or cheap ham
350 g/12 oz pork sausagemeat
$\frac{1}{2}$ teaspoon chopped sage, or pinch dried
50 g/2 oz fresh breadcrumbs
2 eggs
4 tablespoons milk or stock
salt and pepper

Heat the fat and toss the onions for several
minutes. Mince the bacon, then mix with the
onion and remaining ingredients. Grease a 1-
kg/2-lb loaf tin. Press the mixture into
this; cover with greased foil and stand in a bain-
marie. Cook in a moderate oven (160°C,
325°F, Gas Mark 3) for $1\frac{1}{4}$ hours. Serve hot or
cold. **Serves 4–6**

Beef Tacos

3 tablespoons oil
225 g/8 oz minced beef
2 tablespoons chilli sauce
2 teaspoons chilli powder
1 large onion, thinly sliced
1 large carrot, grated
$\frac{1}{2}$ green pepper, seeds removed and shredded
4 tortillas or small pancakes

Heat 2 tablespoons of the oil, add the beef and
fry quickly for 15 minutes, stirring well. Add
the chilli sauce and powder, the onion, carrot
and green pepper and cook for 2–3 minutes, so
the vegetables remain crisp. Meanwhile, heat
the remaining oil and fry the tortillas for 2–3
minutes then drain. Fold each one in half and
fill with the meat mixture. Serve with a fresh,
crisp salad or shredded cabbage. **Serves 4**

Crisp-topped Beans with Two Sauces

225 g/8 oz butter beans, soaked
1 (227-g/8-oz) can tomatoes, chopped
1 small onion, finely chopped
salt and pepper
1 teaspoon chopped fresh sage
300 ml/$\frac{1}{2}$ pint stock
15 g/$\frac{1}{2}$ oz butter
15 g/$\frac{1}{2}$ oz flour
150 ml/$\frac{1}{4}$ pint milk
150 ml/$\frac{1}{4}$ pint single cream
75 g/3 oz cheese, grated
25–50 g/1–2 oz fresh breadcrumbs

Drain the beans and mix with the tomatoes,
onion, seasoning, sage and stock in a large pan
and simmer gently for about 1 hour or until the
beans are nearly tender. Meanwhile, melt the
butter, stir in the flour and cook for 1 minute,
stirring. Gradually add the milk and cream and
cook gently for 2–3 minutes. Then stir in
50 g/2 oz of the cheese and add more seasoning.

Place the beans in the base of an ovenproof
dish and top with the sauce. Mix the remaining
cheese and the breadcrumbs and sprinkle over
the top. Cook in a moderately hot oven
(190°C, 375°F, Gas Mark 5) for about 35
minutes until crisp and golden. Serve as a light
supper or with a meat dish. **Serves 4**

Pastries

There is no secret knack to successful pastry-making, despite what our mothers or grand-mothers may have told us. Some pastries do take a little bit of practice to make perfectly, some are so simple you just can't fail. Just be sure you use the right proportions and keep cool – yes – literally keep all your equipment, ingredients and your hands cool (except of course for choux pastry and hot water crust) and all your pastries will be crisp and light.

Shortcrust Pastry

This is the simplest pastry which can be used for nearly all purposes. It can be frozen or re-frigerated, or stored at the crumbly stage in the refrigerator ready for making into pies or crumble toppings at short notice.

Given below is the standard recipe using half the quantity of fat to flour. You can success-fully make shortcrust pastry with a little less fat if you wish but add more liquid, or use oil (see the All-in-one method page 139). If you prefer a richer, more crumbly version, add a little more fat, or see our recipe below for flan pastry, but this does need more careful handling.

Shortcrust Pastry

Sufficient for an 18–20-cm/7–8-inch flan dish, 10–12 tartlets, pie base or lid. In recipes 200 g/8 oz pastry is that made using 200 g/8 oz flour.

200 g/8 oz plain flour
pinch salt (plus 1 tablespoon castor sugar for sweet dishes)
100 g/4 oz butter, margarine or lard
3–5 tablespoons cold water

Sift the flour and salt into a large bowl. Cut the cold fat into small cubes and rub into the flour until the mixture resembles fine breadcrumbs. Do this by rubbing the mixture gently be-tween the thumb and first two fingers, the palms upwards. If it gets sticky, chill for 10 minutes or so before continuing. Then stir in the water, a spoonful at a time, and mix with a fork or palette knife until the dough just clings together. Turn on to a lightly floured surface and knead lightly until smooth. Chill well.

To roll out the pastry, place on a lightly-floured surface. Flour the rolling pin but avoid adding extra flour, or you will make leathery pastry. Roll in short firm movements, but don't force or stretch the pastry or it will shrink during cooking. Always roll away from you and turn the pastry, not yourself, to roll out evenly. Reroll scraps only once.

Shortcrust pastry need not necessarily be made with white flour. Try half wholemeal flour, or substitute 25 g/1 oz rice or cornflour for a crisper, lighter pastry. For potato pastry, use half flour and half dry mashed potato – add very little extra liquid.

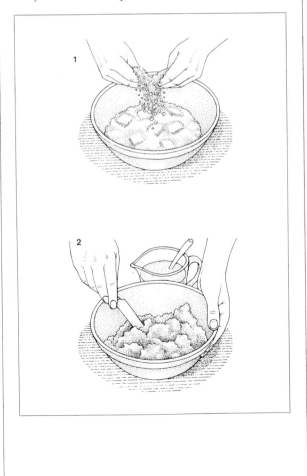

French apple tart (see page 141) and Cooked cheesecake (see page 173)

To Bake Blind

Shortcrust pastry for a flan is best cooked first, to be sure of a crisp crust. Line the flan ring or dish with the pastry and then with greaseproof paper, shaping well into the corners. Fill with baking beans (these can be used again and again) or uncooked macaroni or crusts. Cook in a moderately hot oven (190°C, 375°F, Gas Mark 5) for 15 minutes. Remove the paper and beans and cook for a further 5 minutes, or more if you want to cook the pastry completely.

To Cover a Pie Dish

Roll out the pastry (shortcrust, puff or flaky) to at least 2.5 cm/1 inch wider than the dish. Cut off a 1-cm/½-inch strip all the way round. Brush the edge of the filled pie dish with water. Place the strip of pastry securely on the rim and brush with water again. Then lift the pastry, on rolling pin, over the pie and seal the edges together. Flute the edges with thumb and forefinger, or press with a fork. Decorate with any extra pastry cut into leaves or lattice strips.

To Line a Flan Dish

Roll out the pastry at least 2.5 cm/1 inch wider than the size of the dish. Roll the pastry on to a rolling pin, to lift without cracking, and place over the dish. Gently ease the pastry into the dish, shaping it into the corners and up the sides with your knuckles, but don't stretch the pastry, or it will shrink back during cooking.

Italian trifle and Traditional trifle (see page 174)

All-in-one Pastry

This is a little more difficult to roll than ordinary shortcrust pastry because of its oil content, but if carefully handled it is just as successful. Only oil can be used in this recipe as melted margarine or butter give a heavy pastry that is very difficult to roll.

Sufficient for an 18-cm/7-inch flan or 9 tartlets

175 g/6 oz plain flour
4 tablespoons vegetable oil
2 tablespoons cold water
pinch of salt

Beat the oil and water together in a large basin and gradually work in the flour and salt with a fork. Knead lightly and roll out on a well-floured board (or between two sheets of greaseproof paper if you find it difficult to handle). Bake in a moderate oven (160°C, 325°F, Gas Mark 3) for 5–10 minutes longer than for ordinary shortcrust. This pastry is best used for savoury dishes.

Flan Pastry

This is used for the very rich, crisp, French flans and tarts. It is more like a biscuit than a pastry and is really delicious.

Flan Pastry

Sufficient for an 18–20-cm/7–8-inch flan or 12 tartlets

225 g/8 oz plain flour
pinch salt
25–50 g/1–2 oz icing or castor sugar, sifted
150 g/5 oz butter or margarine
1 or 2 small egg yolks (beaten with 1 tablespoon ice cold water)

This pastry is best made on a cold working surface to prevent it becoming too greasy, but a chilled bowl is often easier. Sift the flour, salt and sugar together. Rub in the fat gently with the fingertips and then add sufficient egg mixture to make a pliable consistency. Knead lightly until smooth and chill for 1–2 hours before using. Roll out gently between two sheets of greaseproof paper if you find this pastry difficult to handle.

Creamy Quiche

200 g/8 oz Shortcrust pastry (see page 136)
75 g/3 oz cream cheese
2 eggs
salt and pepper
pinch garlic salt
150 ml/¼ pint milk
50 g/2 oz cheese, grated
3 tablespoons chopped watercress or spinach

Roll out the pastry thinly on a floured surface and use to line four individual quiche tins or one 18–20-cm/7–8-inch flan tin. Bake blind (see page 139). Beat together the cream cheese, eggs, seasoning, garlic and milk. Add the grated cheese and the watercress or spinach. Fill the quiche cases and bake in a moderate oven (180°C, 350°F, Gas Mark 4) for about 25 minutes, or longer for 1 large quiche, until the filling is just firm and golden. **Serves 4**

Other Quiche Fillings

Bacon quiche omit the cream cheese and watercress. Add 1 small onion, chopped and 4 oz bacon, chopped and fried and an extra 150 ml/¼ pint milk.

Mushroom quiche omit the watercress and add 225 g/8 oz mushrooms, sliced and washed.

Spinach quiche omit the watercress and beat into mixture 225 g/8 oz spinach, quickly cooked, shredded and very well drained.

Tomato quiche omit the watercress, prepare the filled quiche as above then top with 225 g/8 oz tomatoes, thinly sliced and neatly arranged.

To Serve cold

(Illustrated on page 35)

Prepare four individual quiches, as above but omitting the watercress. Chill and top with slices of raw mushroom and grated carrot, or sliced tomato and oranges. Garnish with mustard and cress or watercress.

Charter Pie

3–4 tablespoons oil
1 (1.5-kg/3-lb) chicken, jointed
1 small onion, chopped
300 ml/½ pint thick White wine sauce (see page 185)
300 ml/½ pint double cream
salt and pepper
2 tablespoons chopped parsley
350 g/12 oz Shortcrust pastry (see page 136)
beaten egg to glaze

Heat the oil and fry the chicken and onion until golden.

Put the chicken and onion in a pie dish. Mix the sauce with half the cream and the seasoning. Pour over the chicken and sprinkle with parsley. Roll out the pastry on a floured surface. Cover the pie as described on page 139. Decorate with pastry trimmings and make a small hole in the centre. Glaze with beaten egg and bake in a moderately hot oven (200°C, 400°F, Gas Mark 6) for 20 minutes. Then reduce to moderate (180°C, 350°F, Gas Mark 4) for 1½ hours. Pour in the remaining cream just before serving. **Serves 4–6**

Mediterranean Flan

200 g/8 oz Shortcrust pastry (see page 136)
4 tablespoons olive oil
4 courgettes, sliced
1 red pepper, seeds removed and sliced
1 small aubergine, sliced
1 onion, sliced
1 clove garlic, crushed
3 eggs
150 ml/¼ pint milk
salt and pepper

Roll out the pastry on a lightly-floured surface and use to line a 20-cm/8-inch flan dish. Heat the oil and lightly fry the courgettes, pepper, aubergine, onion and garlic. Drain and transfer to the flan case. Beat the eggs, milk and seasoning together and pour over the vegetables.

Roll out any pastry trimmings and cut into six 5-mm/¼-inch strips. Twist carefully and arrange on the flan in a lattice pattern, damping the end of each strip to ensure it sticks. Bake in a hot oven (220°C, 475°F, Gas Mark 7) for 15 minutes. Reduce to moderate (180°C, 350°F, Gas Mark 4) for 30 minutes. **Serves 5–6**

Treacle Tart

175 g/6 oz Shortcrust pastry (see page 136)
100 g/4 oz treacle or syrup
50 g/2 oz fresh white breadcrumbs
50 g/2 oz medium oatmeal
grated rind and juice of 1 lemon

Roll out the pastry on a lightly-floured surface and use to line a 23-cm/9-inch pie plate. Trim the edges with a sharp knife. Bake blind (see page 139). Heat the treacle and mix in the remaining ingredients. Pour into the pie shell and decorate with the pastry trimmings in a lattice pattern. Bake in a moderate oven (180°C, 350°F, Gas Mark 4) for 15–20 minutes. **Serves 4–6**

Blackberry and Apple Pie

175 g/6 oz Shortcrust pastry (see page 136)
450 g/1 lb cooking apples
450 g/1 lb blackberries
juice of 1 lemon
sugar to taste
milk to glaze

Roll out the pastry on a lightly-floured surface to cover a 20–23-cm/8–9-inch pie plate. Peel, core and roughly chop the apples and put into the pie plate with the blackberries. Sprinkle with the lemon juice and add sugar to taste. Cover the pie with the pastry as described on page 139. Brush with milk and bake in a moderately hot oven (190°C, 375°F, Gas Mark 5) for 35–40 minutes. Sprinkle with more sugar before serving. **Serves 4–6**

French Apple Tart

(Illustrated on page 137)

200 g/8 oz Flan pastry (see page 140)
crème patissière:
25 g/1 oz cornflour
300 ml/½ pint milk
1 vanilla pod or few drops vanilla essence
50 g/2 oz sugar
4 tablespoons double cream
3 egg yolks
topping:
675–900 g/1½–2 lb dessert apples
40 g/1½ oz butter or margarine
25 g/1 oz soft brown sugar

Roll out the pastry on a lightly-floured surface and use to line a 20-cm/8-inch flan ring or a Swiss roll tin. Bake blind (see page 139). To make the filling, mix the cornflour with the milk and add the vanilla pod or essence. Cook, stirring, over a low heat until thickened; remove the pod. Add the sugar, cream and yolks. Beat well but do not go on cooking.

Core and slice the apples. Melt the butter and sugar together and toss the apple lightly in it. Spread the crème patissière over the part-cooked pastry and top with apple slices. Cook in a moderately hot oven (200°C, 400°F, Gas Mark 6) for 25–30 minutes. **Serves 6**

Sweet Mint Pasties

275 g/10 oz Shortcrust pastry (see page 136)
75 g/3 oz sultanas
75 g/3 oz currants
75 g/3 oz seedless raisins, chopped
50 g/2 oz butter
75 g/3 oz brown sugar
½ teaspoon ground mixed spice
2 tablespoons chopped mint
beaten egg or milk to glaze

Roll out the pastry and cut into eight or ten rounds. Mix all the remaining ingredients, except the egg, together. Divide the filling between the rounds, piling it up in the centre. Brush the edges with egg and fold the pastry over to form half-moon shapes. Seal the edges well, brush with more egg and place on a baking tray. Cook in a moderate oven (180°C, 350°F, Gas Mark 4) for about 20 minutes. **Makes 8–10**

Suet Pastry

Suet pastry is quick to make but takes longer to cook than other pastries. Although traditionally steamed, some people prefer suet pastry baked slowly in the oven to give a golden, crisp crust.

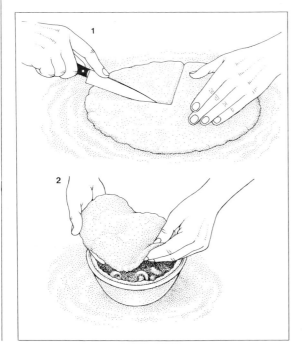

Suet Pastry

Sufficient for a 1.25-litre/2-pint pudding basin. In recipes, 225 g/8 oz pastry is that made using 225 g/8 oz flour.

225 g/8 oz self-raising flour
pinch salt
100 g/4 oz shredded suet
sweet or savoury filling

Sift the flour with the salt. Stir in the suet thoroughly. Add sufficient ice-cold water to make a soft dough. Knead lightly. Roll out on a floured surface, cut out one-third and put it aside. Use the large piece to line a greased 1.25-litre/2-pint pudding basin. Mould the pastry evenly into the corners and seal the join with water. The pastry should come well up to the lip of basin. Fill the pudding with the chosen sweet or savoury filling and roll the remaining third into a circle for the top. Brush the edges with water to seal and press down well to prevent steam and juices from escaping. Cover the basin firmly with greaseproof paper and foil with a pleat to allow rising. Steam over a pan of boiling water for 2–2½ hours. For a crisp crust, place the basin (making sure it is ovenproof) in a moderately hot oven (200°C, 400°F, Gas Mark 6) for the last 30 minutes.

Sausage Suet Pudding

225 g/8 oz Suet pastry (see above)
225 g/8 oz mixed root vegetables, diced
1 tablespoon oil
225 g/8 oz pork sausages
1 large onion, chopped
1 clove garlic, crushed (optional)
salt and pepper
1 teaspoon dried mixed herbs
2–3 tablespoons tomato ketchup

Line a 1.25-litre/2-pint basin as for basic pudding (see above). Boil the vegetables in salted water for 5 minutes and drain. Heat the oil and fry the sausages, onion and garlic until browned. Chop the sausages and mix with the vegetables and onions. Add the remaining ingredients. Fill the pudding, cover with the pastry lid and steam as above. **Serves 4–6**

Hot Water Crust Pastry

This lovely crisp, golden pastry makes the most traditional British 'raised' pies. Originally the pies were shaped (raised) by hand, but there are attractive moulds available or a loose-bottomed cake tin will do just as well.

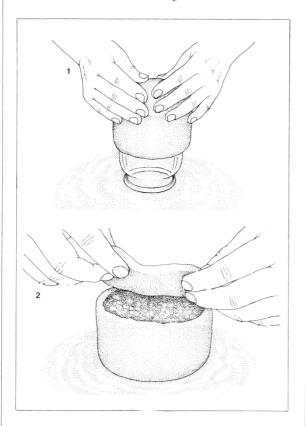

Hot Water Crust Pastry

Sufficient for a 1-kg/2-lb pie mould or an 18-cm/7-inch cake tin. In recipes, 450 g/1 lb pastry is that made using 450 g/1 lb flour.

450 g/1 lb flour
200 ml/7 fl oz water
100 g/4 oz lard
pinch salt
savoury filling
beaten egg to glaze
450/¾ pint stock
15 g/½ oz powdered gelatine or aspic

Sift the flour into a bowl. Bring the water and lard to the boil and add the salt. Pour immediately into the flour and mix well to make a firm dough. If any of the pastry is not going to be used immediately, it must be kept warm to prevent it hardening up. Use two-thirds of the pastry, thinly rolled out on a lightly-floured surface, to line the mould. Make sure it comes right up to the top of the sides. Fill according to choice and cover with the remaining pastry. Seal the edges well and flute. Make a small hole in the top for steam to escape and decorate with any remaining pastry. Glaze lightly with egg and bake in a moderate oven (180°C, 350°F, Gas Mark 4) for 2–2½ hours. Remove the sides of the tin 30 minutes before the end. Glaze the sides of the pie and return to the oven.

Most raised pies have jellied stock poured in when cool, to fill the gaps and help preserve the meat. Use either the liquid the meat was cooked in, or stock, with dissolved gelatine or aspic.

Farmhouse Pies

450 g/1 lb Hot water crust pastry (see above),
using milk and water mixed for the liquid
450 g/1 lb cooked chicken, diced
150 ml/¼ pint chicken stock
grated rind of 1 lemon
salt and pepper
milk or beaten egg to glaze

Divide the pastry into four equal portions. Work three-quarters of each to a thick circle and put aside the remaining pieces for lids. Place a jam jar in the centre of one circle and work the pastry up the sides. Invert the jar and gently pull pastry down if you find this easier – to give a 6.5–7.5-cm/2½–3 inch depth. Let the pastry cool and gently lift out the jar. You must work quickly or the dough will become hard and brittle. Repeat with the other circles.

Mix the chicken with the stock, lemon rind and seasoning and divide between the four pies. Roll or work the remaining pastry pieces to form four lids. Damp the edges and place on top of the pies. Seal and decorate the edges. Make a small hole in the top for steam to escape and glaze with milk or egg. Place the pies on a baking tray and cook in a moderate oven (180°C, 350°F, Gas Mark 4) for 45 minutes–1 hour, until golden and crisp. Glaze the pies again 15 minutes before the end of cooking time. Eat hot or cold. **Serves 4**

Puff Pastry

Sufficient for twelve small or six larger vols-au-vent, one jalousie or galette or about ten vanilla slices. In recipes, 225 g/8 oz puff pastry is that made using 225 g/8 oz flour.

225 g/8 oz plain or strong flour
pinch salt
225 g/8 oz butter or margarine

Sift the flour and salt into a bowl. Mix with sufficient cold water to make a soft dough. Roll out on a lightly-floured surface into a large rectangle and rest for 10–15 minutes. Soften the butter and mould into a 2.5-cm/1-inch thick slab. Place the piece of butter in the middle of the dough. Fold the dough over from each end to cover the butter and then seal the sides. Roll out from the centre to make a rectangle. Fold again into three or four, seal the edges, and give the pastry a quarter turn. Repeat this rolling and folding four more times, resting and cooling each time. Roll out and use as Flaky pastry (see page 145).

Onion and Tomato Puff

450 g/1 lb Puff pastry (see above)
50 g/2 oz butter
1 large onion, sliced
1 teaspoon chopped tarragon or ½ teaspoon dried
3 hard-boiled eggs, coarsely chopped
4 tomatoes, peeled and sliced
75 g/3 oz cheese, grated
salt and pepper
beaten egg and milk to glaze

Roll out the pastry on a lightly-floured surface to a large rectangle about 5 mm/¼ inch thick. Heat the butter and lightly fry the onion until soft. Spread over half the pastry, leaving the edge clear. Sprinkle with the tarragon, egg, tomato, grated cheese and seasoning. Brush the edges with egg and milk. Fold over the other half of pastry, seal well and flute the edges. Make three diagonal cuts across the top and brush all over with egg and milk. Bake in a moderately hot oven (200°C, 400°F, Gas Mark 6) for 20–25 minutes until golden. **Serves 4**

Prawn and Cucumber Vol-au-vent

450 g/1 lb Puff or Flaky pastry (see left and page 145)
beaten egg to glaze
filling:
150 ml/¼ pint White sauce (see page 185)
¼ cucumber, finely chopped
100 g/4 oz frozen prawns
salt and pepper
1 teaspoon chopped chives or ½ teaspoon dried

Roll out the pastry on a lightly-floured board, to about 1 cm/½ inch thick and cut out four large circles or squares. With a cutter 2.5–4 cm/1–1½ inches smaller, make indentations in the centre of each, but don't cut through. Place the vols-au-vent on a baking tray and glaze very lightly with beaten egg. Bake in a moderately hot oven (200°C, 400°F, Gas Mark 6) for about 25 minutes. Meanwhile mix the sauce, cucumber, prawns, seasoning and chives together. Remove the centre lids from the cooked vols-au-vent and fill with the prawn mixture. Replace the lids and return to the oven for 10 minutes. **Serves 4**

Rough Puff Pastry

Although flaky, puff and rough puff pastry give similar cooking results, puff pastry usually rises more and is more impressive but rough puff pastry is by far the easiest to make. It is ideally suitable for meat pies which require longer cooking, as well as many other uses. In recipes, 225 g/8 oz rough puff pastry is that made using 225 g/8 oz flour.

225 g/8 oz plain or strong flour
½ teaspoon salt
175 g/6 oz butter, margarine or lard
cold water to mix

Sift flour and salt into a bowl. Add the fat then cut it into the flour using two knives, until the fat is well distributed but still in fairly large pieces. Add enough water to bind the mixture. The pieces of fat will still be noticeable. Mix using only knives or a fork. Turn on to a lightly-floured surface and roll and fold four times as for Puff and Flaky pastry (see opposite and page 145). Leave to rest after each rolling and folding and chill before use. Bake as for flaky or puff pastry.

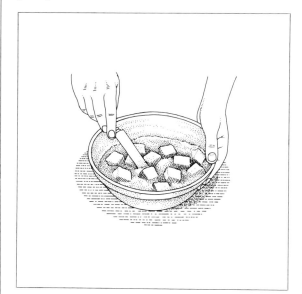

Strawberry Galette

450 g/1 lb Rough puff pastry (see opposite)
300 ml/$\frac{1}{2}$ pint double cream
few drops vanilla essence
1 egg white
2 teaspoons castor sugar
350 g/12 oz strawberries
sifted icing sugar to dust

Roll out the pastry thinly on a lightly-floured surface and cut two rectangles, each 23 × 10 cm/ 9 × 4 inches. Cut the centre from one, leaving a 4-cm/1$\frac{1}{2}$-inch border. Roll out the small rectangle to the same size as the larger one. Transfer the two rectangles and the border to dampened baking trays and bake in a hot oven (220°C, 425°F, Gas Mark 7) for 15 minutes. Cool on wire racks. Trim the edges with a knife. Whip the cream and vanilla essence until thick. Whisk the egg white until stiff and fold into the cream with the castor sugar. Slice some of the fruit and keep the rest whole. Layer the pastry rectangles (thick one on the bottom, thin one in the middle, the border on top) with the cream and sliced strawberries. Fill the top with the whole strawberries and dust with sifted icing sugar. **Serves 6–8**

Croissants

1 teaspoon sugar
450 ml/$\frac{3}{4}$ pint milk and water mixed
15 g/$\frac{1}{2}$ oz dried yeast
575 g/1$\frac{1}{4}$ lb plain flour
salt
260 g/9$\frac{1}{2}$ oz butter
beaten egg to glaze

Dissolve the sugar in 150 ml/$\frac{1}{4}$ pint of the liquid, sprinkle on the yeast and leave in warm place until frothy. Mix the flour and salt with the yeast mixture, 40 g/1$\frac{1}{2}$ oz of the butter, melted and enough liquid to make a soft dough. Knead lightly and roll out to a thin oblong.

Soften the rest of the butter and divide into three. Dot one portion over the top two-thirds of the dough in small pieces and continue as for Flaky pastry (see page 145) until all the fat is added. Then roll and fold twice more. Chill.

Roll out thinly, cut into 23 × 23 × 15-cm/ 9 × 9 × 6-inch triangles. Roll up from the wide end into crescents. Leave for 30 minutes. Glaze and bake in a hot oven (230°C, 450°F, Gas Mark 8) for 15–20 minutes. **Makes 15**

Danish Pastries

Croissant dough (see above), with 200 g/7 oz butter
50–75 g/2–3 oz almond paste
2 tablespoons jam
currants or mixed peel
nibbed almonds
glacé icing

Make up the croissant dough and divide into three. Roll out one-third to a 25-cm/10-inch square and cut into four. Press the points of each square to the centre. Top with a round of almond paste. Roll out one-third as before and halve diagonally. Put a small piece of almond paste at the point of each triangle and roll like croissants. Roll out the rest to a rectangle. Spread with jam, currants and almonds. Roll up from the long side. Cut into 2.5-cm/1-inch slices. Place the pastries on baking trays and leave for 20 minutes. Bake in a hot oven (220°C, 425°F, Gas Mark 7) for about 10 minutes. Brush with glacé icing. **Makes about 15**

Baking

We seem to do less and less baking at home today. There is too little time and there are so many ready-to-eat alternatives that perhaps it's understandable. But if you have a large hungry family to feed, you will save money by doing batches of baking yourself, especially if you use any of the convenience products which are designed to save time. You may also enjoy baking, at the same time knowing that the lucky ones you are feeding will appreciate not only the glorious aroma of baking but also the delicious tastes.

The ingredients you use, the cost and the time taken, are all important to the final result.

Fats

Use butter for its rich taste and colour. Unsalted or slightly salted is best for sweet baking.

Use margarine for a milder flavour and, of course, economy. Do use the soft-blend margarine to save creaming and blending time rather than heating a fat to soften it.

Low-fat and cholesterol-free spreads can be used in baking but not in pastries.

Hard fats can be used in rubbed-in and melted method baking. Lard, in particular gives good crisp pastry when used with other fats.

Oils can be used for most purposes, especially all-in-one speedy methods, but avoid the stronger flavoured ones (coconut, arachide or soya) for sweet baking.

Sugars

Although there is little or no difference between the nutritional value of white and brown sugar, there will be a great deal of difference in the taste and colour of your baking. Interchange them if you wish, with this in mind.

Castor and light or dark soft brown sugars are the best for creaming and quick mixing as they dissolve quickly; therefore they are also best for caramel.

Granulated or demerara (the latter has a slightly larger crystal) can be used for all purposes, but in many cases castor is better.

Icing sugar is essential for icings and is also good for meringues and decorations.

Sugar Substitutes

Honey and syrup, or other sweeteners can replace sugar in breads, cakes and biscuits but not easily in pastries. Allow 1 tablespoon honey or syrup per 25 g/1 oz sugar, or sweetener dissolved according to directions (cut down on liquid accordingly).

Flours

Self-raising flour has a raising agent added. Although good for most things that need a soft, light texture, it's not good for pastries.

Plain flour can be used for all purposes, provided you add an extra raising agent in the form of baking powder where an airy or risen result is required.

Strong flour is designed specially for breadmaking so the mixture can expand as much as possible yet retain its shape and firmness.

There is a brown strong flour for breadmaking too.

Brown flours wheatmeal, wholemeal, wholewheat, granary meal and stoneground – have some or all of the wheat germ and bran left in during milling so they have a coarser texture. They can be used in breads, cakes and pastries but can give a heavy result. Most people prefer to use a half and half mixture of brown and white flour. They are very good in rich cakes and tea breads.

Yeast

Fresh, dried and easy-blend yeast all do the same job in different ways. Fresh yeast needs creaming with sugar to start it working very rapidly. It should be really fresh and crumbly.

Dried yeast needs to be dissolved in warm milk with a little sugar and then given 10 minutes' rest before it becomes frothy and ready to use. Store dry yeast well sealed in a dry place to prevent it absorbing moisture. Easy-blend yeast is ready to use. You can just mix it in with the other ingredients straight away.

Not all breads need to be made with yeast, as you will see in some of these recipes. For speed you could use a bread mix, which usually needs only one resting and rising stage.

Plain White Bread

450 g/1 lb strong white flour
1 teaspoon salt
20 g/$\frac{3}{4}$ oz fat
15 g/$\frac{1}{2}$ oz fresh yeast, 7 g/$\frac{1}{4}$ oz dried yeast or 1 sachet easy-blend yeast
1 teaspoon sugar
300 ml/$\frac{1}{2}$ pint lukewarm water
milk or egg to glaze

Sift the flour into a warmed bowl with the salt. Rub in the fat evenly. Add easy-blend yeast straight to the flour if used. Cream fresh yeast with the sugar, or stir dried yeast into half the liquid with the sugar and leave for 10 minutes until frothy. Stir the yeast and enough water into the flour to give a soft elastic consistency. Turn out on to a lightly-floured surface and knead with the heel and knuckles of your hand for about 10 minutes until firm. Place in a greased bowl, cover with a damp cloth and leave in a warm place to double in size. This takes about 1 hour. Turn out on to a floured surface and knead again until firm. Place in a lightly-greased 0.5-kg/1-lb loaf or cake tin and brush with milk or beaten egg to glaze.

Cover again and leave in a warm place to prove and double in size. Then bake in a hot oven (220°C, 425°F, Gas Mark 7) for about 35 minutes until well risen and hollow sounding when tapped underneath.

If you want to make bread in bulk, remember that 15 g/$\frac{1}{2}$ oz fresh yeast (7 g/$\frac{1}{4}$ oz dried) is sufficient for up to 675 g/1$\frac{1}{2}$ lb flour. For up to 1.5 kg/3 lb flour use 25 g/1 oz fresh yeast (15 g/$\frac{1}{2}$ oz dried). **Makes 1 (0.5-kg/1-lb) loaf**

Different Shapes

Dinner Rolls The above recipe will make about 16. Divide into 16 pieces and shape into rolls, fingers, knots or rings. Prove and bake for only about 25 minutes.

Plaits Roll out the dough to one long thick sausage. Make three slits, leaving one end still attached and plait. Bake as for plain white bread.

Cottage Loaves Divide the dough into 10 pieces. Divide each piece into two, one piece twice the size of the other. Place the smaller ball on top of larger one, push your little finger or a spoon handle through the middle to seal. Glaze and bake as for dinner rolls. Illustrated on the jacket.

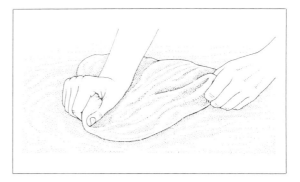

Different Flavours

Doughs can be flavoured before cooking to give interesting results. For instance stir in 100 g/4 oz grated cheese, or 1 finely chopped onion, or 3 tablespoons chopped fresh (1$\frac{1}{2}$ tablespoons dry) mixed herbs, or 1 tablespoon cumin seeds, to the basic bread dough.

Toppings

You don't have to glaze a loaf if you don't want to, just dust it with flour. A little cracked wheat, poppy seeds, or sesame seeds sprinkled on after the glaze give a professional effect and a delicious texture.

Rich Milk Bread

450 g/1 lb strong or plain flour
2 teaspoons salt
15 g/½ oz lard
15 g/½ oz fresh yeast
150 ml/¼ pint milk
2 tablespoons dried milk made up with 150 ml/¼
pint water
little milk for brushing

Sift the flour and salt together and rub in the lard. Cream the yeast with a little of the milk. Add to the flour with the remaining liquid. Mix well. Turn on to a floured surface and knead until smooth – about 10 minutes. Place in a greased bowl, cover with a damp cloth and leave in a warm place until doubled in size – about 45 minutes. Knead again quickly. Divide into three even-sized pieces and place side by side in a greased 1-kg/2-lb loaf tin. This gives the finished ridged effect. Cover and leave in a warm place once again, until doubled in size. Brush with milk. Bake in a moderately hot oven (200°C, 400°F, Gas Mark 6) for 30–35 minutes. **Makes 1 large loaf**

Herb Baps stir in 4 tablespoons chopped herbs with the flour as in the above recipe and shape into 12 flat rounds. Bake as above for 15–20 minutes.

Date and Nut Loaf stir in 75 g/3 oz chopped dates, 50 g/2 oz chopped nuts and 75 g/3 oz brown sugar with the flour as in the above recipe. Bake in a round cake tin as above.

Granary Loaf

100 g/4 oz self-raising flour
½ teaspoon baking powder
pinch salt
100 g/4 oz wholemeal flour
1 egg
milk to bind
15 g/½ oz margarine
1 tablespoon cracked wheat

Sift the self-raising flour, baking powder and salt together. Add the wholemeal flour. Beat the egg and make up to 150 ml/¼ pint with milk. Add the liquid to the dry ingredients.

Melt the margarine and stir in to the other ingredients. Mix to a smooth dough. Shape into a smooth round ball and place on a greased baking tray. Brush with milk and sprinkle with the cracked wheat. Bake in a hot oven (220°C, 425°F, Gas Mark 7) for 30–35 minutes. **Makes 1 small loaf**

Honey Ginger Loaf

275 g/10 oz white bread mix
1–2 teaspoons ground ginger
75 g/3 oz castor sugar
2 tablespoons melted margarine
3 tablespoons honey
75 g/3 oz sultanas

In a large bowl mix together the bread mix, ginger, sugar and margarine. Then stir in 200 ml/7 fl oz hot water and knead until smooth on a floured surface. Roll out until 1 cm/½ inch thick. Spread with 2 tablespoons of the honey, sprinkle with the sultanas and fold over keeping the filling in. Fit into a greased 0.75-kg/1½-lb loaf tin. Leave in a warm place until doubled in size. Bake for 20 minutes in a hot oven (220°C, 425°F, Gas Mark 7). Brush with more honey and return to the oven for a further 10–15 minutes, lowering the heat to moderately hot (190°C, 375°F, Gas Mark 5). **Serves 8–10**

Quick Wheatmeal Loaf

15 g/½ oz lard or butter
225 g/8 oz strong white flour
225 g/8 oz wheatmeal flour
2 teaspoons salt
3 teaspoons sugar
15 g/½ oz fresh yeast or 7 g/¼ oz dried yeast
milk or beaten egg to glaze

Rub the fat into the mixed flours and add the salt and 2 teaspoons of the sugar. Cream fresh yeast with the remaining sugar, or mix dried yeast with the sugar and 2 tablespoons warm water. Leave until frothy. Pour the yeast liquid and about 300 ml/½ pint warm water (or less if using dried yeast) into the flour and mix until it leaves the side of the bowl. Knead on a floured surface for about 5 minutes. Divide in two now if you wish to make two loaves. Shape into one or two rounds and place on a greased baking tray. Cover with greased polythene and leave in a warm place until doubled in size – about 1 hour. Glaze with milk or egg and bake in a hot oven (230°C, 450°F, Gas Mark 8) for 30–40 minutes. To test, knock the underneath of the loaf – it should sound hollow. **Makes 1 small loaf**

Raisin Soda Bread

450 g/1 lb self-raising flour
$\frac{1}{2}$ teaspoon ground mixed spice
1 teaspoon salt
$\frac{1}{2}$ teaspoon bicarbonate of soda
1 tablespoon vinegar
300 ml/$\frac{1}{2}$ pint milk
75 g/3 oz raisins

Sift the flour, spice and salt together. Mix the bicarbonate of soda with the vinegar and milk. Mix into the dry ingredients, adding the raisins, and knead the dough together. Turn on to a floured board and shape into a round ball. Place on a greased baking tray and flatten slightly with the palm of your hand. Using a palette knife, mark a deep lattice on top of the dough. Bake in a moderately hot oven (200°C, 400°F, Gas Mark 6) for 40–45 minutes. Cool before slicing as this bread is very crumbly. **Makes 1 large loaf**

Soda Doughnuts mould the same dough into small balls. Heat oil for deep-frying to 190°C/375°F or until a cube of bread turns golden in 1 minute. Fry until crisp and golden, then toss in castor sugar.

Fruit Tea Loaf

40 g/1$\frac{1}{2}$ oz fresh yeast, or 20 g/$\frac{3}{4}$ oz dried yeast
175 g/6 oz soft dark brown sugar
300 ml/$\frac{1}{2}$ pint warm black tea, strained
350 g/12 oz dried fruit, mixed raisins, sultanas, apricots (soak the apricots in the tea for 1 hour)
275 g/10 oz granary meal
175 g/6 oz strong white flour

Cream the yeast with 1 teaspoon sugar and a little tea. Set aside until frothy. Mix the remaining sugar, tea, fruit and prepared yeast together in a large bowl. Gradually mix in the remaining ingredients and yeast to produce a firm dropping consistency; turn out on to a floured surface. Knead for about 5 minutes until smooth. Place in a greased 1-kg/2-lb loaf tin and leave to rise until doubled in size – 1–2 hours. Sprinkle with a little granary meal and bake in a moderately hot oven (200°C, 400°F, Gas Mark 6) for about 30 minutes, then reduce to moderate (180°C, 350°F, Gas Mark 4) for a further 15 minutes. **Serves 8–10**

Crumpets

450 g/1 lb plain flour
2 teaspoons salt
15 g/$\frac{1}{2}$ oz fresh yeast
1 teaspoon sugar
600 ml/1 pint milk and water mixed
pinch bicarbonate of soda
1 teaspoon warm water

Sift the flour and salt together. Cream the yeast and sugar with a little milk and water. Add this to the flour, then add the remaining milk and water and mix to make to make a smooth batter. Leave to rise until doubled in size. Beat with a wooden spoon. Dissolve the bicarbonate of soda in the water and add to the batter. Leave for 30 minutes. Heat a griddle or heavy frying pan and grease some 9-cm/3$\frac{1}{2}$-inch rings or cutters. Pour a little batter into each ring on the griddle and cook until the batter is set and full of holes. Remove the rings and turn each crumpet when the top is set. **Makes 24**

Cakes

Most cakes are made by the creaming method – where you cream the butter and sugar together first – as in a Victoria sandwich, for instance. This can be done either by hand or with a mixer, using soft fat or oil. Cream all the ingredients together at once. The lightest of all cakes – a true sponge – is made by whisking the eggs and sugar over hot water to partially cook the eggs first. This cake needs no fat, but in the classic Genoese sponge recipe some melted fat is added to give better flavour and keeping qualities. All these methods are given here with many flavour variations.

A Foolproof Victoria Sandwich Cake

Using the correct proportion of ingredients is the vital key to this recipe. Always use double the quantity of fat, sugar and flour to the number of eggs.

For 2 (15-cm/6-inch) sandwich tins, use
2 eggs
100 g/4 oz butter or margarine
100 g/4 oz castor sugar
100 g/4 oz self-raising flour
For 2 (18-cm/7-inch) sandwich tins, use
3 eggs
175 g/6 oz butter or margarine
175 g/6 oz castor sugar
175 g/6 oz self-raising flour

Lightly grease and flour the sandwich tins, or to be on the safe side, cover the base with a circle of greased greaseproof paper. Sift the flour, once or even twice for lightness. Cream the butter or margarine and sugar until pale, light and fluffy. Beat the eggs together and gradually beat into the creamed mixture gently. If it begins to curdle, stir in 1 tablespoon of the flour – then fold in the rest of the flour. Add any flavourings you wish and divide equally between the tins. Smooth the surface and bake in a moderately hot oven (180°C, 350°F, Gas Mark 4) for about 20 minutes. The top should be golden, fairly flat and still springy to the touch. Test with a skewer, which should come

out of the centre of the cake clean, or listen to hear if the cake has stopped crackling and is therefore cooked.

Place on damp cloths, to ease turning out, until nearly cool. Then turn out and invert on a wire rack to cool. Fill and decorate as you wish.

An Economical Speedy Sandwich Cake

For 2 (18-cm/7-inch) tins

225 g/8 oz self-raising flour, sifted twice
175 g/6 oz castor sugar
3 eggs, beaten
6 tablespoons salad oil
2 teaspoons grated orange or lemon rind

Put all the ingredients into a bowl and beat until really smooth, golden yellow and of a thick batter consistency. Add 1–2 tablespoons water if necessary. Divide the mixture between the greased tins and cook as above.

Flavours and Fillings for a Victoria Sandwich

(Quantities for a 2-egg mixture.)

Coffee dissolve 2 teaspoons coffee essence or granules in 1–2 teaspoons boiling water. Add with the flour. Fill the cake with vanilla or chocolate butter cream.

Chocolate replace 25 g/1 oz flour with 25 g/1 oz cocoa powder. Fill the cake with rum or dark chocolate butter cream.

Essences add 2–3 drops of vanilla, lemon, orange, brandy or other essence to the creamed mixture. Fill the cake with lemon or orange butter cream.

Jam sandwich the cakes with jam or any rich conserve or even fresh fruit and a layer of whipped cream.

Jellied strawberries (see page 175)

Toppings

The simplest topping is a fine sprinkling of icing or castor sugar, passed through a sieve. For a pretty design, put a doily on the cake, sprinkle with sugar and remove the doily.

You could also top with butter cream and mark or ridge with a fork or warm knife.

For feather icing cover the top with a layer of one colour of glacé icing. Then in a different colour, pipe thin parallel lines straight across, about 2.5 cm/1 inch apart. With a knife or skewer, score through the icing diagonally to the piping. The lines of piping should drag slightly to give a curved or feathered effect.

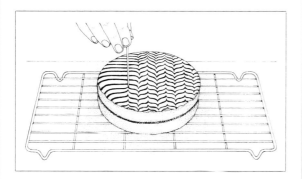

Small Cakes

Use either of the above recipes to make small queen cakes, fairy cakes or butterfly cakes. A 3-egg mixture will make 16–20 cakes. Divide equally between small cake trays or paper cases and bake as above for about 15 minutes. Flavour as you wish and top with glacé icing or fill with butter cream.

Sponge Flans

Use any of these sponge recipes to make a sponge flan. You will need the special flan tin which has a raised centre and deep sides. Grease and flour it, then place a circle of greaseproof paper in the centre. Use a 3-egg mixture for a standard 18-cm/7-inch tin and cook for 10 minutes longer. Cool slightly then turn out.

Victorian plum pudding (see page 163)

Whisked Sponge

For 2 (20-cm/8-inch) sandwich tins

75 g/3 oz plain flour
3 large eggs
100 g/4 oz castor sugar

Sift the flour twice into a large bowl. Whisk the eggs and sugar together until very pale and thick enough to leave a trail when you take out the whisk. Do this over simmering water if you are using a hand or rotary whisk. If using an electric beater, there is no need to heat the mixture. Remove the bowl from the heat and gently fold in the flour. Use a large metal spoon or spatula to cut through and fold over, slowly, until you have a smooth batter-like mixture. Spoon evenly into greased 18–20-cm/7–8-inch tins and bake in the centre of a hot oven, preferably both on the same shelf, (220°C, 425°F, Gas Mark 7) for about 8 minutes. Test as above, cool and turn out.

For a Genoese sponge, which is slightly richer, fold 25 g/1 oz melted butter into the egg mixture with the flour. Take extra care to do this slowly and evenly.

Flavour, fill or decorate as above, but use less flavouring for this mixture.

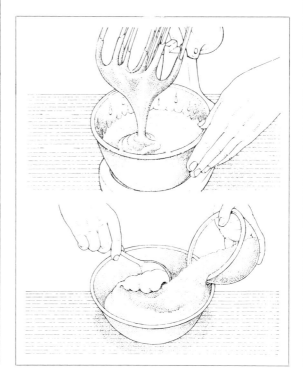

Orange Yogurt Cake

100 g/4 oz self-raising flour
150 g/5 oz castor sugar
½ teaspoon salt
grated rind of 2 small oranges
5 tablespoons oil
4 tablespoons water
6 tablespoons natural yogurt
3 egg whites
pinch cream of tartar
100 g/4 oz icing sugar, sifted

Sift the flour, sugar and salt into a bowl. Mix half the orange rind, oil, water and 4 tablespoons of the yogurt and stir into the dry ingredients to make a smooth batter. Whisk the egg whites with the cream of tartar until just peaking, then fold in the batter using a metal spoon. Mix quickly but gently and pour into an ungreased 0.75-kg/1½-lb loaf tin. Bake in a moderate oven (160°C, 325°F, Gas Mark 3) for 1–1¼ hours, until springy to the touch. Cool in the tin for 20 minutes, then turn out to cool on a wire rack.

To decorate, mix the icing sugar, with the remaining yogurt and grated rind until smooth and pour over the cake. **Serves 6–8**

Angel Layer Cake

100 g/4 oz plain flour
250 g/9 oz castor sugar
10 egg whites (about 300 ml/½ pint)
pinch salt
½ teaspoon cream of tartar
½ teaspoon vanilla essence
50 g/2 oz plain dessert chocolate
600 ml/1 pint whipped cream
3 tablespoons lemon curd
cherries and angelica to decorate

Sift the flour and sugar together. Whisk the egg whites, salt and cream of tartar until stiff. Fold in the flour, sugar and essence. Divide between four 18-cm/7-inch ungreased sandwich tins and bake in a cool oven (140°C, 275°F, Gas Mark 1) for 15 minutes, increasing to moderate (160°C, 325°F, Gas Mark 3) for a further 10 minutes. Melt the chocolate in a bowl over hot water and mix with half the cream. Mix the lemon curd with the remaining cream. Spread each filling on two layers and sandwich alternate layers together. Top with the cherries and angelica. **Serves 6–8**

Chocolate Swiss Roll

Line an 18 × 28-cm/7 × 11-inch Swiss roll tin with lightly-greased greaseproof paper. Make the mixture as above substituting 15 g/½ oz flour with 15 g/½ oz cocoa. Spoon evenly into the tin and bake as above.

Meanwhile sprinkle a clean cloth with castor sugar. When the sponge is cooked turn it immediately on to the cloth. Remove the greaseproof paper and cut away any crisp edges. Make a cut 2.5–3.5 cm/1–1½ inches from one narrow end to start rolling easily. If you are going to fill with jam, spread this on now. Butter cream and other cream mixtures would melt so roll up the cake carefully, using cloth as a support. Chill until cool, unroll, spread with filling and roll up again. A Swiss roll can be covered with butter cream if you wish or just dredged with sugar.

Sponge Fingers either use a sponge finger tray or pipe 5-cm/2-inch lines with a plain nozzle, well apart, on a greased and floured baking tray. Bake for about 10 minutes, remove and toss in castor sugar, or, when cool, dip the ends in melted chocolate.

Sponge Drops drop dessertspoons of the mixture well apart on a greased baking tray. Cook for 8–10 minutes and when cool dust with icing sugar.

Sponge Horns bake as for sponge drops, but have metal horn tins ready greased and wrap each hot sponge drop around or curl inside the tins. Leave until cool and set and fill with whipped cream.

Black Forest Gâteau

(Illustrated on page 115)

225 g/8 oz chocolate cake covering
6 eggs
½ teaspoon vanilla essence
225 g/8 oz castor sugar
50 g/2 oz plain flour
50 g/2 oz cocoa powder
150 g/5 oz unsalted butter, melted
syrup:
175 g/6 oz sugar
6 tablespoons cold water
4 tablespoons kirsch
to assemble the gâteau:
750 ml/1¼ pints double cream
65 g/2½ oz icing sugar, sifted
3 tablespoons Kirsch
1 (425-g/15-oz) can cherries, drained and stoned
175 g/6 oz fresh or maraschino cherries

Use 100 g/4 oz of the chocolate cake covering (at room temperature) to make curls. With the blade of a vegetable peeler, shave off thin narrow curls. Handle the covering as little as possible to prevent melting. Refrigerate until required. Grate the remaining chocolate coarsely.

Grease and flour three 18-cm/7-inch sand-wich tins. Whisk together the eggs, vanilla and sugar until very thick and fluffy. Sift the flour and cocoa together and fold in very gently with the melted butter, 2 tablespoons at a time. Don't overmix. Spread evenly in the prepared tins and bake in a moderately hot oven (180°C, 350°F, Gas Mark 4) for 10–15 minutes. Allow to cool slightly then turn on to wire racks to cool.

Dissolve the sugar in the water over a gentle heat. Bring to the boil and boil briskly for 5 minutes. Cool and add the Kirsch. Prick the bases of the sponges with a skewer or cocktail stick, then trickle the syrup over them. Leave for 5–10 minutes to soak up the liquid.

Whip the cream until stiff, then gradually whip in the icing sugar and Kirsch. Put one sponge on a plate and spread it with one-fifth of the cream and half the canned cherries. Top with a second sponge, adding more cream and the remaining canned cherries. Put the third sponge on top of that. Using a large palette knife, cover the sides of the gâteau with cream then press on the grated chocolate. Spread the

remaining cream on top. Top with fresh or maraschino cherries, chocolate curls and sifted icing sugar. **Serves 8–10**

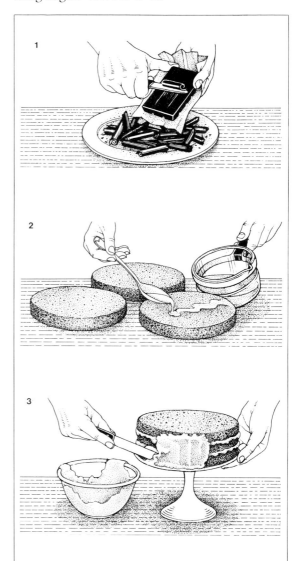

Simple Cookie Mixture

50 g/2 oz margarine, softened
75 g/3 oz castor sugar
1 egg
½ teaspoon vanilla essence
225 g/8 oz plain flour
1 teaspoon baking powder

Cream the margarine and sugar together until light and fluffy. Then gradually beat in the egg and vanilla essence. Fold and knead in the sifted flour and baking powder until well mixed. Chill until required. Divide, flavour to taste then cut into shapes. Arrange on a baking tray and cook in a moderate oven (180°C, 350°F, Gas Mark 4) for 10–15 minutes. **Makes about 40**

VARIATIONS

Add 2 teaspoons lemon rind, roll into small balls and coat in coconut. Flatten, put a little lemon curd in the centre and bake as before.

Add the grated rind of half an orange. Roll out between sheets of greaseproof paper and cut into fingers. Bake and sandwich together with orange butter cream.

Add almond essence, divide into balls and mould each one round half a glacé cherry. Coat in nibbed almonds and bake as before.

Apricot Bars

175 g/6 oz plain flour
1 teaspoon baking powder
225 g/8 oz soft brown sugar
275 g/10 oz medium oatmeal
¼ teaspoon salt
175 g/6 oz butter or margarine
2–3 tablespoons apricot jam

Mix together the flour, baking powder, sugar, oatmeal and salt. Rub in the butter until evenly mixed. Press two-thirds of the mixture evenly over the base of an 18 × 28-cm/7 × 11-inch Swiss roll tin. Cover with the jam and press the crumble on top. Bake in a cool oven (150°C, 300°F, Gas Mark 2) for about 35 minutes. Cut into squares while warm. **Makes about 36**

Almond Brownies

250 g/9 oz margarine
3 tablespoons cocoa powder
250 g/9 oz soft dark brown sugar
3 eggs
75 g/3 oz plain flour
75 g/3 oz almonds or other nuts, blanched and roughly chopped
icing sugar to dust

Melt 75 g/3 oz of the margarine and stir in the cocoa powder. Beat the remaining margarine, sugar and eggs together for 2–3 minutes until smooth. Stir in the melted margarine and cocoa mixture, then fold in the flour and nuts. Turn into a greased and lined 23-cm/9-inch square cake tin and smooth the surface. Bake in a moderately hot oven (190°C, 375°F, Gas Mark 5) for about 45 minutes. Cut into 5-cm/2-inch squares and dust with sifted icing sugar. **Makes about 16**

Peanut Blossoms

200 g/7 oz plain flour
1 teaspoon baking powder
½ teaspoon salt
75 g/3 oz granulated sugar
75 g/3 oz soft light brown sugar
100 g/4 oz butter or margarine
100 g/4 oz peanut butter
1 egg
2 tablespoons milk
1 teaspoon vanilla essence
about 48 chocolate dots

Sift the flour, baking powder and salt together. Stir in the sugars, and mix in the butter and peanut butter. Mix to a soft dough with the egg, milk and vanilla. Chill. Roll into about 48 (2.5-cm/1-inch) balls and place on ungreased baking trays. Cook in a moderately hot oven (190°C, 375 F, Gas Mark 5) for about 12 minutes. Cool on a wire rack and press a chocolate dot in the centre of each before they are cool. **Makes about 48**

Puddings and Desserts

Whether you have to make a pudding every day for supper, or only just for special occasions, it still needs to be exciting to look at, and eat, as well as reasonably simple to make. We all run out of ideas occasionally so there are lots in this chapter for you to choose from – warming and economical puddings as well as refreshing summer specials.

Cider and Orange Pudding

225 g/8 oz self-raising flour
pinch salt
100 g/4 oz margarine
100 g/4 oz castor sugar
2 eggs
100 g/4 oz sultanas
grated rind of 1 small orange
4 tablespoons cider
3 tablespoons marmalade

Sift the flour and salt. Cream the margarine and sugar together until light and fluffy. Add the eggs to the creamed mixture, one at a time, beating well. Fold in the flour, sultanas and orange rind. Gently mix in the cider to produce a stiff dropping consistency. Spoon into a greased 1.25-litre/2-pint pudding basin. Cover with greased greaseproof paper with a pleat in and steam for $1\frac{1}{2}$–2 hours. Melt the marmalade and pour over the turned out pudding just before serving. **Serves 6–8**

Victorian Plum Pudding

(Illustrated on page 156)

350 g/12 oz fresh white breadcrumbs
675 g/1$\frac{1}{2}$ lb raisins
100 g/4 oz currants
225 g/8 oz chopped mixed peel
100 g/4 oz soft dark brown sugar
350 g/12 oz shredded suet
$\frac{1}{2}$ teaspoon ground cinnamon
$\frac{1}{2}$ teaspoon grated nutmeg
$\frac{1}{2}$ teaspoon ground allspice
4 eggs
wine glass brandy, rum or port
2–3 tablespoons treacle

Put the breadcrumbs, raisins, currants, peel, sugar, suet, cinnamon, nutmeg and allspice into a large bowl. Beat the eggs lightly to break up well, then gradually stir into the fruit mixture with the brandy, rum or port (use half brandy and half sherry if you wish). Add the treacle, using a hot spoon for ease, and mix well for about 5 minutes. Place in a greased 1.75-litre/3-pint pudding basin or wrap in a floured clean cloth for the traditional round shape. Pull up the corners of the cloth as tightly as possible and tie with string. Pull the corners again. Place the pudding in a steamer over a pan of boiling water and steam for 5–6 hours – topping up with boiling water occasionally. If the pudding is to be stored, steam again for about 2 hours to reheat. Serve with custard, cream or brandy butter. **Serves 8–10**

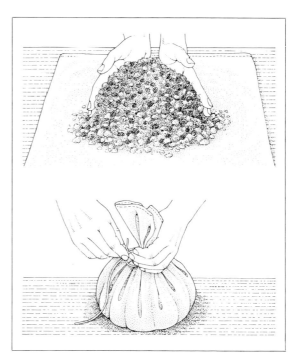

Plum Doughnuts

50 g/2 oz butter
225 g/8 oz self-raising flour
milk to bind
1 (533-g/1 lb 3½-oz) can plums, drained
oil for deep-frying
75 g/3 oz castor sugar

Rub the butter into the flour until the mixture resembles fine breadcrumbs. Bind with milk to make a soft dough. Divide into 10–12 pieces. Roll out each piece thinly and wrap around the well-drained plums. Seal well. Heat the oil to 190°C/375°F, or until a cube of bread turns golden in 1 minute. Fry the doughnuts until golden and crisp, 4–5 minutes. Drain on absorbent kitchen paper and dredge in castor sugar. Serve hot with the can juice thickened as a sauce. **Serves 5–6**

Pineapple Savarin

25 g/1 oz castor sugar
6 tablespoons lukewarm milk
15 g/½ oz dried yeast
225 g/8 oz strong plain flour
pinch salt
4 eggs, lightly beaten
100 g/4 oz butter, softened
1 (227-g/8-oz) can pineapple rings
2–3 tablespoons rum
150 ml/¼ pint cream, whipped

Dissolve 1 teaspoon of the sugar in the milk and sprinkle over the yeast. Leave until frothy – about 10 minutes. Sift the flour and salt into a bowl. Pour in the yeast mixture and remaining sugar, eggs, butter and two pineapple rings, drained and chopped. Beat well. Pour into a greased 1.75-litre/3-pint savarin tin or mould and leave until the dough rises to fill two-thirds of the mould. Bake in a moderately hot oven (200°C, 400°F, Gas Mark 6) for about 40 minutes. Turn out and prick all over with a skewer or cocktail stick. Mix the pineapple juice from the can with the rum and pour over the savarin while still hot. Chop the remaining pineapple rings. Top the savarin with pineapple and piped cream. **Serves 8**

Rice and Orange Pudding

3 small oranges, peeled and sliced
225 g/8 oz round-grain rice
750 ml/1¼ pints milk
200 g/7 oz sugar
6 tablespoons water

Arrange half the orange slices around the sides and base of a 1.25-litre/2-pint ovenproof dish. Simmer the rice and milk in a heavy-based pan for 40 minutes or until the rice is soft. Stir in 75 g/3 oz of the sugar and leave to cool. Dissolve the remaining sugar in the water in a heavy-based frying pan (without stirring) then boil it steadily until the sugar syrup turns a light golden brown colour. Pour this over the orange slices immediately and leave to set. When set, pour in the rice pudding. Arrange the remaining orange slices on top. (If you wish, you could make a second quantity of caramel, pour it over the oranges on the top and leave to set before serving.) As a variation, omit the oranges and sugar for glazing and add 100 g/4 oz sultanas to the rice, milk and sugar. Cook in a moderate oven (180°C, 350°F, Gas Mark 4) for 1½–2 hours. Illustrated on pages 86–7.

Pasta Roma

225 g/8 oz noodles or short-cut pasta
100 g/4 oz butter
50 g/2 oz soft brown sugar
100 g/4 oz marshmallows
2 tablespoons top of the milk
few drops vanilla essence

Cook the pasta in boiling salted water until just tender then drain. Put the butter, sugar, marshmallows and milk in a saucepan and stir over a moderate heat until melted. Bring to the boil and boil for 2 minutes. Stir in the vanilla. Add the pasta and heat through, stirring. Serve hot or chilled with ice cream. **Serves 6**

Right: Pork korma (see page 68)

Overleaf: Beef and game pie (see page 191)

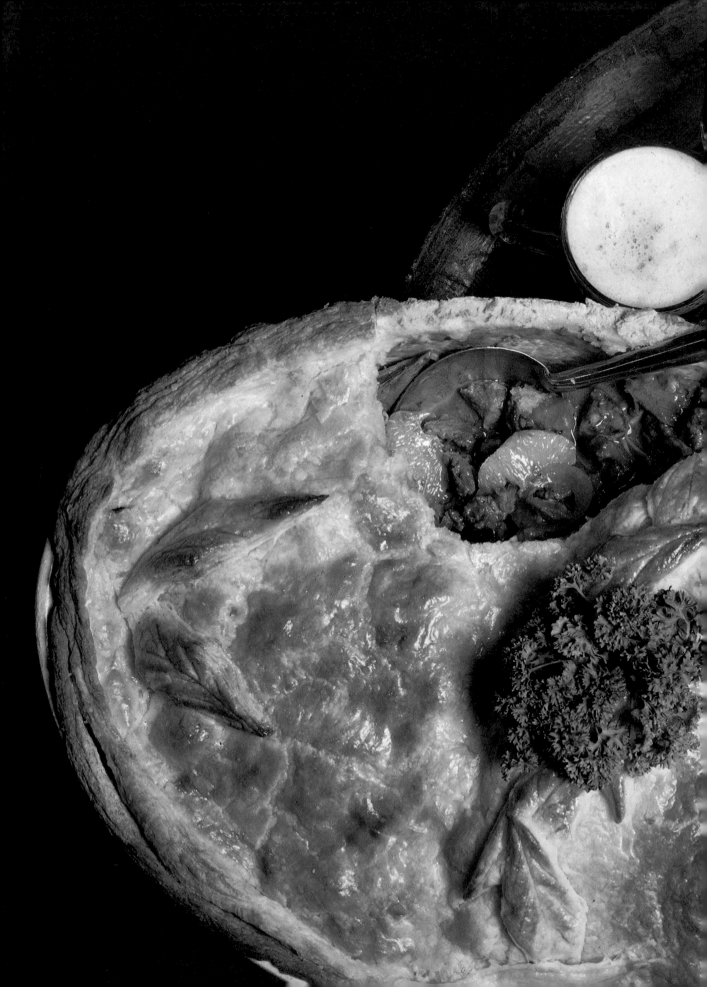

Floral Pear Pudding

3 small pears
grated rind and juice of ½ lemon
1 tablespoon granulated sugar
50 g/2 oz soft margarine
50 g/2 oz castor sugar
1 egg
50 g/2 oz self-raising flour
½ teaspoon baking powder
6 teaspoons raspberry jam
few blanched almonds

Peel, halve and core the pears. Put in a pan with the lemon juice, sugar and just enough water to cover. Bring to the boil and simmer very gently until just tender. Drain, reserving the liquor.

Beat together the margarine, castor sugar, egg and lemon rind. Sift the flour with the baking powder and beat with the creamed mixture for 2–3 minutes until smooth and creamy. Line the base of an 18-cm/7-inch sandwich tin with greased greaseproof paper and grease the sides of the tin. Arrange the pear halves, flat side downwards, in the tin to form a flower pattern.

Spoon the creamed mixture on top and smooth over with a palette knife. Bake in a moderate oven (160°C, 325°F, Gas Mark 3) for 35–40 minutes until well risen. Turn out of the tin on to a serving plate and fill the core cavities with jam. Arrange a few blanched almonds in the centre and serve hot. If liked, thicken the cooking liquor with arrowroot, adjust the sweetness to taste and serve as a sauce with the pudding. **Serves 4–5**

Rice Aigrettes

175 g/6 oz flaked pudding rice
600 ml/1 pint milk
75 g/3 oz sugar
2 eggs, separated
oil for deep-frying
350 g/12 oz jam
50–75 g/2–3 oz castor sugar

Simmer the rice and milk together for 30 minutes until soft and creamy. Remove from the heat, stir in the sugar and egg yolks and beat well. Whisk the egg whites until light and stiff, and carefully fold them into the rice mixture. Heat the oil to 190°C/375°F, or until a cube of bread turns golden in 1 minute, and drop dessertspoons of the rice into the fat. Turn them as they brown, and fry for 3–5 minutes. Drain on absorbent kitchen paper and keep hot until all the aigrettes are cooked. Melt the jam with a few tablespoons of water to make a smooth sauce; pour over the aigrettes and sprinkle with sugar. **Serves 4–5**

Apple Amber Pie

200 g/8 oz Shortcrust pastry (see page 136)
450 ml/¾ pint warm custard
2 large dessert apples, cored and sliced
2 tablespoons brown sugar
2 egg whites
75 g/3 oz castor sugar

Make the pastry according to the recipe and use to line an 18-cm/7-inch flan ring, dish or cake tin. Layer the custard, apple and brown sugar in this. Bake in a moderate oven (180°C, 350°F, Gas Mark 4) for 30 minutes. Whisk the egg whites stiffly, fold in the sugar and spoon the meringue over the pie. Return to the oven for 10–15 minutes until the meringue is crisp and golden. **Serves 4–6**

Tournedos Marseillais (see page 59)

Pineapple Flambé

50 g/2 oz butter
50 g/2 oz sugar
2 tablespoons orange juice
1 (339-g/12-oz) can pineapple rings
1–2 tablespoons liqueur
25 g/1 oz flaked almonds, toasted

Melt the butter in a frying pan. Add the sugar, allow to dissolve and then heat until it turns to caramel. Add the orange juice and pineapple with its juice and heat through. Flambé the pineapple by pouring the liqueur into a warmed spoon and lighting it with a match. Add this to the pan and leave until the flames die down. If you prefer you can simply add the liqueur and heat through. Simmer for 10 minutes and serve topped with the almonds.
Serves 4

Lemon Poached Pears

2 lemons
175 g/6 oz castor sugar
pinch grated nutmeg
300 ml/½ pint dry white wine
6 firm, ripe pears
little extra castor sugar
6 tiny bay leaves

Using a potato peeler, remove the rind from one of the lemons. Shred the zest, without the pith, finely. With the pointed end of the peeler, or a cannelle knife, remove the rind from the other lemon in six long pieces. Squeeze the juice from the lemons and place in a saucepan with the six pieces of rind, the shredded rind and the sugar, nutmeg and wine. Heat until the sugar is dissolved. Peel the pears, leaving the stalks on if possible, and poach in the lemon syrup, turning frequently, until almost tender. Transfer the pears to a serving dish. Simmer the syrup until it thickens slightly, remove the long strips of rind and pour the syrup over the pears. Dip the pieces of rind in the extra castor sugar and use with the bay leaves to decorate the pears. Serve with whipped cream. **Serves 6**

Meringues

The most crucial thing about making meringues is whisking to the right texture and stiffness.

Always whisk the egg whites (at room temperature) in a really clean dry bowl until crisp and almost dry in texture. The white should stand in gentle peaks. Sprinkle on half the sugar and whisk until really stiff, smooth and glossy. Then fold in the remaining sugar using a metal spoon. You should be able to invert bowl without the meringue moving.

If you like a chewy-centred meringue with a crisp outside, fold in 2 teaspoons cornflour and 1 teaspoon vinegar, with the last of the sugar.

Then bake in a cool oven (140°C, 275°F, Gas Mark 1) for 1½–2 hours. If you prefer a really crisp meringue, omit the cornflour and vinegar and bake in a very cool oven (110°C, 225°F, Gas Mark ¼) for 3–4 hours, or even leave overnight with the oven door slightly open.

To prevent meringues sticking, cook them on greased greaseproof paper or damp rice paper.

Meringue Layer Gâteau

(Illustrated on page 205)

6 egg whites
350 g/12 oz castor sugar
75 g/3 oz ground almonds
75 g/3 oz chopped hazelnuts
filling:
175 g/6 oz butter
275 g/10 oz icing sugar, sifted
1 egg white
75 g/3 oz plain chocolate, melted
450 ml/¾ pint whipped cream

Whisk the egg whites until stiff then whisk in half the sugar and continue until stiff and glossy. Fold in the remaining sugar and the nuts with a metal spoon. Mark three 23-cm/9-inch circles on rice paper on baking trays. Spread the meringue between the three rounds. Cook in a moderate oven (160°C, 325°F, Gas Mark 3) for 35–40 minutes.

To make the filling, beat the butter, sugar and egg white together until fluffy. Beat in the cooled melted chocolate. Sandwich the meringues together with chocolate filling and cream between the layers. Spread a layer of cream on top. **Serves 12**

Meringue Gâteau

3 egg whites
175 g/6 oz castor sugar
50 g/2 oz nibbed almonds
600 ml/1 pint double cream
450 g/1 lb small strawberries
2 teaspoons Kirsch or rum (optional)

Cover two baking trays with greaseproof paper and mark each with a 20-cm/8-inch circle. Grease both papers thoroughly. Whisk the egg whites until stiff. Add half the sugar and continue whisking until glossy. Fold in the remaining sugar together with the almonds. Spread the mixture to fill the circles marked on the paper. Bake in a very cool oven (110°C, 225°F, Gas Mark $\frac{1}{4}$) for 3–4 hours, until dry. Carefully remove from the paper and transfer to a wire rack.

Not more than 1 hour before serving, whip the cream until stiff. Hull the strawberries and reserve 12 for decoration. Roughly chop the remainder and mix with a quarter of the cream. Stir in the Kirsch or rum if used. Spread the mixture over one of the meringues. Place the second meringue on top and pipe or spread on the remaining cream. Decorate with the remaining strawberries. **Serves 6**

Meringue Shapes

The above mixture will make about six baskets. Using a large piping bag with large star nozzle, pipe a round or oval base, then pipe one or two more layers on the outer circle of the base to form the sides. Bake according to the meringue recipe and fill with ice cream and fresh fruit or with cream and nuts or any other mixture.

Large meringues can be piped or spooned on to lined and greased trays in whatever shape you wish. The above mixture makes about 12.

Small meringues are nicest piped into tiny rosettes for decorating meringue gâteaux, trifles or ice cream.

Meringues, large or small, will keep well in an airtight container for up to 2 weeks. They can also be lightly coloured with a few drops of colouring added when folding in the sugar.

Charlotte Louisa

(Illustrated on the jacket)

50 g/2 oz muscatel raisins
2 tablespoons rum
16–20 sponge fingers
1 egg white, lightly beaten
175 g/6 oz unsalted butter
175 g/6 oz castor sugar
175 g/6 oz ground almonds
50 g/2 oz hazelnuts, toasted and crushed
50 g/2 oz bitter chocolate, coarsely grated
(optional)
300 ml/$\frac{1}{2}$ pint double cream
angelica and crystallised fruits to decorate

Soak the raisins in the rum for 2–3 hours, drain, reserving the rum and put to one side. Fit a circle of lightly-oiled greaseproof paper in the bottom of a 15-cm/6-inch charlotte mould or cake tin. Line the sides with the sponge fingers lighty dipped in the egg white. Cream the butter and sugar until light and fluffy and all the sugar granules have dissolved. Beat in the rum and ground almonds. Whip the cream and fold in most of it alternately with the hazelnuts, chocolate (if used) and raisins. When the mixture is well distributed, spoon into the lined mould, making sure it is pressed well down into the bottom and sides. Cover with paper or foil and chill until quite set. Turn out and remove the bottom paper, decorate with the reserved whipped cream and the crystallised fruits. **Serves 8–10**

No-bake Cakes

These are ideal for quick desserts, and for using up leftovers of almost any sweet ingredients. They freeze very well too. This first one is really very rich, so don't be too generous with the portions.

Chilled Chocolate Cake

450 g/1 lb crumbs, from sweet biscuits or any type
of plain cake
100 g/4 oz ground almonds
50 g/2 oz glacé cherries, halved
50 g/2 oz walnuts, chopped
50 g/2 oz plain chocolate, melted
6 tablespoons pineapple jam
1 tablespoon brandy
to decorate:
350 g/12 oz plain chocolate
225 g/8 oz butter or margarine
450 g/1 lb icing sugar, sifted
50 g/2 oz cocoa powder
1 tablespoon hot water
6 glacé cherries

Put the crumbs in a large bowl and mix in the
almonds, cherries, walnuts and chocolate. Melt
the jam in a saucepan and stir into the crumbs
with the brandy to make a fairly sticky
mixture. Spoon into a greased and lined 18-
cm/7-inch loose-bottomed cake tin. Press
down well. Leave for 1 hour in the freezer or
for 2 hours in the refrigerator. Remove from
the tin.

To decorate the cake, melt the chocolate in a
basin over hot water. Pour half of it over the
cake to coat evenly. Allow to set. Cream
together the butter and icing sugar, then stir in
the remaining melted chocolate and the cocoa.
Mix in the hot water. Decorate the sides and
top with piped chocolate butter cream and
decorate with glacé cherries. **Serves 8–10**

Flans and Cheesecakes

As the base for a flan or a cheesecake you can
use either sponge, shortbread, shortcrust or
sweet pastry, or a biscuit crumb base. The
simplest is a biscuit crumb base – usually
175 g/6 oz sweet or semi-sweet biscuits of any
sort, crushed and mixed with 75 g/3 oz melted
butter is sufficient for an 18–20-cm/7–8-inch
tin. This type of base only needs chilling.

Gelatine

Many flans need gelatine to make them set, but
it can be difficult to handle. There are two ways
to dissolve gelatine – in a basin with 1–2
tablespoons water over a pan of boiling water,
or simply add 1–2 tablespoons very hot but not
boiling water to the gelatine and stir. Then
leave for 2–3 minutes.

The first method is foolproof; the second
method is quicker and successful as long as you
don't use really boiling water and ruin the
gelatine. It should be clear, not grainy, when
you use it. If necessary sieve the mixture to
remove any lumps.

Chocolate Lime Flan

175 g/6 oz wheatmeal or plain biscuits, crushed
75 g/3 oz plain dessert chocolate, melted
25 g/1 oz butter
filling:
2 packets white marshmallows
150 ml/¼ pint milk
finely grated rind and juice of 2 limes or lemons
300 ml/½ pint cream, lightly whipped
to decorate:
grated chocolate
slices of lime

Mix the biscuit crumbs, melted chocolate and
butter in a pan. Press into the base and sides of a
20-cm/8-inch pie plate or flan tin. Chill.

To make the filling, melt the marshmallows
with the milk in a basin over hot water. Then
lower the basin half-way into a bowl of chilled
water to cool quickly.

Stir in the lime or lemon rind and juice. When
cool, fold in the cream and pour over the
crumb base. Leave to set in the refrigerator.
Decorate with the grated chocolate and lime
slices. **Serves 6–8**

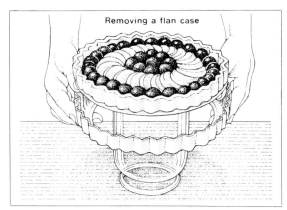
Removing a flan case

Strawberry Cheesecake

50 g/2 oz unsalted butter
100 g/4 oz crushed biscuits or cereal
350 g/12 oz cottage cheese
finely grated rind and juice of 1 small lemon
75 g/3 oz sugar
2 eggs, separated
1 tablespoon powdered gelatine
3 tablespoons water
150 ml/¼ pint cream, whipped
225 g/8 oz strawberries, hulled and sliced

Melt the butter and add the biscuit crumbs. Press into the base of a 20-cm/8-inch loose-bottomed cake or flan tin. Force the cottage cheese through a sieve or liquidise then mix with the lemon rind. Beat the sugar and egg yolks together until light and fluffy.

Dissolve the gelatine in the water over a pan of boiling water and add the lemon juice. Stir into the egg mixture. Add the cheese and stir well to mix evenly. Whisk the egg whites until stiff. Fold the egg whites, cream and half the strawberries into the cheese mixture. Pour into the prepared base, smooth the surface and leave to set. When set, use the remaining strawberries to decorate the top. Serve with cream. **Serves 6**

Cooked Cheesecake

(Illustrated on page 137)

25 g/1 oz butter or margarine
50 g/2 oz castor sugar
1 egg
50 g/2 oz flour
1 teaspoon baking powder
for the filling:
50 g/2 oz butter or margarine
50 g/2 oz castor sugar
grated rind and juice of 1 lemon
1 egg
50 g/2 oz plain flour
100 g/4 oz dried mixed fruit
450 g/1 lb curd cheese or sieved cottage cheese
150 ml/¼ pint double cream

First make the base. Cream the margarine and the sugar together, beat in the egg and fold in the flour and baking powder. Spread over the base of a greased and lined loose-bottomed 20-cm/8-inch cake tin.

For the filling, cream the margarine, sugar and lemon rind. Thoroughly beat the egg with the lemon juice, then fold into the creamed mixture with the flour and mixed fruit.

In a separate bowl, beat the cheese and cream until smooth and fold into the mixture. Pour on top of the sponge base and bake in a moderate oven (160°C, 325°F, Gas Mark 3) for 1¼–1½ hours. Allow to cool, then remove from the tin. **Serves 8**

Quick Orange Cheesecake

for the base:
150 g/5 oz plain flour
pinch salt
25 g/1 oz ground rice
50 g/2 oz castor sugar
100 g/4 oz butter or margarine
for the filling:
½ packet orange jelly
225 g/8 oz cream or curd cheese
300 ml/½ pint thick sweetened custard
finely grated rind of 1 orange
for the topping:
1 orange, peeled and sliced
few mint leaves or pieces angelica

Sift together the flour, salt and ground rice. Add the sugar and rub in the butter. Press the mixture into an 18–20-cm/7–8-inch flan dish and bake in a cool oven (150°C, 300°F, Gas Mark 2) for about 1 hour until firm. Cool.

Make the jelly up to 300 ml/½ pint with boiling water and stir well to dissolve. Beat the cheese, custard and orange rind together and whisk in the setting jelly. Spoon into the prepared base and chill until firm. Top with orange slices and mint leaves or angelica. **Serves 4–6**

Blackberry Crisp

(Illustrated on page 196)

100 g/4 oz butter or margarine
100 g/4 oz castor sugar
100 g/4 oz golden syrup
100 g/4 oz plain flour
1 teaspoon ground ginger
1–2 tablespoons brandy
1 (500-ml/17.6-fl oz) block vanilla ice cream
300 ml/½ pint whipped cream
225 g/8 oz blackberries

Grease four large baking trays. In a large saucepan, melt the butter, sugar and syrup together. Allow to cool slightly then beat in the flour, ginger and brandy. Divide the mixture evenly between the baking trays and bake, two trays at a time, in a moderate oven (160°C, 350°F, Gas Mark 4) for about 10 minutes. Cool the first two while the other trays cook. When ready to serve, layer the brandy crisps with ice cream, whipped cream and blackberries. As the ice cream will soften quickly, you could prepare two layers with cream and fruit in advance. If you have room in the freezer, prepare two layers with ice cream, and assemble just before serving. **Serves 6**

Italian Trifle

(Illustrated on page 138)

175–225 g/6–8 oz pink or white angel cake
175 g/6 oz fresh or frozen raspberries or 1 (312-g/11-oz) can raspberries
200 ml/7 fl oz double cream
3–4 tablespoons Maraschino, brandy or rum
2 egg whites
100 g/4 oz icing sugar, sifted
few sprigs mint or pieces angelica to decorate

Cut the sponge into small cubes. Hull or thaw the raspberries. (If using canned raspberries, drain well and reserve the liquid.) Pile the sponge and most of the raspberries on to a flat serving dish. Whip the cream until almost stiff and then slowly whip in the liqueur and a little of the raspberry juice. Whip until very thick. Spread the cream evenly over the fruit and sponge, piling it high. Chill. Whisk the egg whites with the sugar in a bowl over hot water until thick and white. (This takes about 15 minutes.) Remove from the heat and keep whipping until cool. Spoon this frosting over the cream. Chill and decorate with a few raspberries and mint or angelica before serving. **Serves 6**

Traditional Trifle

(Illustrated on page 138)

750 ml/1¼ pint Egg custard sauce (see page 189)
225 g/8 oz macaroons
½ packet trifle sponges
3 tablespoons mixed sherry and brandy
1 (425-g/15-oz) can apricots
150 ml/¼ pint cream, whipped
glacé cherries
ratafia biscuits
angelica

Mix the custard and macaroons together. Put half the sponges in the bottom of a glass bowl and sprinkle with half the sherry and brandy mixture. Purée the apricots without the juice and pour half the purée over the sponges. Then add a layer of half the custard. Repeat with the remaining sponges, sherry and brandy, purée and custard. Spread or pipe the cream over the trifle. Decorate with the cherries, ratafias and angelica and chill before serving. **Serves 6**

Caramel Custards

125 g/4½ oz sugar
150 ml/¼ pint water
600 ml/1 pint milk
50–75 g/2–3 oz sugar
4 eggs, beaten

Dissolve the sugar in the water and heat gently, without stirring, until the sugar darkens. Pour into six individual ramekins or pudding moulds and allow to cool. Warm the milk gently with the sugar, pour over the beaten eggs, stirring, and strain. Pour the milk mixture into the moulds then place them in a roasting tin half-filled with water. Bake in a moderate oven (160°C, 325°F, Gas Mark 3) for 40–45 minutes until set. Chill well, preferably overnight, and turn out. **Makes 6**

Chocolate Cup Cakes

175 g/6 oz plain chocolate
2 trifle sponges, crumbled
grated rind and juice of ½ lemon
juice of ½ orange
150 ml/¼ pint cream, whipped
sugar to taste
2 teaspoons drinking chocolate powder

Melt the chocolate in a bowl over a pan of hot water. Using a brush, coat the insides of six greased paper cake cases with chocolate. Leave to set and repeat the process. When firm, carefully remove the paper cases. Divide the crumbled sponges equally between the chocolate cases. Fold the lemon rind and fruit juices into the cream with the sugar. Spoon this mixture on to the cake crumbs in the chocolate cases and chill. Just before serving, sift a little drinking chocolate powder over each one. **Serves 6**

Jellied Strawberries

(Illustrated on page 155)

1 packet strawberry jelly
300 ml/½ pint orange juice
1 tablespoon orange liqueur
450 g/1 lb strawberries

Make up the strawberry jelly according to the instructions on the packet, using the orange juice and 150 ml/¼ pint water, topped up with liqueur. Wash, hull and halve the strawberries, reserving a few whole ones for decoration. Pour a little jelly into a wetted jelly mould and set a few halved strawberries in it. Continue layering with jelly and strawberries, setting between layers, until the mould is full. When set, turn out and decorate with the remaining whole strawberries. **Serves 4–6**

Peach Syllabub

4 ratafia biscuits
1 (227-g/8-oz) can sliced peaches
50 g/2 oz sugar
2 teaspoons lemon juice
150 ml/¼ pint white wine
300 ml/½ pint double cream
2 egg whites
grated nutmeg to decorate

Arrange the ratafias in the bases of four serving glasses. Drain off the peach juice and simmer the fruit with the sugar, lemon juice and wine until soft. Purée the peaches then chill. Whip the cream stiffly and then whip in the peach purée. Stiffly whisk the egg whites, fold in the peach mixture and spoon into the glasses. Chill and top with nutmeg before serving. **Serves 4**

Mexican Creams

100 g/4 oz plain chocolate
1–2 teaspoons instant coffee powder
450 ml/¾ pint custard, sweetened
150 ml/¼ pint cream, whipped or dessert topping
few whole almonds, toasted

Melt the chocolate with the coffee and 1 teaspoon water in a bowl over a pan of boiling water. Whip into the custard. Fold in most of the cream or topping and spoon into four glasses. Pipe the remaining cream on top and decorate with the almonds. Chill before serving. **Serves 4**

Cold Chocolate Soufflé

5 small eggs, separated
50 g/2 oz castor sugar
2 tablespoons water
3 teaspoons powdered gelatine
2 tablespoons cocoa powder
100 g/4 oz plain chocolate, melted
1 tablespoon brandy or rum
250 ml/8 fl oz double cream
100 g/4 oz flaked almonds, toasted

Tie a band of lightly-greased greaseproof paper around the outside of a 1.25-litre/2-pint soufflé dish so that it comes 7.5 cm/3 inches above the rim. Put the egg yolks in a mixing bowl with the sugar and water and whisk over a pan of hot water until thick and the whisk leaves a trail when lifted. Dissolve the gelatine in 5 tablespoons of water in a bowl over a pan of hot water. Whisk into the egg mixture together with the cocoa, chocolate and brandy or rum. Leave until on the point of setting. Whip the cream until thick. Whisk the egg white until stiff but not peaking. Fold the cream and egg whites into the chocolate mixture. Turn into the prepared soufflé dish and leave until quite set. Remove the paper carefully from the soufflé. Press the almonds on to the sides of the soufflé. Serve with cream. **Serves 8**

Apricot and Yogurt Mousse

1 (425-g/15-oz) can apricot halves
2 (15-g/½-oz) envelopes powdered gelatine
2 tablespoons fresh orange juice
sugar to taste
150 ml/¼ pint natural yogurt
2–3 tablespoons cream, whipped
Chocolate sauce (see page 189)

Drain the apricots and liquidise or sieve to make a purée. Dissolve the gelatine in the orange juice in a bowl over a pan of hot water. Stir into the purée, with sugar to taste, and the yogurt. Then fold in the whipped cream. Turn into a wetted 1.25-litre/2-pint mould. Chill until firm then turn out and top with trickles of chocolate sauce. **Serves 4–6**

Strawberry Mousse

450 g/1 lb ripe strawberries, hulled
sugar to taste
150 ml/¼ pint cream, whipped
1 tablespoon powdered gelatine
3 tablespoons water
2 egg whites
extra whipped cream to decorate

Purée the strawberries and mix with the sugar and cream. Dissolve the gelatine in the water in a bowl over a pan of hot water. Stir quickly into the strawberry mixture and leave until on the point of setting. Whisk the egg whites until stiff and fold into the mixture. Turn into a serving bowl or individual dishes and leave until set. Serve chilled, decorated with whipped cream.

Prepare a mould or four ramekin dishes as for the chocolate mousse, if you wish, with paper to support the sides, but this does give larger individual portions. **Serves 5–6**

Lamb en croûte (see page 63)

Buttered Oranges

(Illustrated on page 128)

8 large juicy oranges
5 egg yolks
50 g/2 oz castor sugar
1 teaspoon triple-strength rose water
100 g/4 oz unsalted butter, cut in cubes
150 ml/¼ pint double cream
1 large piece soft candied peel
to decorate:
6 roses on cocktail sticks
extra whipped cream

Reserve six even-sized oranges so that the stalk ends are at the base. Cut off the new top, no more than 1 cm/½ inch down. Scoop out all the flesh from both shells and lids. Grate the rind from the remaining two oranges to make about 1 tablespoon when pressed down. Sieve the flesh to get out as much juice as possible. Mix the juice, rind, egg yolks and sugar in a bowl over a pan of hot water and stir, cooking gently, until it has thickened like a custard. As the mixture begins to 'ribbon', remove the bowl to a pan of cold water and continue stirring until cool. Add the rose water. Remove the bowl from the cold water. Add the pieces of butter, one at a time, to the mixture. Whisk until they are all incorporated. Half whip the cream and fold into the mixture. Cut the soft candied peel into tiny pieces and add as the mixture thickens, stirring so they don't sink. Fill the orange shells with the mixture. Decorate the lids with a fresh rose on a cocktail stick. Pipe a swirl of cream at one side of the rim and top with the 'lid'. **Serves 6**

Crown roast of lamb (see page 50)

Scarlet Fruit Cocktail

350 g/12 oz strawberries, hulled
¼ section water melon, seeds removed and cut in cubes
100 g/4 oz Victoria plums, stoned and chopped
100 g/4 oz redcurrants
100 g/4 oz raspberries
100 g/4 oz cherries, stoned
300 ml/½ pint rosé wine
100 g/4 oz sugar

Halve, or if large, quarter, the strawberries. Mix in a bowl with the remaining fruit. Pour the wine over the fruit and sprinkle with the sugar. Leave to stand for 1 hour, stirring occasionally. Serve with cream. **Serves 6**

Caribbean Fruit Salad

1 (298-g/10½-oz) can mandarin oranges
1 (425-g/15-oz) can mangoes or pineapple
1 (425-g/15-oz) can guava halves
2 bananas, sliced
½ teaspoon ground cloves
pinch grated nutmeg

Drain all the canned fruit and reserve the syrup. Mix the bananas with the canned fruit, cloves and nutmeg, taking care not to break the fruit. Add as much of the reserved syrup as you wish and chill for at least 4 hours. **Serves 4–6**

Pure Dairy Ice Cream

450 ml/¼ pint Egg custard sauce (see page 189)
300 ml/½ pint double cream, whipped

For speed, you can use the same quantity of custard made from a packet. Strain the custard and fold in half the cream. Add flavourings if you wish (variations are given overleaf) and pour into a freezing tray. When partly frozen, turn into a large bowl and gradually stir in the remaining whipped cream. Freeze again until solid. **Makes about 750 ml/1¼ pints**

Pawpaw

Also called papaya, it's very much like a melon in texture though sweeter in taste. To use as a starter, cut the flesh roughly and serve fresh with cream. Remove the dark seeds from the centre. Avoid dried up or blemished fruits. Available most of the year.

Passion Fruit

This is an unattractive-looking fruit with very wrinkled purplish skin. However, the centre is deliciously sweet and juicy with a slight tang of orange. It also has tiny black edible seeds. Best eaten straight from their skins or scooped out and sieved to make a sauce for ices and cream desserts. Available in small quantities most of the year.

Persimmons

These look like large tomatoes but are pinky orange in colour. The soft juicy flesh inside is of a similar colour and has a sharp flavour. Eat on their own, add to salads or use for ices and sauces. A winter fruit, not widely available.

Pomegranates

A very tough-skinned fruit, about the size of an apple. Inside are hundreds of small very juicy red seeds, separated by flimsy pieces of papery skin. They are difficult to eat unless you suck out the juice, or pick out the seeds. The juice can be squeezed out, though, for use in other ways. Available in autumn and winter.

Sauces

Toss pasta in a shrimp sauce; serve poached eggs with a Hollandaise sauce; liven up cold meats with a little Cumberland sauce and you have created something special using ordinary ingredients. That is the wonder of sauces – and what is more they are easy to make with many storecupboard ingredients and good to store in the refrigerator or even freeze in small quantities.

Mayonnaise

Make large quantities when you have some spare egg yolks or lots of eggs and keep in the refrigerator in a screw-top jar for 2–3 weeks.

1 tablespoon vinegar or lemon juice
3 egg yolks or 1 egg and 1 yolk
½ teaspoon salt
pinch white pepper
few grains sugar
600 ml/1 pint salad or other good quality oil

Mix the vinegar, eggs, seasoning and sugar together. Add the oil very slowly, beating it in with a whisk – or blend the mayonnaise in the liquidiser, pouring in the oil in a slow trickle with the machine running until thickened to the consistency you wish. If it is too thick, add a little water. Should the mixture curdle, start again with a fresh egg yolk and pour in the curdled mixture as in the recipe, beating continuously. **Makes 750 ml/1¼ pints**

Vinaigrette Dressing

(French Dressing)
1 teaspoon French mustard
3 tablespoons vinegar (white, wine or cider)
pinch sugar
salt and pepper
6 tablespoons corn oil

Mix the mustard, vinegar, sugar and seasoning. Whisk in the oil until well mixed. Store in the refrigerator in a screw-top jar. Shake before serving. **Makes 300 ml/½ pint**

Ways to Flavour Salad Dressings

These flavourings will add a fillip to a mayonnaise or vinaigrette dressing.

Cheese add grated, cream or sieved cottage cheese to the dressing.

Curry beat a little curry paste into the dressing.

Garlic crush or chop 1–2 cloves garlic and add to the dressing. If this is too strong, halve a clove, leave it in the dressing for a short time, then remove.

Green Mayonnaise add chopped herbs or watercress to the mayonnaise, crushing them enough to produce a green colour.

Herb add freshly chopped herbs to the dressing.

Horseradish add grated horseradish or horseradish cream to the dressing.

Lemon add extra lemon juice instead of vinegar when making the dressing, plus finely grated lemon rind.

Mint add finely chopped mint or melt and cool a little mint jelly and beat into the dressing.

Mustard mix the dressing with extra mustard.

Tartare Sauce add finely chopped parsley, chopped gherkins and capers to the mayonnaise.

Tomato add either fresh tomato pulp, purée or ketchup to the dressing.

Fruit use a mixture of fruit juices – apple, orange or apricot, for example to add variety and a little sweetness to dressings.

Thickened and Enriched Sauces

Liquids from casseroles, or thin sauces can be thickened by the addition of beurre manié, (flour and butter) or enriched and slightly thickened by the addition of a liaison (eggs and double cream).

Beurre Manié

Rub together equal quantities of flour and butter until crumbly. This can be stored in the refrigerator until required. Add to sauces, or casserole liquid in knobs, beating well as the butter melts and thickens the liquid by drawing in the flour. Continue until thickened to the required consistency.

Liaison

Beat together 2 egg yolks and 3–4 tablespoons double cream. Add this to 300 ml/$\frac{1}{2}$ pint sauce or casserole liquid and cook gently in a double saucepan or in a bowl over hot water until slightly thickened.

Quick White Sauce

15 g/$\frac{1}{2}$ oz cornflour
300 ml/$\frac{1}{2}$ pint milk
15 g/$\frac{1}{2}$ oz butter
salt and pepper

Mix the cornflour with a little of the milk. Then add the rest and pour into a pan. Bring to the boil, stirring all the time, then cook for 1–2 minutes. When thickened, stir in the butter and seasoning and beat until glossy. **Makes 300 ml/$\frac{1}{2}$ pint**

Brown Sauces

The simplest and most commonly used brown sauce is gravy, which should be rich and brown with no additions necessary.

Transfer the joint to its serving dish and drain off all but 1 tablespoon of the fat and the meat sediment. Pour in 300 ml/$\frac{1}{2}$ pint hot vegetable stock (reserve the vegetable cooking liquids) and boil briskly, scraping down the sediment from the side of the tin. Serve when slightly reduced and thickened.

If you prefer a thickened gravy, work in beurre manié to the right consistency, or stir 2–3 teaspoons cornflour into a little vegetable stock, stir in the remaining stock and add to the roasting tin.

Espagnole Sauce

This sauce uses a brown roux and can be the basis for almost any other dark, rich meat sauce. It's also very good as it is!

25 g/1 oz butter
25 g/1 oz streaky bacon, chopped
1 shallot or piece of onion, finely chopped
25 g/1 oz mushrooms, chopped (use just stalks if you have them)
1 small carrot, chopped
20 g/$\frac{3}{4}$ oz flour
300 ml/$\frac{1}{2}$ pint beef stock
1 bouquet garni
2 tablespoons tomato purée
salt and pepper

Melt the butter and fry the bacon for 2–3 minutes, then add the onion, mushroom and carrot and cook for 2 minutes, or until golden. Stir in the flour and cook, stirring until lightly browned. This is best done slowly and gently. Off the heat, gradually stir in the stock. When well mixed, return to the heat and cook, stirring, until thickened. Then add the bouquet garni, tomato purée and seasoning to taste. Simmer gently over a very low heat for at least 30 minutes until reduced by half. Strain and use as required.

Espagnole sauce is the perfect base for a red wine or Madeira sauce. Add up to 150 ml/$\frac{1}{4}$ pint red wine or Madeira to the above sauce and simmer until slightly reduced. It can also be flavoured with orange juice, port, redcurrant jelly or other ingredients to make rich sauces for red meat, venison or game. For a simple brown sauce to serve with beef, add 300 ml/½ pint fresh beef stock to 300 ml/½ pint espagnole sauce and simmer until thickened again and glossy. This is a quick version of the classic demi-glace sauce. **Makes about 300 ml/½ pint**

Keeping Sauces

If you are going to make one of these more time-consuming classic sauces why not make at least double quantities and either refrigerate or freeze the rest? It will save work next time you need a really good sauce.

Any thickened sauce will form a skin on cooling. To minimise this, cover very closely with greased paper, or reserve some of the liquid and pour over the top during cooling. This can be whisked in when reheating.

Chestnut Sauce

300 ml/½ pint thick gravy or Espagnole sauce (see opposite)
225–350 g/8–12 oz cooked or canned chestnuts
2 tablespoons sherry
salt and pepper
2 tablespoons cream

Pour the gravy or sauce into a liquidiser and add 100 g/4 oz of the chestnuts and the sherry. Liquidise then chop the remaining chestnuts. Add to the sauce in a saucepan and bring to the boil. Season to taste and stir in the cream. **Makes 600 ml/1 pint**

Cumberland Sauce

pared rind and juice of 1 orange
pared rind and juice of 1 lemon
2 tablespoons redcurrant jelly
½ teaspoon prepared mustard
2 tablespoons vinegar
2–3 glacé cherries, chopped
4–5 tablespoons port

Shred the orange and lemon rind thinly and boil in 5 tablespoons water for 5 minutes. Cool and strain, reserving the rind. Add all the remaining ingredients, bring to the boil and simmer until reduced and slightly thickened. **Makes 300 ml/½ pint**

Gooseberry Sauce

225 g/8 oz gooseberries
15 g/½ oz sugar
½ teaspoon cornflour
salt and pepper
25 g/1 oz butter

Top and tail the gooseberries and simmer, with the sugar and 5 tablespoons water until very soft. Purée through a sieve or in a liquidiser. Mix the cornflour with a little water and stir in. Season and bring to the boil, stirring until thickened. Beat the butter into the sauce and serve hot with pork, mackerel or other white fish. **Makes 300 ml/½ pint**

Mint Sauce

4 tablespoons boiling water
2 tablespoons chopped fresh mint
1½ tablespoons castor sugar
4 tablespoons vinegar

Pour the boiling water on to the mint and add the sugar. Stir until the sugar has dissolved then add the vinegar. Leave to stand for several hours. Serve with roast lamb or lamb chops. **Makes about 150 ml/¼ pint**

Italian Tomato Sauce

25 g/1 oz butter
2 large onions, chopped
1 clove garlic, crushed
2 teaspoons dried basil
1 (425-g/15-oz) can tomatoes, chopped
salt and pepper

Melt the butter and fry the onion and garlic until tender. Stir in the basil and tomatoes, bring to the boil and simmer for about 5 minutes, until slightly reduced. Season to taste. **Makes 600 ml/1 pint**

Low-calorie Sauces

Many sauces can be made successfully without butter, flour or cream. The most important thing is to start with a good basic flavour – a fresh, well-flavoured stock or casserole juices. Cook sufficiently to reduce to a thickened consistency and then, if you wish add fromage blanc, yogurt or a vegetable purée to give a thicker creamy texture. Fromage blanc is a very fresh, French cheese, mild and creamy in taste. If you can't buy it, liquidise 80 g/3½ oz cottage cheese with 125 g/4½ oz natural yogurt and 3 tablespoons lemon juice until smooth, shiny and slightly thick.

Yogurt needs to be 'stabilised' before it can be used successfully in sauces as it separates when boiled. Mix 1 tablespoon cornflour with 600 ml/1 pint natural yogurt and bring slowly to the boil, stirring. When smooth, allow to cool. Chill and use as required.

Many vegetable purées can make excellent sauces, very quickly. Carrots, onions, leeks, celery, tomatoes, asparagus, spinach, courgettes, and many others (even canned varieties) are ideal. Mix together equal quantities of purée and fresh stock with seasoning and then simmer to the required consistency. Add fromage blanc or yogurt if you wish before serving.

Carrot Purée Sauce

1 (283-g/10-oz) can carrots
200 ml/7 fl oz beef stock
1 teaspoon dried rosemary
salt and pepper
5 tablespoons fromage blanc

Drain most of the liquid from the carrots. Purée or liquidise the carrots with a little juice. Transfer to a saucepan and add the stock and rosemary. Simmer until reduced by half. Season to taste and stir in the fromage blanc. Heat but do not boil. Serve hot with lamb, chicken or veal. **Makes about 300 ml/½ pint**

Sweet Sauces

Many delicious sweet sauces can be made using a white sauce, sweetened and not seasoned, or custard. However arrowroot or cornflour are invaluable for turning delicious fruit juices into lightly-thickened sauces, for glazing flans or serving with puddings. Although they both thicken in the same way, remember that arrowroot becomes clear and is therefore more suitable for glazing attractive fruit flans.

Brandy Sauce

300 ml/½ pint unseasoned Basic white sauce (see page 185)
5–6 tablespoons brandy
sugar to taste
2 tablespoons double cream
pinch grated nutmeg

Mix the sauce, brandy and sugar in a saucepan. Bring to the boil and simmer until quite thick. Mix in the cream and nutmeg. This sauce is good with Christmas pudding. Rum or whisky can also be used. **Makes 300 ml/½ pint**

Chocolate Sauce

300 ml/½ pint unseasoned Basic white sauce
1 tablespoon cocoa powder or 100 g/4 oz cooking
chocolate, grated or chopped
sugar to taste

Make the sauce as prescribed in the basic recipe (see page 185) either with the cocoa mixed into the milk or with the chocolate melted into the thickened sauce. Sweeten to taste.

VARIATION

To make a coffee sauce, make up the basic white sauce, unseasoned, using half milk and half strong black coffee. Stir in 1 tablespoon double cream and sugar to taste. **Makes 300 ml/½ pint**

Egg Custard Sauce

300 ml/½ pint milk
1 vanilla pod
small piece lemon rind
2–3 egg yolks
25 g/1 oz castor sugar

Bring the milk to the boil with the vanilla pod and lemon rind. Leave to stand for a few minutes. Beat the egg yolks with the sugar and strain the milk over the mixture, whisking continuously. Transfer to a double saucepan or a bowl over hot water and cook gently, stirring until slightly thickened. It should coat the back of the wooden spoon. Serve hot or cold.

If liked, bake the same mixture in a *bain-marie* in a moderate oven (180°C, 350°F, Gas Mark 4) for 45 minutes. This serves two, for four servings, use 3 whole eggs (whites included) and 600 ml/1 pint milk. **Makes 450 ml/¾ pint**

Easy Custard

300 ml/½ pint milk
few drops vanilla essence
25 g/1 oz castor sugar
2 teaspoons cornflour
1 egg
sherry to taste (optional)

Heat all but 3 tablespoons of the milk with the vanilla and sugar. Mix the remaining milk with the cornflour and whisk into the hot milk with the egg. Heat without boiling, stirring until thick. Add sherry if liked. **Makes 300 ml/½ pint**

Jam Sauce

4 tablespoons jam
150 ml/¼ pint water
1 teaspoon cornflour
few drops lemon juice

Heat the jam with the water until melted and thinned. Mix the cornflour with a little water then stir into the jam. Stir over a low heat until thickened and add a few drops of lemon juice. Serve hot with puddings, ice creams or cakes or sieve and use as a glaze. **Makes 300 ml/½ pint**

Lemon or Orange Sauce

finely grated rind and juice of 2 oranges or
finely grated rind and juice of 1 lemon
sugar to taste
1–2 teaspoons whisky or brandy
1 teaspoon cornflour

Place the orange or lemon rind and juice in a saucepan with 300 ml/½ pint water. Simmer gently until the rind is softened. Sweeten to taste and add the whisky or brandy. Mix the cornflour with some water and stir into the sauce. Stir over a low heat until thickened. If preferred, omit the cornflour and boil until reduced and slightly thickened. **Makes 300 ml/½ pint**

Melba Sauce

225 g/8 oz fresh, frozen or canned raspberries
150 ml/¼ pint raspberry liquid from can or water
sugar to taste
1 teaspoon cornflour

Place the raspberries and liquid in a saucepan and boil until tender. If using canned raspberries, there is no need to cook. Purée or sieve and return to the pan. Sweeten to taste and heat. Mix the cornflour with some water and stir into the purée. Bring to the boil, stirring until thickened. **Makes 300 ml/½ pint**

Entertaining

Some people enjoy entertaining and carry it off with ease, but many get into a flap just at the thought. However, it can be simple if you follow these golden rules.

Never cook a complicated dish that you haven't tried before – have a trial run.

Plan, shop and even cook as much in advance as possible. If you are not sure of your guests' likes and dislikes, choose popular foods, or have an alternative available.

Choose your guests carefully too, so that they will all get on well and have something in common. This is particularly important if you are only inviting a few people.

Informal Suppers

Informal, spur-of-the-moment entertaining can be great fun if you keep the preparation simple and divide the responsibilities. If you are going to cook, try to get your co-host, husband, flat-mate, or even another couple to join in and help either with the shopping or organising the drinks. Use storecupboard foods or ones you can buy at the last minute from a supermarket. Don't be over ambitious with the food. Choose one main dish, as our party ideas here suggest, which is easy to prepare in large quantities rather than several smaller more complicated items. Then finish off with cheese or fruit. Ten to twelve people is normally the ideal number to manage and, if necessary, ask your friends to bring extra plates or cutlery along.

Sausage and Cider Party

Sausages are good party fare and always popular, but will be even more so in this cassoulet, which can be left to cook by itself. Serve with different types of cider (allowing three glasses per head), mustard croûtons and green salad. **Serves 10**

Sausage Cassoulet

(Illustrated on page 195)

350 g/12 oz haricot beans
350 g/12 oz red kidney beans
1–2 tablespoons oil
1.5 kg/3 lb sausages, pork, beef or herb
3 large onions, sliced
3 cloves garlic, crushed
1 (793-g/1 lb 12-oz) can tomatoes
600 ml/1 pint dry cider
900 ml/1½ pints chicken stock
1 tablespoon chilli powder
1 (64-g/2¼-oz) can tomato purée
1 teaspoon prepared mustard
4 teaspoons dried mixed peppers
2 tablespoons chopped parsley
1 tablespoon cornflour

Soak all the beans for 3–4 hours in cold water. Heat the oil and fry the sausages gently. Remove and slice thickly. Drain the beans and put into one very large or two to three smaller ovenproof dishes with most of the juices from the sausages and all the remaining ingredients except the sausages. Stir well, cover and cook in a moderate oven (180°C, 350°F, Gas Mark 4) for 1½ hours or until the beans are tender. Add the sausages and cook for a further 1 hour.

Mustard Croûtons

4 French loaves
225 g/8 oz butter, softened
4 tablespoons mustard relish

Slice the loaves thickly, then toast. Mix the butter and mustard, spread on the toast, then put under a hot grill until the butter melts. Serve with the cassoulet.

Green Salad

Make a green salad of lettuce (use two heads), watercress, chunks of cucumber, sliced courgettes and sliced green pepper. Serve tossed in a Vinaigrette dressing (see page 183).

Beef and Beer Party

A good, wholesome beef pie makes a change from the more usual party foods. Serve this one with a salad, herb bread and plenty of beer or lager (allowing 3–4 glasses per head), and you have the ideal menu for an autumn or winter party. **Serves 10**

Beef and Game Pie

(Illustrated on page 166–167)

4 wood pigeons or 1 (2-kg/4½-lb) boiling fowl
600 ml/1 pint water
½ onion, halved
salt and pepper
1.5 kg/3 lb stewing steak, cut in cubes
4 tablespoons flour
4 tablespoons oil
4 oranges
225 g/8 oz onions, sliced
225 g/8 oz button mushrooms, sliced
2 (368-g/13-oz) packets frozen puff pastry,
thawed
milk to glaze

Simmer the pigeons or boiling fowl in the water with the onion and seasoning for about 1 hour. Remove with a draining spoon, cool, then take the flesh from the bones. Reserve the cooking liquor. Toss the steak in the flour. Heat the oil and fry the steak until brown. Stir in the reserved liquor from the birds and bring to the boil. Grate the rind of one orange. Segment all the oranges and put aside. Add the rind to the pan with the pigeon flesh and onions. Season, cover and simmer for 1½–2 hours. Leave to cool. Add the orange segments and mushrooms and turn into an ovenproof dish. Roll out the two pastry pieces. Use to cover the pie (see page 139), overlapping them in the centre. Moisten and seal the edges together. Use the trimmings to decorate the top. Knock up the edges and flute. Glaze with milk and bake in a hot oven (220°C, 425°F, Gas Mark 7) for 15–20 minutes. Reduce to moderately hot (190°C, 375°F, Gas Mark 5) for 35–40 minutes, until cooked through.

Herb Bread

2 French loaves
225 g/8 oz butter
4 cloves garlic, crushed
1 tablespoon dried mixed herbs

Cut the loaves in 2.5-cm/1-inch slices, nearly through to the base. Mix the butter, garlic and herbs and spread over both sides of each slice. Wrap in foil and cook in a moderately hot oven (190°C, 375°F, Gas Mark 5) for about 20 minutes.

Tomato and Onion Salad

Toss 900 g/2 lb sliced tomatoes in Vinaigrette dressing (see page 183) with 1 chopped onion and trimmed spring onions.

Curry Party

Curries are so popular nowadays that it makes an ideal supper party dish. However, be sure it is not too hot, unless you really know the tastes of your guests. One meat curry dish is sufficient but if you have time you could also make a vegetable curry. Serve with plain rice, poppadums (or chapatis warmed through if you can buy them locally), and a selection of relishes and side dishes. It is best to serve lager or other long cool drinks with curry. **Serves 12**

Coconut Beef Curry

This is a mild, slightly sweet curry called a Rendang.

1.5 kg/3 lb cooked beef
150 g/5 oz unsweetened desiccated coconut
900 ml/1½ pints milk
3 tablespoons soy sauce
6 tablespoons vinegar
2–3 tablespoons oil
4 cloves garlic, crushed
4 onions, quartered
salt and pepper
1 tablespoon chilli powder
1 tablespoon ground coriander
1 tablespoon ground turmeric
1 tablespoon ground ginger

Cut the beef into chunks and put into a shallow dish. Heat the coconut in the milk until nearly boiling. Cool slightly and then liquidise or pound. Add the soy sauce and vinegar and pour the liquid over the beef. Leave, stirring occasionally, for 3–4 hours or overnight. Heat the oil and fry the garlic and onion until golden. Then stir in the seasoning, chilli, coriander, turmeric and ginger and fry for 2 minutes. Transfer to a casserole, stir in the meat and liquid and mix well. Cook in a moderately hot oven (190°C, 375°F, Gas Mark 5) for about 1 hour until the meat is tender.

If you use uncooked braising steak it will need about 2½ hours cooking time.

Vegetable Curry

4–5 tablespoons oil
2 large onions, sliced
1 tablespoon curry paste
300 ml/½ pint chicken stock
1 large cauliflower, cut in florets and lightly cooked
350 g/12 oz frozen peas
150 ml/¼ pint natural yogurt

Heat the oil and fry the onion until transparent. Stir in the curry paste and cook for a further 1–2 minutes. Stir in the stock, cauliflower and peas and cook for 5–8 minutes, or until the peas are heated through. Stir in the yogurt at the last minute and heat through.

This curry can be prepared using other left-over vegetables if you prefer. Use about 900 g/2 lb of mixed vegetables. **Serves 12**

Curry Side Dishes

Mango or peach chutney, piccalilli or other sweet relishes are ideal. If you wish, serve side dishes of sliced banana or other fruits dipped in lemon juice, sliced onions, tomatoes, or nuts.

Fondue Party

Fondues are an ideal and easy way to entertain two to four people and they're great fun too. Although you can obviously buy special fondue equipment, there's no need to invest in anything expensive unless you plan to do this frequently. All you need is a small table hotplate or burner, long fondue forks or skewers and a heavy-based metal pan for an oil fondue or a flameproof casserole for cheese.

Give everyone their own plate of meat and knife and fork. Arrange bowls of salads, sauces, pickles and extras on the table and let people help themselves. Everyone can then cook or dip their own food, on a fork or skewer, in the liquid but be careful with meat straight from the fondue – it will be hot, and so will the fork!

Cheese Fondue

1 clove garlic (optional)
225 g/8 oz Emmental or Edam cheese, grated
450 ml/¾ pint dry white wine or dry cider
225 g/8 oz Gruyère or Gouda cheese, cut in cubes
2–3 tablespoons kirsch
1 teaspoon cornflour
freshly ground black pepper

Halve the clove of garlic and rub round the inside of the fondue pot. Chop the garlic finely or crush and add to the Emmental in a heavy-based pan. Mix well and add the wine. Heat gently, stirring all the time in the shape of a figure-of-eight, using a wooden spoon. Add the Gruyère and stir until melted. Mix the kirsch and cornflour and add to the cheese. Season with pepper and stir until thickened and creamy. Transfer to the table burner. Keep the cheese bubbling gently. Serve cubes of French bread and fruit and vegetables speared on forks to dip into the cheese. **Serves 4**

Fondue Bourguignonne

Pieces of steak are skewered and dipped into hot oil and left to cook at the table. Be sure the table burner stands firmly and always use fresh oil for the best flavour. Although more expensive than other fondues, this is a delicious way to serve tender juicy steak. If you marinate the meat, or cut it very small you could get away with using cheaper meat. Include sausages and meatballs to make the steak go further. Serve with tangy sauces and crisp vegetables or a salad, baked potatoes or chips.

675 g/1½ lb rump steak
12 sausages
900 ml/1½ pints oil
for the meatballs:
450 g/1 lb minced beef
pinch grated nutmeg
1 egg, beaten
2 teaspoons fresh breadcrumbs
salt and pepper
1 medium onion, finely chopped

Mayonnaise home-made or bought.

Cream Sauce mix whipped cream with crushed garlic and seasoning. Chill.

Tomato Sauce fry 1 large chopped onion in 2 teaspoons oil; sieve 1 (227-g/8-oz) can tomatoes. Add the flesh and juice to the onion and season with salt, pepper and dried thyme. Cook until thick.

Apple-horseradish Sauce mix 2 grated apples with 1 tablespoon grated horseradish and 2 teaspoons lemon juice; add 1 small onion, chopped, 1 teaspoon oil and seasoning to taste.

Herb Sauce mix 150 ml/¼ pint natural yogurt with 2 tablespoons chopped parsley, 2 tablespoons chopped chives, 2 tablespoons chopped

dill and a few sliced stuffed olives. Add 1 teaspoon oil and cover.

Cut the steak into bite-sized cubes and chill. Cut or twist the sausages into similarly-sized pieces. Mix all the ingredients for the meat balls together and roll into 20 balls using wet hands. Chill.

Heat the fondue pan of oil on your cooker and then very carefully transfer it to the lighted table burner. The oil should be at a temperature of 190°C/375°F (a 2.5-cm/1-inch cube of bread should brown in 1 minute). Maintain this temperature throughout the cooking time. Guests cook pieces of meat in the oil and help themselves to the sauces, salads and baked potatoes or bread. **Serves 6**

Catering for Large Numbers

This is a guide to the quantity of food that you will need when cooking for 25 or 50 people.

Baked foods	For 25	For 50
Bread (white, 24 slices)	1¼ loaves	2½ loaves
(wholewheat, 16 slices)	1¾ loaves	3½ loaves
Cakes (20-cm/8-inch round), fruit	1¾	3½
Cakes (20 cm/8-inch round), sponge	2½	5
Pies (20-cm/8-inch)	4½	9
Pastry (for 20-cm/8-inch pie top)	1.25 kg/ 2½ lb	2.25 kg/5 lb
Filling (for 20-cm/8-inch pie)	3.5 kg/ 8 lb	7.25 kg/ 16 lb
Pudding (100-g/4-oz portion)	2.85 kg/ 6¼ lb	5.75 kg/ 12½ lb

Continued overleaf

Continued from previous page

Catering for Large Numbers

Drinks	For 25	For 50
Instant coffee	35 g/1¼ oz	65 g/2½ oz
Tea	50 g/2 oz	100 g/4 oz
Soft drinks	1.25 litres/ 2¼ pints	2.5 litres / 4½ pints
Wine (1 glass per person)	4½ bottles	8½ bottles
Sherry (1 glass per person	2 bottles	4 bottles
Milk for tea/coffee	750 ml/1¼ pints	1.4 litres/2½ pints

Vegetables	For 25	For 50
Potatoes – whole – to mash	4 kg/9 lb 3.25 kg/ 7 lb	8 kg/ 18 lb 6.25 kg/ 14 lb
Green or other	2.75 kg/ 6 lb	5.5 kg/ 12 lb
Salad – lettuces	6	12
– tomatoes	2.75 kg/ 6 lb	5.5 kg/ 12 lb
– cucumbers	4½	9
– coleslaw	2.75 kg/ 6 lb	5.5 kg/ 12 lb
– rice (uncooked)	1.5 kg/ 3 lb	2.75 kg/ 6 lb

Fruit	For 25	For 50
Fresh fruit (100 g/4 oz per person)	2.75 kg/ 6 lb	5.5 kg/ 12 lb
Puddings	3.5 kg/ 8 lb	7.25 kg/ 16 lb
Dried	1.75 kg/ 4 lb	3.5 kg/ 8 lb

Meat	For 25	For 50
With bone	6.75 kg/ 15 lb	13.5 kg/ 30 lb
Without bone	3.75 kg/ 8½ lb	7.5 kg/ 17 lb
Offal/sausages	3.25 kg/ 7 lb	6.25 kg/ 14 lb

Fish	For 25	For 50
Boneless fillets	3.75 kg/ 8½ lb	7.5 kg/ 17 lb
Whole fish	6.75 kg/ 15 lb	13.5 kg/ 30 lb
Shellfish	2.25 kg/ 5 lb	4.5 kg/ 10 lb

Sausage cassoulet (see page 190)

Hard Ball (120–130°C/245–265°F) the same test as above produces a firm ball of syrup. Use for caramels, marshmallows and nougat.

Soft Crack (135–145°C/270–290°F) drops of syrup in cold water will separate into threads which are hard but not brittle. Use for toffees.

Hard Crack (150–155°C/300–310°F) when tested as above it forms threads which are hard and brittle. Use for hard toffees, rock and humbugs.

Caramel (155°C/310°F) the syrup becomes golden brown. This is used for caramel toppings. Add chopped nuts and 1 teaspoon cream of tartar to the golden syrup. Shake well and pour on to foil to make praline (illustrated on the jacket).

Peppermint Humbugs

450 g/1 lb soft light brown sugar
1 tablespoon golden syrup
50 g/2 oz butter
$\frac{1}{4}$ teaspoon cream of tartar
few drops peppermint essence

Place all ingredients except the peppermint, in a large pan with 150 ml/$\frac{1}{4}$ pint water. Dissolve the sugar gently and then bring to boil. Boil to 140–145°C/280–290°F or to the small crack stage then add about $\frac{1}{2}$ teaspoon peppermint essence. Pour on to a large, well-oiled surface. Leave it until it forms a skin. Grease your hands and a scraper so that you can handle the mixture withouts its sticking.

When cool enough to handle, start folding the mixture into the centre with a scraper until it begins to firm up. Then start pulling with your hands, folding, then pulling again. Work quickly as the mixture will harden rapidly. When quite ready it should develop a sheen and still be just malleable. Pull it into a rope about 1.5 cm/$\frac{3}{4}$ thick. Quickly cut into small pieces with oiled scissors. To give the sweets the traditional half-twisted humbug shape, give the rope a quarter turn each time before cutting. Wrap each one in greaseproof paper to prevent their sticking together. **Makes about 350 g/12 oz**

Vanilla Fudge

450 g/1 lb granulated sugar
1 (397-g/14-oz) can condensed milk
50 g/2 oz margarine
1 teaspoon vanilla essence
150 ml/$\frac{1}{4}$ pint plus 2 tablespoons water

Put all the ingredients into a saucepan with the water. Heat until the sugar dissolves. Boil to 115°C/238°F or the soft ball stage. Remove from the heat and beat until thick. Pour into a greased tin, cool and cut in squares. **Makes 24**

Gooey Chocolate Fudge

50 g/2 oz clear honey
50 g/2 oz raisins
100 g/4 oz plain chocolate
100 g/4 oz butter
50 g/2 oz granulated sugar
225 g/8 oz sweet biscuits

Heat all the ingredients except the biscuits in a saucepan until the sugar dissolves. Crush the biscuits and mix into the fudge. Pour into a tin, cool then cut into squares. **Makes 24**

Marshmallows

275 g/10 oz granulated sugar
2 teaspoons glucose
20 g/$\frac{3}{4}$ oz powdered gelatine
1 egg white
1–2 tablespoons rose-hip syrup
few drops pink colouring (optional)
icing sugar for dredging

Dissolve the sugar and glucose very slowly over a low heat in 150 ml/$\frac{1}{4}$ pint water. When clear, bring to the boil and heat to 120°C/260°F. Meanwhile, dissolve the gelatine in 150 ml/$\frac{1}{4}$ pint hot water in a basin over hot water. Whisk the egg white until stiff. Whisk the gelatine into the sugar syrup with the egg white, rose-hip syrup and a few drops of colouring if used. Continue whisking for 15 minutes until the mixture leaves a thick trail. Pour immediately into a tin which has been greased and dredged with icing sugar. When the mixture is set, cut in cubes and dredge with more icing sugar. Leave to dry for 24 hours. This mixture can be stored in an airtight tin, but only for 1 week. **Makes 350 g/12 oz**

Bonbons

225 g/8 oz marzipan
100 g/4 oz cherries, soaked in Kirsch
apricot jam, warmed and sieved
desiccated coconut
glacé icing (optional)

Mould a piece of marzipan round each cherry. Dip each one in the apricot glaze and toss in the coconut. To vary, dip half the bonbons in thick icing and top with coconut. **Makes 14**

Coconut Ice

150 ml/¼ pint condensed milk
350 g/12 oz icing sugar, sifted
175 g/6 oz desiccated coconut
few drops pink colouring
icing sugar for dredging

Mix the condensed milk and sugar together and heat gently to dissolve. Boil to 115°C/240°F to the soft ball stage, and remove from the heat. Stir in the coconut and spread half the mixture over the base of a greased tin. Colour the rest of the mixture pink and pour over the top. Mark into squares when cool. Dredge with icing sugar.

Working with Chocolate

Unfortunately there isn't one chocolate that combines all the ideal qualities needed in cooking. Use which you prefer or can afford. Dessert chocolate has the better flavour – not surprisingly, since it's made from cocoa beans.

Cooking chocolate is not actually chocolate; it's a mixture of vegetable fats and flavourings which is best described as chocolate-flavoured cake covering. It's easier to work with and as it's not as brittle, is excellent for coating cakes or moulds or making decorative shapes. To get the best of both worlds use half and half.

Always melt chocolate in the top of a double boiler or in a basin over a pan of hot, not boiling, water. Be careful not to wet the chocolate – chocolate and water don't mix. If you want to thin it, add a knob of butter.

Chocolate Cup Sweets

275 g/10 oz chocolate
25 tiny paper sweet cases

Melt the chocolate, cool slightly and then brush or paint thickly round the inside of the paper cases. Cool and then chill for 10 minutes before removing the chocolate cases. Fill with some of the following ideas and top with more melted chocolate to seal if you wish. **Makes 25**

Fondants mix 6 tablespoons sifted icing sugar and a very little egg white to a smooth consistency. Colour and flavour as you wish. This will fill 25 cases. Top with melted chocolate.

Rum 'n' Raisin soak 4 tablespoons raisins in a little rum until swollen. Fill 25 chocolate cups, top with melted chocolate and decorate with halved glacé cherries.

Orange Creams flavour 200 ml/7 fl oz whipped cream with 1 teaspoon grated orange rind, and 1 tablespoon brandy or orange liqueur. Fill 25 cups and top with melted chocolate and pieces of candied orange peel. These could be served like iced sweets.

Chocolate Fruits

(Illustrated on page 208)

For very special occasions and luscious after-dinner petit fours, coat a selection of fruits in chocolate. Strawberries, raspberries, cherries, grapes and dates are best. If possible, leave the stalk or calyx on, to dip into the chocolate with, or place gently on the end of a cocktail stick. Dip into cool melted chocolate and either rest on wire racks or spike the sticks into a potato, until the chocolate has set. Chill and put in cases.

Preserving

Making your own preserves at home can be very economical and rewarding and need not take up too much time. Use foods that are in good supply or when there is a glut. Always make sure the ingredients are of a good quality. Only choose foods and recipes that you know your family like, unless of course you will be giving it all away!

This section includes many recipes for marmalades, jams, jellies, curds and butters, pickles, chutneys and relishes as well as several time-saving tips. Have a look at these tips before you start and do make sure you have the right equipment.

Equipment

You will need a large preserving pan or extra large saucepan, scales, lots of jars of any size with lids or jam pot covers and elastic bands; some recipes require muslin; several wooden spoons, ladles, a thermometer (you don't have to have one but it is accurate and does save time), storage space and labels.

Bottling and Storing

Pour the preserve into jars which have been well washed and rinsed. Dry them in a cool oven and use while still hot so that they do not crack from the heat of the jam.

Fill right to the top of the jars and cover with wax discs, wax side down, and cellophane jam pot covers or lids. Kilner jars can also be used. Label and date the jars. Store in a cool dark place; warmth encourages fermentation and mould, sunlight bleaches out colour and vitamins. Rotate your store of preserves each year.

How to Make Perfect Marmalade

From the chart or recipe suggestions select the type of marmalade you wish to make and also the quantities – remembering that total weight of fruit and sugar gives you an estimate of the final weight of marmalade or jam. For instance, 450 g/1 lb fruit and 450 g/1 lb sugar will give about 800 g/1¾ lb marmalade.

Remove the orange rind (discarding the white pith) and cut, shred or mince it or leave in large chunks, depending on the texture required. Halve the fruit and remove the pips. Tie the pips in a piece of muslin for extra flavour and to extract all the setting agent. Squeeze the juice and put aside. Soak the rind and pips overnight in the specified amount of water (see chart on page 210). Next day, tip the fruit, water, rind and bag of pips into a large pan. Simmer gently until the rind is tender, or use a pressure cooker (see page 209). Add the sugar, lemon and fruit juice.

Stir until the sugar is dissolved. Boil the marmalade rapidly until setting point is reached.

Ways to Test for Setting Point

1 A sugar thermometer should reach 104°C/220°F for a light set, 105°C/222°F for a very firm set.

2 Put a little marmalade on a saucer to cool and push your finger across the surface to see if it wrinkles. If not, continue boiling.

3 Take a spoonful of marmalade from the pan and allow it to drip until the marmalade hangs in flakes. If not, continue boiling.

4 Weigh the preserving pan (if you have large enough scales) when empty and make a note of the weight for later. Then weigh with the marmalade in, when you think it has reached setting point. If it is the correct weight for the quantity of fruit and sugar used, then the marmalade is ready (after deducting the weight of the pan of course!). Remember it is better to

Meringue layer gâteau (see page 170)

Above: Fresh orange cocktail (see page 198); Hoarders' cocktail (see page 198); Nice 'n' spicy (see page 199); Lemon and lime mixer (see page 198) and strawberry whip (see page 198)

Right: Hangover Harry (see page 201); Rose hip sip (see page 200) and Pooh's nightcap (see page 200)

test early. Once you have passed the setting point some marmalade may never set.

When you are sure the marmalade is ready, remove the bag of pips and allow to cool until syrupy. Then stir gently to make sure the rind is evenly distributed (not too vigorously or you get air bubbles in the marmalade). Fill the prepared jars, seal and label.

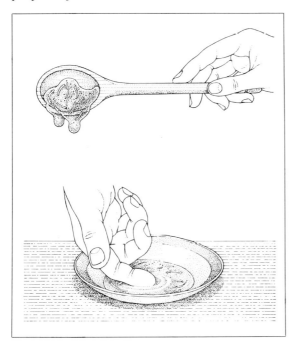

Why it Refuses to Set

1 You have not extracted enough pectin from the orange pips and rind, or you've omitted the lemon juice. Both these provide the pectin essential for setting.

2 You over-boiled the marmalade and so passed the setting point.

3 The marmalade never reached a sufficiently high temperature. Once sugar has completely dissolved, boil the marmalade rapidly – always use a big pan to prevent boiling over. If the marmalade boils too slowly the liquid will not reduce sufficiently to allow it to set.

Chocolate fruits (see page 203)

How to Put It Right

1 Set the marmalade with gelatine. Allow 7–15 g/¼–½ oz powdered gelatine to each 450 g/1 lb marmalade, depending on how runny it is. Soak the gelatine in 1 tablespoon lemon juice then stand it in a bowl over boiling water until dissolved. Heat the marmalade for a few minutes and stir in the dissolved gelatine. Allow to set. Do not treat too large a quantity of marmalade in this way at one time, as gelatine encourages the growth of mould over a long period.

2 If the marmalade has been badly over-cooked and is therefore very sweet as well as runny, mix it with apple preserve. Dice peeled and cored cooking apples – allow 450 g/1 lb apples to each 450-g/1-lb pot of marmalade. Simmer the apples in 2–3 tablespoons marmalade until soft. Add 225 g/8 oz sugar and 1 tablespoon lemon juice. Stir over a moderate heat until the sugar dissolves. Add the rest of the marmalade. Boil briskly for 2–3 minutes, cool slightly, stir and pour into the warm jars.

Using a Pressure Cooker

With a pressure cooker, you can speed up the initial cooking and softening stages considerably. Use the pressure cooker as you would your preserving pan. Prepare the fruit or vegetables in the usual way. Add the water (usually only one-third to half the quantity of water is required) and the muslin bag of pips or pickling spices. Cover with a lid and bring up to pressure according to the time given below. Allow the pressure to drop, remove the cover and continue in the normal way with your recipe.

Timing at Pressure

For most fruits, use Medium/10 lb pressure or, if you have only one pressure setting, reduce times given here by 1 minute. Do not pressure cook very soft fruit.

Marmalade times Lemons: 8 minutes. Tangerines: 6 minutes. Oranges: 12–15 minutes depending on the chunkiness of the rind.

Jam times Apples and blackberries: 7 minutes. Apricots, plums and greengages: 4 minutes. Blackcurrants: 3–4 minutes. Damsons: 5 minutes. Gooseberries: 4–5 minutes.

Chutney times allow 10–15 minutes at High/ 15 lb pressure. Pickles can also be cooked if you wish, at High/15 lb pressure for 1 minute only.

Manufactured Pectin

Pectin is the setting agent vital to any marmalade, jam, jelly or preserve. It is found in most fruits, but some have a higher content than others (see the chart below). You can buy pectin from most chemists in a liquid form. This is added after a very brief boiling time. There is no need to boil to the setting point: just mix in and boil for 1–2 minutes. With manufactured pectin you can make an uncooked jam.

Preserving Chart – A Brief Guide to Quantities

Fruit (for 0.5 kg/1 lb)	Water	Sugar	Pectin
Marmalades:			
Seville – bitter	1.15 litres/2 pints	900 g/2 lb	2 tablespoons lemon juice
– less bitter	1.15 litres/2 pints	1.25 kg/2½ lb	3 tablespoons lemon juice
– sweet	1.75 litres/3 pints	1.5 kg/3 lb	3 tablespoons lemon juice
Grapefruit	1.15 litres/2 pints	900 g/2 lb	2 large lemons
Lemon/Lime	1.15 litres/2 pints	900 g/2 lb	—
Tangerine	800 ml/1⅓ pints	450 g/1 lb	2 large lemons
Jams:	Water	Sugar	Pectin
(Use extra 50 g/2 oz fruit if stones are included)			
Deficient in pectin: ripe apricots, peaches, blackberries, dessert cherries, marrow, strawberries (put cracked stones in muslin bag)	only enough water to cook fruit in or none at all	400 g/14 oz	2 tablespoons lemon juice or 4 tablespoons redcurrant juice or 100 g/4 oz cooking apple
Rich in pectin: cooking apples, blackcurrants, damsons, green gooseberries, redcurrants, cooking cherries	8–12 tablespoons water depending on ripeness	500–575 g/1 lb 2 oz–1 lb 4 oz for very tart fruits	—
Adequate pectin – ripe gooseberries, plums, raspberries, loganberries	4–8 tablespoons water or none	450 g/1 lb	—

Summer Marmalade

(Illustrated on page 248)

1 grapefruit
2 large sweet oranges
2 lemons
1.75 kg/4 lb sugar
1 bottle pectin

Remove the rind from all the fruit and chop finely. Discard the pith, chop the flesh and tie the pips in a muslin bag. Place the fruit rind and muslin bag in a large bowl and cover with 1.15 litres/2 pints water. Leave for 2–4 hours.

Simmer the fruit, bag and water for about 2 hours in a preserving pan until the rind is tender. Remove the muslin bag when the marmalade is cool enough to allow you to squeeze out the excess juice. Add the sugar, stirring until dissolved. Stir in the pectin, boil for 1 minute, then cool and bottle according to the instructions on page 204. **Makes about 1.6 kg/3½ lb**

Whisky Three-fruit Marmalade

(Illustrated on page 248)

1.5 kg/3 lb mixed citrus fruit
3 litres/5 pints water
2.75 kg/6 lb sugar
150 ml/¼ pint whisky

Wash, peel and halve the lemons. Squeeze the juice into a preserving pan and place the lemon rind in a muslin bag. Wash and thinly peel the oranges and grapefruit using a vegetable peeler. Shred the rind and place in the pan. Tie up the pith in the muslin bag.

Segment the oranges and grapefruit and place in the preserving pan with the water and muslin bag. Simmer, uncovered for about 2 hours until the rind is tender and the water has reduced by half. Add the sugar, stir until dissolved, then bring to the boil until setting point is reached (see page 204). Add the whisky and boil for a further 5 minutes. Remove the muslin bag, cool and bottle according to the instructions on page 204. **Makes 2.75 kg/6 lb**

Rum 'n' Raisin Marmalade

1.75 kg/4 lb Seville oranges
3 lemons
450 g/1 lb raisins
3 litres/5 pints water
2.75 kg/6 lb preserving sugar
2 teaspoons black treacle
150 ml/¼ pint rum

Wash and roughly chop the oranges and lemons. Place in a pan with the raisins and water. Bring to the boil and cook, uncovered, for 1 hour or until the fruit is tender and the liquid is reduced by half. Add the sugar and treacle, stir until dissolved then boil rapidly until setting point is reached (see page 204). Stir in the rum and boil for a further 3–5 minutes. Allow to cool for 10 minutes and bottle according to the instructions on page 204. **Makes 2.75 kg/6 lb**

Green Tomato Marmalade

5 lemons
900 g/2 lb green tomatoes, peeled
1.6 kg/3½ lb granulated or preserving sugar

Wash, peel and halve the lemons and squeeze out the juice. Finely shred the lemon rind. Place the rind in a pan with 600 ml/1 pint water; simmer, covered, for 30 minutes. Quarter the tomatoes, remove the cores and seeds and tie in a muslin bag.

Thinly slice the tomato flesh and place in a preserving pan with the muslin bag, the lemon peel and the juice made up to 1.75 litres/3 pints with water. Simmer until tender. Add the sugar, stir until dissolved and boil rapidly until setting point is reached (see page 204). Remove the muslin bag and allow the marmalade to cool for 10 minutes. Bottle according to the instructions on page 204. **Makes 1.75–2.25 kg/4–5 lb**

Jam Making

The basic method for making jam is exactly the same as for marmalade. The fruit has to be cooked until sufficiently softened. The sugar is added and dissolved, then cooked until setting point is reached. As well as the recipes here the chart on page 210 gives proportions for simple jams.

Melon Ginger Jam

900 g/2 lb honeydew melon flesh
4 lemons
100 g/4 oz preserved ginger
450 g/1 lb sugar

Dice the melon flesh. Squeeze the juice from the lemons then tie the lemon rind in a muslin bag. Chop the ginger finely, and place all together in a pan with the sugar. Heat gently until the sugar has dissolved, then boil rapidly until setting point is reached (see page 204). Remove the muslin bag and leave to cool for 5 minutes. Bottle according to the instructions on page 204. **Makes 900 g/2 lb**

Tomato and Apple Jam

1.5 kg/3 lb firm red or green tomatoes, peeled
900 g/2 lb cooking apples
25 g/1 oz fresh root ginger
2 sticks cinnamon
grated rind and juice of 3 lemons
1.75 kg/4 lb sugar

Wash and quarter the tomatoes. Peel core and roughly chop the apples. Bruise the ginger and tie in a muslin bag with the cinnamon. Place the tomatoes, apples, muslin bag and lemon rind and juice in a pan with just enough water to cover the fruit. Boil until the fruit has softened slightly. Add the sugar, heat gently until dissolved then simmer until setting point is reached (see page 204). Remove the muslin bag and bottle according to the instructions on page 204. **Makes 1.75 kg/4 lb**

Freezer Jam

575 g/1¼ lb strawberries, raspberries or blackberries
900 g/2 lb castor sugar
2 tablespoons lemon juice
½ bottle pectin

The fruit must be very ripe and soft but not blemished. Crush the fruit and mix with the sugar, lemon juice and pectin. Leave for 24 hours for the sugar to dissolve (or cook the mixture slowly). Stir well, then bottle according to the instructions on page 204. Refrigerate or pack into plastic containers, leaving a space between the fruit and the lid, and freeze immediately. **Makes about 1.6 kg/3½ lb**

Jellies

Fruit jellies are made by the same principle as jams and marmalades, but you do need either a jelly bag or a large piece of double thickness muslin to strain the fruit through. Refer to the chart for lemon juice or pectin quantities.

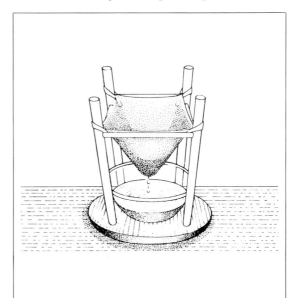

Orange Jelly

6 large sweet oranges
2 lemons
3.5 litres/6 pints water
preserving sugar (see method)

Peel and slice the oranges and lemons thinly, removing and reserving the pips; tie these in a muslin bag. Put the fruit, rind and pips into a preserving pan with the water. Simmer until the liquid has reduced by half, about 3–4 hours, or until the fruit is really tender. Remove the muslin bag then turn into a jelly bag over a large bowl. Leave to drain until the next day. Do not stir, or the jelly will be cloudy. Measure the resulting juice and allow 450 g/1 lb sugar to each 600 ml/1 pint. Dissolve gently and then boil rapidly until it reaches setting point (see page 204). Cool slightly, pour into warm jars and seal. **Makes about 1.15 litres/2 pints**

Conserves

Conserves are a richer, more luxurious type of jam. The fruit is marinated with sugar overnight to draw out the juice. No liquid need be added, so the flavour is more concentrated. Delicious for gâteaux and ice cream sauces.

Peach, Lemon and Kumquat Conserve

(Illustrated on page 245)

450 g/1 lb peaches
1.5 kg/3 lb castor sugar
100 g/4 oz kumquats, or 1 large orange
juice of 3 lemons
½ bottle pectin

Stone and chop the peaches. Layer with a little of the sugar in a bowl and leave overnight.

Quarter the kumquats (or remove the rind if using an orange, cut away and shred the pith and chop the flesh). Simmer the kumquats, or shredded orange rind, with 150 ml/¼ pint water, or more if necessary, until tender and most of the liquid has evaporated. Add to the peaches, with the orange flesh (if used), sugar and lemon juice in a large pan. Heat until the sugar dissolves then stir in the pectin. Bring to the boil for 2 minutes, cool and bottle according to the instructions on page 204. **Makes about 1.5 kg/3 lb**

Fruit Butters and Cheeses

These are the same mixture, but cooked to different consistencies. A butter should be cooked until there is no liquid left and a wooden spoon leaves a mark. A fruit cheese is cooked until much thicker – so that a wooden spoon will cut through, leaving a mark. Put into greased moulds, turn out and serve cut into slices or pieces.

Lemon Curd

3 lemons
225 g/8 oz loaf sugar (lump sugar) or castor sugar
100 g/4 oz unsalted butter
2 eggs, beaten

Wash and dry the lemons. Rub the lumps over the rind to remove all the zest, or, if using castor sugar, finely grate the rind. Squeeze out the lemon juice. Put the sugar, rind (if used) and butter in the top of a double saucepan over boiling water. Add the lemon juice. When the butter has melted, add the eggs and cook very slowly, stirring frequently until the mixture is thick enough to coat the back of a wooden spoon. Pour into hot jars and seal. **Makes about 450 g/1 lb**

Orange Curd use 2 oranges (or for extra flavour, use the rind of 3 oranges and ½ lemon, plus the juice of 1¼ oranges and ½ lemon) and follow the above method.

Tangerine Curd use the rind of 4–5 tangerines and juice of 2, plus the juice of ½ lemon and follow the above method.

Grapefruit Curd use the rind of 2 grapefruit and the juice of 1½ large or 2 small grapefruit and follow the above method.

Plum Butter

675 g/1½ lb ripe plums
600 ml/1 pint cider, white wine or fruit juice
castor sugar (see method)
½ teaspoon ground cinnamon

Wash the plums, remove the stones and cut into quarters. There is no need to peel them. Simmer with the cider, wine or fruit juice in a covered pan until the fruit is pulpy. Rub through a sieve. Weigh the purée and allow 350 g/12 oz sugar for every 450 g/1 lb purée. Put both purée and sugar in the pan with the cinnamon, and heat slowly to dissolve the sugar. Then boil rapidly until thick and creamy. Put into hot jars immediately and seal. **Makes about 1.5 kg/3 lb**

Damson Cheese

2.75 kg/6 lb damsons
300 ml/½ pint water
castor sugar (see method)

Wash, trim and stone the damsons. Put into a large pan with the water. Cover, bring to the boil and simmer until the fruit is pulpy. Rub through a fine sieve. Weigh the purée and return to the pan. Bring to the boil again and cook, uncovered, until thickening. Then add the sugar, allowing 450 g/1 lb for each 450 g/1 lb purée. Dissolve the sugar and continue to cook, stirring frequently until very thick. Pour into hot moulds or jars and cover immediately. **Makes about 3.25 kg/7 lb**

Chutneys and Pickles

These are quick and easy to make successfully if you use unblemished foods and the right equipment. Be sure to use an enamel or stainless steel pan, use wooden spoons and nylon or stainless steel sieves. Avoid using aluminium unless it is well scrubbed and scoured first. Never use aluminium or metal lids next to the chutney when potting.

Beetroot and Cabbage Chutney

100 g/4 oz salt
450 g/1 lb sugar
1.15 litres/2 pints vinegar
50 g/2 oz peppercorns
50 g/2 oz mustard seed
900 g/2 lb white cabbage, finely chopped
225 g/8 oz onions, minced
900 g/2 lb raw beetroot, finely diced

Put the salt, sugar and vinegar in a large pan. Tie the peppercorns and mustard seed in a muslin bag and crush roughly with a hammer or rolling pin. Add the bag to the vinegar mixture. Heat gently to dissolve the sugar and then bring to boil. Add the vegetables and simmer until tender and most of the liquid has evaporated. Remove the muslin bag. Cool and bottle according to the instructions on page 204. **Makes about 1.75 kg/4 lb**

Mango and Carrot Chutney

(Illustrated on pages 246–7)

2 large mangoes, peeled and sliced
900 g/2 lb carrots, sliced
2 medium onions, sliced
50 g/2 oz crystallised ginger, chopped
1 tablespoon grated lemon rind
225 g/8 oz granulated sugar
1 tablespoon salt
½ teaspoon ground cloves and dry mustard mixed
1 teaspoon ground ginger
1 teaspoon cayenne pepper
900 ml/1½ pints white vinegar

Place the mango, carrot and onion in a pan and add all the remaining ingredients. Heat gently to dissolve the sugar. Cook for about 1½ hours or until thickened. Cool and bottle according to the instructions on page 204. **Makes about 900 g/2 lb**

Sweet Tomato Chutney

(Illustrated on pages 246–7)

1.5 kg/3 lb ripe tomatoes, chopped
1 cucumber, peeled and chopped
1 green pepper, seeds removed and sliced
2 medium onions, sliced
1 tablespoon rock salt or sea salt
275 g/10 oz soft brown sugar
900 ml/1½ pints malt vinegar
1 knob fresh root ginger, bruised
1 clove garlic
2 bay leaves
6 cardamoms
6–8 black peppercorns
6–8 cloves

Place the tomato, cucumber, pepper and onion in a pan with the salt, sugar and vinegar. Tie the remaining ingredients in a small muslin bag. Add the bag to the pan and marinate for 24 hours.

Stir well, then simmer gently for 1¼ hours. Remove the lid and boil until thick. Remove the muslin bag. Cool and bottle according to the instructions on page 204. **Makes about 900 g/2 lb**

Corn and Pineapple Pickle

(Illustrated on pages 246–7)

1.25 kg/2½ lb fresh or canned sweetcorn
4 sticks celery, finely chopped
2 red and 2 green peppers, seeds removed and chopped
1 onion, chopped
100 g/4 oz carrots, cut in matchsticks
1 (200-g/7-oz) can pineapple chunks, drained
450 g/1 lb soft brown sugar
3 teaspoons salt
750 ml/1¼ pints white vinegar
3 teaspoons dry mustard
¾ teaspoon ground coriander
¾ teaspoon ground turmeric

Place all the ingredients in a pan. Bring to the boil and simmer for 20 minutes. Bottle according to the instructions on page 204. **Makes about 2.75 kg/6 lb**

Marrow Chutney

(Illustrated on pages 246–7)

1.5 kg/3 lb marrow
50–75 g/2–3 oz salt
675 g/1½ lb dates, chopped
350 g/12 oz cooking apples, peeled and chopped
350 g/12 oz onions, chopped
600 ml/1 pint vinegar
15 g/½ oz mustard seed
2 teaspoons ground ginger
2 teaspoons ground allspice
1 teaspoon ground cinnamon
1 teaspoon ground mace
450 g/1 lb castor sugar

Peel the marrow, remove the seeds and chop the flesh. Layer the flesh with the salt in a large bowl. Cover and leave for several hours. Rinse and drain thoroughly. Place the dates, apple, onion, vinegar and all the spices in a pan. Cook gently for 1½ hours until tender.

Stir in the sugar and marrow and cook for a further 1 hour. If there is still too much liquid, boil briefly with the lid off to reduce. Bottle according to the instructions on page 204. **Makes about 1.5–1.75 kg/3–4 lb**

Gooseberry Relish

900 g/2 lb gooseberries
350 g/12 oz seedless raisins
450 g/1 lb onions, sliced
225 g/8 oz brown sugar
1 tablespoon prepared mustard
1 tablespoon ground ginger
2 tablespoons salt
¼ teaspoon cayenne pepper
1 teaspoon ground turmeric
600 ml/1 pint vinegar

Top, tail, wash and drain the gooseberries. Chop or mince them with the raisins and onions, then put into a preserving pan with the remaining ingredients. Slowly bring to the boil and simmer for 45 minutes. For a chunky texture, bottle at this stage. For a thick sauce, rub through a coarse sieve. **Makes about 1.25 kg/2½ lb**

Garden Pickle

(Illustrated on pages 246–7)

450 g/1 lb cauliflower, cut in florets
450 g/1 lb cucumber or courgettes, chopped
450 g/1 lb large onions, quartered
25 g/1 oz rock salt
1.75 litres/3 pints vinegar
15 g/½ oz pickling spice or a mixture of bay leaves,
black peppercorns, cloves, crushed root ginger
and cardamoms

Place the cauliflower, cucumber or courgette and onion in a large bowl, sprinkle with the salt and leave overnight. Drain and pack into jars with the loose spices or, if using powdered pickling spice, add this to the vinegar. Top up the jars with vinegar and seal well. Store for 1 month before using as required. **Makes about 1.75 g/4 lb**

Bottling

Hard fruits such as pears, apples, peaches, plums and greengages are best preserved in syrup, or simply water for slimmers. Soft fruits like raspberries, strawberries, black and red currants or other berries can be bottled in their own syrup – this means they are bottled in layers with sugar which dissolves to give a fruit-flavoured syrup. Some fruits – apples, apricots and plums are the best – make excellent purées which can be bottled.

Little equipment is needed other than strong glass jars and a large pan or preserving pan. Either collect jars and lids from everyday products to use with sealing rings (to make the lids completely airtight) or, if you have no lids use a commercial sealing film. You can also use Kilner jars with their own screw-top or flip-top lids.

First make the syrup, which needs to cool before use. Allow 100, 175 or 225 g/4, 6 or 8 oz castor sugar to 600 ml/1 pint water, depending on the sweetness of the fruit. Heat gently until the sugar has dissolved, then flavour with lemon juice (this is important for keeping pears or apples white), or add a little brandy or whisky for special occasions.

To Prepare the Fruit

Apples and pears need to be dipped immediately after cutting into a salt-water solution (1 tablespoon salt to 1.15 litres/2 pints water) and then rinsed in cold water: or place in jars and cover with lemon syrup immediately.

Peaches need peeling (dip into boiling water for 2 seconds to make this easier) then halve or slice. Plums and other hard fruit should be wiped and stoned if you wish, and damsons should have the skins pricked so the syrup can penetrate. Soft fruit should be picked over, washed in cold water and drained.

To Bottle

Pack the fruit neatly into jars using the handle of a wooden spoon to guide. Add any spices, fruit rinds, nuts or other flavourings you wish and cover with cold syrup. Fill to the top of the jar. For fruits in their own syrup, layer neatly with a generous quantity of sugar but do not add any liquid. Seal the jars loosely as they expand on heating and could crack.

Stand the jars on a rack in a large pan, or on a wad of newspaper or thick cloth. Fill with water up to the neck of the jars. Bring the water to between 74.5 and 79.5°C/165 and 175°F slowly, taking about 1½ hours. Maintain this temperature for 10 minutes for most fruits, or 20 minutes for large jars of solid fruit, such as raspberries. If you have no thermometer, an occasional bubble on the water surface will show when this temperature is reached. For pears, bring the water to 82–87.5°C/180–190°F and maintain this for 30 minutes, this is a slow simmer. Remove the jars, stand on a dry surface and allow to cool. Tighten the seals as soon as possible to form suction on cooling. After 24 hours, check the seal by testing the suction of the lid.

To Bottle Purées

Cook the fruit with sugar to taste. Purée and pack into sterilised jars. Seal down as above, place in a pan of boiling water on a rack and boil steadily for 10 minutes (or 20 minutes for tomato purée). Tighten the lids and check the seal as above.

Savoury cheesecake (see page 225)

Freezing

Freezing is an uncomplicated way of preserving foods for substantial periods. The food is kept at such a cold temperature that no bacteria can grow and it is preserved in its present state. However, food must be frozen to be put into the freezer in good condition, either raw and very fresh, or freshly cooked and cooled. The food must also be handled hygienically during preparation and packaging. Food will not go 'off' in the freezer, it just remains in the same state, but if there was anything harmfully wrong with the food before freezing, this won't change either.

On thawing, the food warms up, allowing the dormant bacteria to resume working. Food then carries on its normal ageing process, from the stage at which it was frozen. Hence it is vitally important to treat thawed food as carefully as food which is just about to be frozen.

Refreezing

This is never recommended for any food and will always impair the flavour and texture. However, if it is really necessary and done with care, no harm should come to the food. Note that certain foods, particularly meats, should never be refrozen (see below).

The food should have been refrigerated and treated as fresh. In many cases you will have to repack – always state on the label that the food has been refrozen.

Never refreeze poultry and game, vegetables and fish dishes. Whenever possible cook the food before refreezing.

Dhall (see page 223); Salmon mayonnaise (see page 224); Peppered liver spread (see page 224) and Avocado spread (see page 223)

There are many very good books available that thoroughly explain the technicalities of freezing. Any new freezer owner would be well advised to buy one. However, this section covers some of the areas often left out of books, as well as simple reminders, tips and easy reference charts which both new and experienced freezer owners will find very useful.

Packaging

There are several ways to package most items, so you can choose whichever suits you best. The real purpose of packaging is to exclude air from the foods and freeze them quickly for the very best results.

Foods that are wrapped in foil or film should either be double-wrapped or you should use heavy-duty freezer wrap or polythene.

If you are using wax or foil cartons for liquids such as soups and sauces, leave about $1 \text{ cm}/\frac{1}{2}$ inch at the top to allow the liquid to expand.

Many cartons and wrappers can be re-used if thoroughly washed, and much of the packaging from shop-bought foods can be used to freeze in too.

Some foods are 'open' or 'tray' frozen. For instance, soft berry fruits which would stick to each other in a bag; or gâteaux where the decoration would spoil if wrapped. Freeze without a cover, or set well apart on a tray, before packing.

Colour code groups of foods, like meat, pastries or vegetables, for quick recognition. Store foods like vegetables, sauces, rashers of bacon, chops or steaks in small or separate packs for speedy thawing. Slice cakes, flans and gâteaux (but wrap them whole) before freezing so you can just take out one slice.

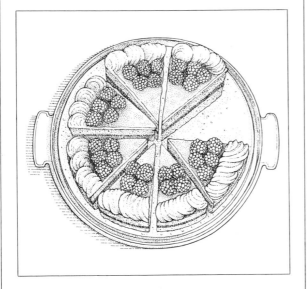

Blanching

This is important for the successful freezing of most vegetables and fruits.

The idea behind blanching is to scald the food, halting the enzyme action that causes spoilage, and preserving the colour, texture and nutritional value. It's quite a time-consuming business, but it's worth it, especially if you've got a good crop of home-grown or locally-picked produce.

For best results, freeze tender young vegetables which aren't blemished. Unlike fruit, which is best frozen when ripe, you'll find vegetables are sweeter and more tender before they are fully mature.

Bring a large pan of water (about 2.25 litres/4 pints) to a rapid boil. Put in the vegetables (not more than 450 g/1 lb at a time, or the temperature of the water will drop too much), using a wire basket. Bring back to the boil and start timing from this moment (see the chart on the right for times). As soon as the time is up, take out and immerse in cold water chilled with ice cubes. Drain and pack when quite cold.

Blanching Times

Celery	
hearts	5 minutes
5-cm/2-inch lengths	3 minutes
Courgettes, sliced	1 minute
Peas	1 minute
Corn on the cob	
small	5 minutes
large	8 minutes
Runner beans	
cut	2 minutes
sliced	1 minute
French beans, whole	3 minutes
Broad beans	2 minutes
Broccoli	3–4 minutes
Sprouts	3 minutes
Cauliflower, cut in florets	3 minutes
Carrots and root vegetables	
small whole	5 minutes
sliced, diced	2 minutes
Spinach, lettuce	$\frac{1}{2}$ minute
Cabbage	2 minutes

Foods that Cannot be Frozen Successfully

Raw eggs freeze whites and yolks separately.

Cooked eggs soft or hard-boiled eggs, even in sandwich fillings, become hard and leathery. Remember this when thinking of freezing dishes like raised pies or Scotch eggs.

Single cream or anything like a soup or sauce that has cream in. The cream will separate. Double cream won't separate out on freezing but even so you will get a better result by adding the cream later.

Jellies gelatine and aspic mixtures do not freeze well, unless they contain double cream or the quantity of jelly is very small.

Egg custards these will separate during thawing. However, you could freeze a custard containing at least 50% single or double cream, or freeze the custard liquid in a fireproof container so you can cook from frozen.

Crisp salad ingredients such as lettuce, celery, spinach and radishes, lose their crispness, but can be used in cooked dishes.

Real mayonnaise made with egg yolks and oil has a tendency to curdle.

Certain flavourings such as garlic, curry, and wine do not improve with freezing, so add when reheating or check the flavour then. They can also taint other foods in the freezer unless really thoroughly wrapped.

Butter and cheese although they freeze well they also keep well in the refrigerator so don't waste freezer space unnecessarily.

Short Cuts to Freezing

1 Vegetables and fruit do not have to be blanched if they are only for short-term storage, 2–3 months at the most.

2 Freeze oranges and lemons whole when cheap – grate the rind from frozen and squeeze the juice when thawed.

3 Freeze stock, egg yolks or whites, tiny portions of gravies and sauces in ice-cube trays then transfer them to a polythene bag so you can use one at a time.

4 If you haven't time to make jams and marmalades when fruits are in season, then freeze the fruit in bags. When you come to make the preserve, add an extra 10% of fruit to your normal recipe to make up for the pectin lost through freezing. Marmalade fruits could be cooked and then frozen, so all you have to do is thaw them and add the sugar.

What to Cook from Frozen

Vegetables and fish (unless the portions are large or the fish are whole) cook very well from frozen. Chops and steaks can be slowly cooked from frozen but should never be left rare. Start cooked dishes such as stews, pies with cooked fillings, soups and sauces in a moderate oven (160°C, 325°F, Gas Mark 3) and once thawed, increase to moderately hot (200°C, 400°F, Gas Mark 6) until well heated through. Breads can be heated through gently.

Joints of beef and lamb can be cooked from frozen, but be sure they are well cooked. Place the meat in a cold oven and bring slowly to the required temperature. Do this in two stages if using gas. Allow at least 30 minutes per 0.5 kg/1 lb and 30 minutes over. To prevent overcooking the outside when the centre is still uncooked, use a meat thermometer, or cover with a lid or foil.

Never cook raw chicken from frozen. Then be sure that cooked casseroles, once thawed, are heated through very thoroughly.

Chain Cooking

If you want to fill your freezer with home-prepared foods the easiest way is to chain-cook. You start with one basic ingredient or mixture, and use it to make a variety of dishes. Freeze the dishes as ready-to-cook or ready-to-eat, and possibly freeze some of the basic ingredients, too, in convenient amounts to use later.

Apart from the obvious advantage of working with just one basic item, chain-cooking also gives you variety. The alternative is to cook one particularly popular recipe in large quantities and freeze it in portions.

Minced beef is an obvious choice as the basic ingredient in a chain because it's so versatile. Try 2.25 kg/5 lb as a workable amount to start with. Turn it into Meatballs (see page 63), beefburgers, simple mince for the base of a pie, and spaghetti sauce.

Pastry also makes a good basis for many dishes and is well worth making in large quantities, like 2.25 kg/5 lb. Freeze in 225- or 450-g/8-oz or 1-lb packs, or store some in the refrigerator in its crumb state ready to mix and crumble over dishes. This large batch would cover one or two pie tops, make a flan case, tartlets, and other things – all ready for freezing.

Chart to Home Freezing

Food and Storage Time	Preparation	Packing and Freezing	Thawing and Using
Root vegetables (10–12 months)	Purée or cut up for stew packs and blanch.	Polythene bags, foil, or containers.	Cook from frozen or thaw for 4–6 hours.
Potatoes	Tray freeze par-cooked chips or duchesse potato.	Polythene bags, foil or containers.	Cook from frozen or thaw for 4–6 hours.
Carrots	Blanch small whole, sliced or diced.	Polythene bags, foil or containers.	Cook from frozen or thaw for 4–6 hours.
Firm greens (3–6 months)	Wash, top and tail, or slice. Blanch.	Polythene bags, foil or containers.	Cook from frozen or thaw for 4–6 hours.
Leafy greens (3–6 months)	Wash and trim. Blanch in small amounts. Drain well, shred or purée.	Bags or containers.	Cook from frozen.
Tomatoes (10–12 months)	Stew, purée or keep whole peeled.	Boxes or containers.	Cook from frozen.
Soft fruits – best only (6–8 months)	Wash, hull and dry. Tray freeze or layer with sugar or in sugar syrup.	Bags or containers.	Cook from frozen or after 6–7 hours in the refrigerator.
Firm fruits (9–12 months)	Peel and cut. Dry sugar or syrup.	Boxes or containers.	Cook from frozen or after 4–6 hours in the refrigerator.
Fish – only very fresh (white – 6 months, oily – 4 months)	Clean, trim and skin. Whole – open freeze, dip occasionally in iced water to coat. Fillets, steaks – dip white fish in salt solution and oily varieties in ascorbic acid solution.	Wrap tightly in foil or polythene. Separate with foil, then wrap tightly.	Cook after 6–8 hours per 0.5 kg/1 lb in the refrigerator. Cook after 4–6 hours per 0.5 kg/1 lb in the refrigerator or from frozen.
Shellfish (1–2 months)	Freeze freshly cooked either whole or shelled.	Bags, foil or containers.	Cook after 10–12 hours per 0.5 kg/1 lb in the refrigerator or from frozen.
Meat Beef, lamb, poultry, (8–10 months) Veal, pork (6 months) Ham, bacon (1 month) Mince, offal, sausages (3 months)	Large joints – wash and dry, or bone. Small joints, steaks – cut in sensible portions. Offal – trim, mince and divide in portions ready for cooking.	Wrap tightly in foil or polythene. Separate with foil then wrap tightly. Wrap tightly in foil or polythene.	Cook after 6–8 hours per 0.5 kg/1 lb in the refrigerator. Cook after 4 hours per 0.5 kg/1 lb in the refrigerator. Cook after 10–12 hours per 0.5 kg/1 lb in the refrigerator.
Cream – double or whipping only (6 months)	Lightly whip with sugar or pipe rosettes and open freeze.	In wax cartons or polythene bags.	Thaw for 12 hours per 600 ml/1 pint. Beat to restore the consistency.
Cheese (soft – 6 months, hard – 3 months)	In suitable portions or ready grated.	Wrap tightly in foil or polythene.	Thaw for 12 hours per 0.5 kg/1 lb, then bring to room temperature to eat.
Eggs (see page 220) (beaten – 6 months separated – 9 months)	Lightly beat with seasoning or freeze whites and yolks separately.	Small wax containers.	Thaw at room temperature for 2–3 hours.
Uncooked doughs (bread – 8 weeks, pastry – 4 months)	In quantities to suit recipes – 225 g/8 oz or 450 g/1 lb. Indicate on label.	Wrap in foil or polythene.	Thaw overnight in the refrigerator or for 3–4 hours at room temperature.
Pastries – uncooked or cooked (storage time depends on fillings)	Cook the filling if you wish but don't overcook. Tray freeze either if sweet and decorated.	Wrap in foil or polythene. Support the base with cardboard or use foil tins.	Cook or reheat from frozen or after 3–4 hours in the refrigerator.
Cakes, breads, scones – cooked (3–4 months)	Cool thoroughly. Slice and put back together if wished, or halve.	Wrap in polythene, foil or containers.	Reheat breads from frozen. Thaw for 1–4 hours at room temperature.
Decorated cooked flans, gâteaux (3–4 months)	Open freeze until solid. Add sauces or delicate decoration later.	Wrap in foil, or put in suitable boxes or wax containers.	Thaw at room temperature for 1 hour for small, 4–8 hours for large or fruit cakes.
Soups, stocks, sauces (2–3 months, less if highly spiced)	Ready to serve, or as the basis – ready to cook with or add to a dish.	When cold in upright wax containers. Leave 1 cm/½ inch space.	Cook from frozen or after 2–3 hours at room temperature.

Days in the country or by the seaside; caravanning or camping; or just eating in the garden – whatever the occasion, the food needs extra care and planning. It should be easy to transport and eat, suitable for keeping out of the refrigerator for some time, and be quick and simple to prepare.

For quick impromptu picnics, simple cold or smoked meats, salad and hunks of bread and cheese will always satisfy hungry appetites. If you have a little more time, there are many delicious spreads and potted meats that can be made from storecupboard foods.

When you can really plan a picnic in advance, the food can be more adventurous. The recipes here suit all occasions and many can be frozen in advance so you can take the food out and thaw it overnight or en route.

Packing is important. Wrap sandwiches in cling film, then in foil or polythene; or for longer times, wrap in damp kitchen paper first. Carry liquids, dressings, sauces and drinks in screw-top bottles, tall plastic jars with a close seal or yogurt or cottage cheese pots with their own lids. Boxes, tins and large sealed plastic containers are ideal for cooked dishes, cakes and salads – wrap first in polythene.

Don't forget damp cloths, in a polythene bag, for sticky hands, and take a large bag for the rubbish.

Avocado Spread

(Illustrated on page 218)

2 ripe avocados
100 g/4 oz cottage cheese
juice of $\frac{1}{2}$ lemon
$\frac{1}{2}$ teaspoon chopped parsley
salt and pepper
$\frac{1}{4}$ teaspoon Worcestershire sauce
2–3 walnuts to garnish

Discard the skin and stones from the avocados and mash the pulp thoroughly (or liquidise) with the cottage cheese and lemon juice. Stir in the chopped parsley, reserving some for garnish. Add seasoning and Worcestershire sauce to

taste. Spoon the spread into pots or containers with lids, cover and chill. Garnish with pieces of walnut. Serve with biscuits or rye bread or use for sandwich fillings. **Serves 4–5**

Dhall

(Illustrated on page 218)

100 g/4 oz lentils or chick peas
1 large onion, finely chopped
2 tablespoons desiccated coconut
$\frac{1}{2}$ teaspoon ground turmeric
$\frac{1}{2}$ teaspoon chilli powder
$\frac{1}{2}$ teaspoon garam masala
$\frac{1}{2}$ teaspoon mustard seed
$\frac{1}{2}$ teaspoon cumin seed
salt

Soak the lentils or chick peas in cold water overnight. Drain. Put in a pan with cold water to cover and simmer, covered, for 1 hour or until tender, adding more water if necessary to give a soft consistency. When tender, liquidise or mash thoroughly with a fork. Add the onion, coconut, turmeric, chilli, garam masala, mustard and salt and continue cooking for 15–20 minutes until the onion is cooked and most of the liquid has evaporated. Store frozen in foil or wax containers for up to 2 months and then thaw for 2–3 hours. Serve with smoked meats or crisp raw vegetables. **Serves 6**

Peanut and Bacon Spread

175 g/6 oz peanut butter
4 tablespoons thick mayonnaise
$\frac{1}{4}$ teaspoon salt
100 g/4 oz cooked bacon, chopped

Mix together all the ingredients. Use as a spread or for sandwich fillings. **Serves 2–3**

Salmon Mayonnaise

(Illustrated on page 218)

1 (212-g/7½-oz) can pink salmon
6 tablespoons thick mayonnaise
juice of ½ lemon
1½ teaspoons tomato purée
salt and pepper
few black olives
wedges of lemon

Drain the salmon and discard the skin and bone. Mash the flesh then mix with the mayonnaise, lemon juice, tomato purée and seasoning. Chill. Serve with the black olives and lemon wedges on crusty bread. **Serves 4–6**

Peppered Liver Spread

(Illustrated on page 218)

1 fresh green chilli (optional)
2 red peppers, seeds removed
1 green pepper, seeds removed
1 medium onion
1 clove garlic
100–175 g/4–6 oz lamb's liver
salt and pepper
2 tablespoons dark brown sugar
2 tablespoons vinegar
3 tablespoons water

Carefully remove and discard seeds from the chilli if used, then wash hands thoroughly as the seeds sting. Pass the chilli, peppers, onion, garlic and liver through a fine mincer then put into a saucepan with the remaining ingredients. Bring to the boil and simmer for 30 minutes, stirring occasionally. Freeze in foil or wax containers for up to 1 month. Thaw for 2 hours. Serve with fresh bread, tomatoes and celery. **Serves 4–6**

Chunky Sandwiches

Use large sections of French bread, pitta bread or baps and fill generously with various fillings. Wrap individually. Pitta bread is ideal for picnics because it has ready-made pockets and keeps well. Some of these sandwiches can be served hot for barbecues too.

Beefburger and Pepper Filling

6 beefburgers
2 tablespoons oil
1 red pepper, seeds removed and sliced
1 green pepper, seeds removed and sliced
2 cloves garlic, crushed (optional)
½ teaspoon dried oregano
2 tablespoons tomato purée
2 tablespoons water
salt and pepper
3 pitta breads, halved or 6 chunks French bread

Cook the beefburgers in the oil (or grill without extra fat if preferred). Keep warm and sauté the peppers with the garlic and oregano for 10 minutes. Add tomato purée, water and seasoning and stir well. Cook for 5 minutes and then return the beefburgers to the pan. Cover, and heat through for about 10 minutes, then spoon a beefburger and some tomato and pepper mixture into the split breads; or cool and use to fill the sandwiches as required. **Makes 6**

Ham and Aubergine Salad

(Illustrated on page 235)

1.25 kg/2½ lb aubergines
salt
2 tablespoons oil
2 large cloves garlic, crushed
50 g/2 oz flour
freshly ground black pepper
225 g/8 oz ham, chopped
marinade:
4 tablespoons olive oil
4 tablespoons wine vinegar
juice of 1 lemon
pinch dried chervil
pinch ground mace
pinch grated nutmeg
pinch ground ginger
3 bay leaves
to garnish:
few lettuce leaves
chopped parsley
sliced green pepper

Slice the aubergines, sprinkle with salt and leave for 30 minutes. Rinse and drain the slices. Heat the oil and fry the aubergine and garlic until tender. Stir in the flour and cook for 2–3 minutes. Season well and cool. Mix all the marinade ingredients together and add the aubergine. Cover and leave for several hours or overnight. Just before serving, mix in the ham and arrange in a dish with the lettuce, parsley and green pepper. **Serves 4**

Chicken Terrine

(Illustrated on page 236)

1 (2-kg/4½-lb) roasting chicken with giblets
275 g/10 oz lean bacon, rinds removed
4 chicken livers
50 g/2 oz butter, melted
salt and freshly ground black pepper
6 tablespoons Madeira or brandy
1 egg
pinch grated nutmeg
pinch ground bay leaf
2 teaspoons dried tarragon
2 teaspoons dried thyme
2 teaspoons dried oregano
75–100 g/3–4 oz fresh white breadcrumbs
4 slices ham
to garnish:
clarified butter
slices of lemon
bay leaves

Remove the flesh from chicken in neat pieces and arrange pieces of chicken breast in the base of a 1.75-kg/4-lb terrine or large ovenproof casserole dish. Mince the remaining chicken finely with the gizzard, heart and chicken livers. Beat in the butter, seasoning, Madeira or brandy, egg, nutmeg, bay, tarragon, thyme and oregano, and enough breadcrumbs to make a soft mixture. Spoon into the terrine and top with the ham. Cover with foil and bake in a moderately hot oven (190°C, 375°F, Gas Mark 5) for 1½–2 hours. Weight the mixture and leave to cool. Cover with a layer of clarified butter or lard. Garnish with lemon slices and bay leaves.

Chill well and if possible, leave for 2 days in the refrigerator before serving. To carry, leave in the terrine and cover with cling film and foil. To freeze, cook in a foil container, or wrap tightly. Store for up to 1 month. Thaw for 6–8 hours. **Serves 8–10**

Cream Cheese Pâté

(Illustrated on page 86)

450 g/1 lb cream cheese
2 hard-boiled eggs
40 g/1½ oz brown rice, cooked
75 g/3 oz cucumber, diced
2 tablespoons chopped parsley
½ red pepper, seeds removed and diced
2 tablespoons chopped walnuts
salt and pepper
8 savoury biscuits or crackers
assorted salad to garnish

Turn the cream cheese into a bowl and chop the eggs. Mix in the rice, cucumber, parsley, pepper, nuts and seasoning.

Line a 1-kg/2-lb loaf tin with greased greaseproof paper and arrange the biscuits around the base and sides. Put the pâté mixture into the tin and chill well. Turn out and garnish with assorted salad. **Serves 6–8**

Savoury Cheesecake

(Illustrated on page 217)

100 g/4 oz savoury biscuits or crackers
40 g/1½ oz butter or margarine, melted
75 g/3 oz butter or margarine
salt and pepper
pinch celery salt
pinch cayenne pepper
2 eggs, separated
5 tablespoons single cream
350 g/12 oz Cheddar, grated
100 g/4 oz salted peanuts, chopped
few drops Tabasco sauce
sliced cucumber to garnish

Crush the biscuits into crumbs and mix with the butter or margarine. Use to line the base and sides of a 20-cm/8-inch flan dish.

Cream the butter or margarine with all the ingredients but the cucumber. Whisk the egg whites until stiff and fold into the filling. Spoon into the flan and cook in a cool oven (150°C, 300°F, Gas Mark 2) for 1 hour or until firm. Garnish with cucumber. **Serves 4–6**

Cook's Tips

You don't need to be a Cordon Bleu cook to produce nice-tasting, good-looking food without too much fuss. You do, however, need to know one or two 'tricks-of-the-trade' to help you through awkward moments.

Saving a Disaster

All good cooks have disasters now and then but the more experienced you are, the easier it is to find a way of hiding that disaster, turning it into something that still looks good, or preventing a disaster in the first place.

Unrisen soufflés

You probably beat the egg whites into the basic mixture instead of folding them in, therefore knocking out all the air trapped in the egg whites. Or you may not have beaten the egg whites stiffly enough.

There is nothing you can do to change this once cooked, so try to serve it as nicely as you can, a) in the kitchen, not at the table, b) in small individual dishes so it looks bigger, c) top it with a suitable ingredient or sauce, for example sliced tomatoes and a little homemade mayonnaise, or ratafia biscuits and whipped cream for a sweet soufflé.

Sunken fruit cake

This could mean that the mixture was too soft before baking – it should drop slowly from a wooden spoon for the correct uncooked consistency. It may contain too much raising agent, so it would rise too quickly and then fall in the centre. Don't be tempted to add extra raising agent. If the cake is really unpresentable, slice it and serve it buttered, or use it in a cooked pudding.

Sticky rice

Rice easily goes sticky if it is overcooked, or kept warm before serving. Always test rice and pasta early and then keep testing until just 'al dente'. Once drained, toss well in oil or butter and keep hot over a pan of simmering water. If you need to put it in the oven, be generous with the oil.

If the rice comes out of the pan in big lumps when you come to serve it, rinse once again in boiling water very quickly, stirring with a fork to break it up, then drain well and add oil and seasoning.

Sunken or soggy pastry

When used on top of a pie, the filling needs to be higher than the edges of the dish, to prevent the pastry falling in and absorbing the liquid. Use a pie funnel or egg cup as a support if necessary. Pastry will become soggy if put on top of hot fillings.

If you think the pastry has really become inedible, remove it quickly and top the filling with one of these standbys. Either use quickly-made instant potato and sliced onions or tomatoes and pop under the grill; or for a sweet dish, use a crumbled topping, crushed biscuits or slices of bread, buttered and sugared, and quickly grilled.

Whisked sponges that remain flat and biscuit-like

The eggs and sugar have not been whisked until thick and firm enough – the mixture should leave a definite trail in the mixing bowl, or on adding the flour, you have beaten too quickly instead of folding in.

This won't make a tempting tea-time treat if really crisp and heavy. Try moistening it quickly with a little fruit juice and sherry mixed. Then put together with canned fruit and cream to make it look taller. Or use the sponge for a trifle or baked Alaska pudding.

Flat meringues

The egg whites were not stiff enough. They should not move when the bowl they are whisked in is turned upside down. Do use a really clean, dry bowl.

In most cases, meringues will be perfectly usable and delicious if generously topped with whipped cream and fruit. If very sticky, portion out in the kitchen first.

Badly-turned-out moulds

Be sure to loosen the edges with your thumb

first to allow air in, then dip in water. Use very hot water for thick china moulds and hold in this for 5–10 seconds. Use fairly hot water for metal moulds and just dip in for 1 second. Always invert on to a wetted plate so you can slide it into the centre if necessary.

A cracked or rough edged mould can sometimes be rectified by quick and clever garnishing, or decorating round the edge, or giving a light topping of shredded lettuce or toasted nuts. If it has completely collapsed, because it was too heavy for the setting agent, or not set enough, use chopped in other ways, for example for a trifle or vegetable salad, or place in individual bowls and disguise it with some other exciting ingredient or sauce – the more interesting it is, the more you will detract from your disaster.

Disintegrated fish

Poached, fried or grilled fish will easily break up (especially if the pieces are large), if you handle them too roughly or overcook them. Cook in a foil parcel to be sure of success and turn over gently with the help of two fish slices.

There is little you can do to quickly improve the appearance of badly cooked fish other than cover it. Always have handy an ample supply of green leaf garnish such as parsley, watercress or mustard and cress, or thinly sliced lemons or tomatoes or a tasty sauce, to put on top.

Lumpy sauces

This usually means the flour and butter base has not been sufficiently cooked or mixed, or the liquid has not been well whisked in. Remember to whisk or beat frequently while bringing the liquid to the boil.

This is easily rectified; most quickly by sieving and then beating in a little extra liquid before serving; or by liquidising. If it is an egg sauce that has curdled, stir in a little cornflour blended with water or milk and cook gently, stirring frequently, until thickened (2 teaspoons per 300 ml/$\frac{1}{2}$ pint should be sufficient).

Overcooked vegetables

Drain them and return to the heat to dry. Add a large knob of butter, 1–2 tablespoons cream or top of the milk and seasoning. Then mash until

smooth and serve sprinkled with parsley, or form into firm croquettes and fry gently.

Undercooked meat casseroles

Whether your timing was wrong, or the meat was extra tough, or your oven temperature wrong, you cannot serve tough meat and will just have to cook it longer. However, you can speed up the process by either putting the casserole into a pressure cooker or microwave oven for 1–2 minutes, or remove all the meat and cut it up smaller then continue to cook.

Burned food

On occasions when food is severely burnt, obviously it has to be wasted. However, on some occasions it has only just begun to burn, or catch at the bottom of the pan. If this is the case, transfer the food to a clean dish immediately and cut off any badly burnt pieces.

Vegetables that require more cooking should be put into fresh boiling water with a little milk and cooked until tender. Burned vegetables that are cooked enough should be mashed with a little garlic, butter, seasoning and herbs to disguise the burnt flavour.

If it is a casserole, add a few peeled potatoes and extra liquid and simmer gently until the potatoes are cooked. Then discard the potatoes – they should have absorbed most of the burnt or strong salty flavour by then. It's worth overcooking meat under these circumstances to try and eliminate the taste. If it still persists, add some other sweet, or disguising flavour – curry or some suitable fruit.

Soggy chips or roast potatoes

This usually means the fat was not hot enough when you started cooking or you have kept them warm for too long.

Dry them very thoroughly on absorbent kitchen paper. Then sprinkle with salt and dry fry, slowly in an ungreased frying pan, increasing the heat after a few minutes until the potatoes are really golden, hot and crisper.

Soft pork crackling

Always rub the pork skin with oil and/or salt before roasting and increase the heat to moderately hot (200°C, 400°F, Gas Mark 6) for the last 15 minutes to crisp up. If still not well-

Pasta and rice

These both make good bases for salads (see page 119). They can be bound together with flour, eggs and breadcrumbs to make savoury or sweet fritters, rissoles and dumplings; or can be fried with lots of flavourings to make a delicious vegetable or a quick pudding.

Pastry

Uncooked pastry corners can be gently kneaded together, refrigerated (or frozen) and used very thinly rolled for toppings to flans, pies, breads or hot cross buns. Pastry ends can be made into just a few cheese straws, jam tarts or sausage rolls.

Sauces, soups and gravies

Even one spoonful is worth keeping, if you can add it to another sauce or soup, or even a casserole, to give a little more flavour. Use very small quantities as a sauce for individual portions of meat or fish.

Stuffings

Don't use again with uncooked meats, but do turn into rissoles or savoury bites to serve with a spicy sauce or dip.

Vegetables

Add to soups; purée to make sauces; add at the last minute to cooked casseroles; fry up into a golden vegetable hash or omelette; use to fill out quiches or pastries; mash and turn into potato or vegetable cakes; or season well and make into unusual salads.

————————————·————————————

Using convenience foods

Convenience foods have great merit in our busy world, for making quick family meals, or for coping with surprise guests. But there's an art to cheating with convenience foods so that no-one would ever guess how you've prepared a meal so quickly, and so that you will still get the greatest compliments. If you are prepared to pay the price of convenience, make use of these foods wisely.

Using convenience foods to their best advantage

1 Canned meats can produce almost instant pies and casseroles, but be careful not to overcook as the meat is usually very tender.

2 Canned and packet sauces often have very overpowering flavours, so add with care.

3 Frozen foods don't always have to be thawed – in fact fish and vegetables are better cooked from frozen, as are many ready meals, such as pasta dishes.

4 An old favourite like corned beef can produce a surprisingly good pâté for a change – add just a touch of brandy for a special flavour.

5 Canned fruits – the firmer ones like mandarins, peaches and pineapples – make very good additions and stretchers for casseroles or meat pies. For savoury use, choose fruit canned in its own juice rather than in syrup, as it is less sweet.

6 Top cooks often use frozen puff pastry, but for extra puffiness, thaw two (212-g/7½-oz) packets, sandwich together with a little butter and use as required.

7 Canned tomatoes are one of the most invaluable vegetables you could keep in the cupboard. Use for casseroles, sauces, soups, pies and barbecue bastes.

————————————·————————————

Ham and aubergine salad (see page 224) and Koulibiac of salmon (see page 39)

Cod and Shrimp Mousse

Ready-to-serve packaged meals such as fish in sauce can provide the base for a good fish pie, chowder or tasty mousse. With the addition of egg yolks and whisked egg whites, the same ingredients could be turned into a delicious mousse.

4 (170-g/6-oz) packets cod in shrimp sauce
15 g/½ oz powdered gelatine
150 ml/¼ pint double or whipping cream, whipped
2 tablespoons tomato purée
2 egg whites
salt and pepper

Cook the fish according to the instructions on the packet and, when cool enough, liquidise or mash. Dissolve the gelatine in 2 tablespoons hot water in a small bowl over hot water and stir into the fish. Cool and fold in the cream and tomato purée. Whisk the egg whites and fold in with a metal spoon. Season to taste. Turn into a 1–1.5-litre/2–3-pint mould and chill. When set, turn out and serve with cucumber or a fresh green salad. **Serves 6–8**

Chicken terrine (see page 225)

Beef in Red Wine Pie

1 (396-g/14-oz) can stewing steak
1 (283-g/10-oz) can red wine sauce
2 tablespoons red wine or brandy (optional)
2 tablespoons oil
2 onions, sliced
1 clove garlic, crushed
225 g/8 oz mushrooms, halved
1 teaspoon dried mixed herbs
1 (370-g/13-oz) packet frozen puff pastry, thawed
beaten egg to glaze
3 tablespoons soured cream

Mix the meat and sauce in a pie dish. If you wish, add the extra wine or brandy. Heat the oil and fry the onion and garlic until golden. Stir in the mushrooms and then mix with the meat mixture and the herbs. Roll out enough pastry to cover the pie (see page 139), sealing and trimming the edges. Decorate with any extra pastry and cut a large hole in the centre for steam to escape. Brush with beaten egg and bake in a hot oven (220°C, 425°F, Gas Mark 7) for 35–40 minutes, or until puffed up and golden. Just before serving, pour the soured cream into the centre of the pie. **Serves 4**

Tongue in Madeira Sauce

Canned meats are useful for quick meals, but they can just as easily be turned into a special dish. Tongue is particularly handy and the combination of soup, stock and tomato purée gives a very rich sauce.

1 packet savoury vegetable rice
1 (680-g/1 lb 8-oz) can pressed tongue
½ (440-g/15½-oz) can oxtail soup
300 ml/½ pint beef stock
3 tablespoons tomato purée
2–3 tablespoons Madeira or sweet sherry
1–2 tablespoons double cream
¼ teaspoon dried sage

Cook the rice according to the instructions on the packet, and place on a heated dish. Cover with foil. Meanwhile, cut the tongue into strips. Heat together the soup, stock, tomato purée and Madeira or sherry and bring to the boil. Then add the tongue and simmer for about 10 minutes. Add the cream and sage and pour over the prepared rice. **Serves 6**

Iced Rice Cake

Rice and semolina puddings can be used to add texture, bulk and goodness to many hot and cold dishes. Top with crushed biscuits, cereals, meringue, or nuts for a crunchy texture, or stir into fruit mixtures or flavoured sauces. In this particular recipe the rice is liquidised to give a creamier, smoother texture, but you may prefer not to. Incorporate the suggested liqueur into the mixture at an earlier stage if you wish.

15 g/$\frac{1}{2}$ oz powdered gelatine
1 (439-g/15$\frac{1}{2}$-oz) can creamed rice pudding
1 (64-g/2$\frac{1}{4}$-oz) packet dessert topping
150 ml/$\frac{1}{4}$ pint milk
1 (396-g/14-oz) jar apricot pie filling
2 egg whites
cocoa powder to dust
few canned apricots to decorate
Drambuie, brandy or rum

Dissolve the gelatine in 2 tablespoons hot water in a small bowl over hot water. Liquidise the canned rice with the gelatine, dessert topping mix and milk. If you don't have a liquidiser, beat them all together thoroughly in a large bowl. Then beat in the pie filling. Whisk the egg whites stiffly, fold into the mixture and turn into a greased and base-lined 20-cm/8-inch cake tin or mould. Freeze for about 2 hours until very cold and firm but not completely frozen. Turn out on to a serving dish and dust with cocoa powder. Decorate with a few apricot halves and serve with a teaspoon of liqueur poured over each portion. **Serves 6–8**

Swiss Alaska

Packet cakes and biscuits, which keep for a long time, can provide more than just the basis for a trifle. This recipe is like an Alaska without the ice cream, but the Swiss roll could just as easily be used to form the base for a cheesecake, or custard or fruit tart.

1 (227-g/8-oz) can pineapple rings
1 (74-g/2$\frac{1}{2}$-oz) packet instant chocolate dessert
150 ml/$\frac{1}{4}$ pint milk
1 chocolate Swiss roll
2 egg whites
100 g/4 oz castor sugar
few flaked almonds

Drain the pineapple, reserving the juice, and arrange on a heatproof serving dish to approximately the size of the Swiss roll. Make up the chocolate dessert according to the instructions on the packet, using the milk and spread a little over the pineapple. Slice the Swiss roll and sprinkle with a little of the pineapple juice. Then sandwich slices of roll together with the prepared dessert and shape into a long log. Place lengthways on the pineapple slices. Chill. Meanwhile, whisk the egg whites until stiff, whisk in half the sugar, then fold in the rest. When shiny and forming peaks, spoon the meringue over the log. Sprinkle with the almonds and bake in a hot oven (220°C, 425°F, Gas Mark 7) for about 15 minutes until golden. Serve immediately or chill. **Serves 6**

When you are starting up a kitchen you need the minimum of equipment to see you through all jobs. As you become more experienced and have more money to spare, other helpful items can be added to your list – but let's start with the basics.

Saucepans
1 frying pan
1 milk pan
2 vegetable pans
(make sure one is really large enough for pasta or steamed puddings – about 3.5 litres/ 6 pints)

Choose pans that are either good-quality non-stick or heavy duty aluminium or stainless steel pans. Cheap pans are not an economy and will certainly not help your cooking.

Cooking tins
1 roasting tin
1 baking tray
(these usually come with a new oven)
1 pair sponge sandwich tins
1 deep cake tin or loaf tin
1 wire rack
1 pie plate or dish
2 casseroles with lids

Electrical equipment
kettle – with automatic switch off
mixer blender/liquidiser/or beaters
(see page 228 and 229 for further details).

Small utensils
set of 4 knives
1 (7.5–10-cm/3–4-inch) vegetable knife
large cook's knife
(for carving, chopping and cutting large items)
bread knife
palette knife
(for the easy lifting of flat foods)

Once again, don't buy cheap knives, they never last. Choose stainless steel for easy care, but with a very firmly-secured handle. Very flexible knives will not cut well!

2 wooden spoons
(one for sweet and one for savoury)
perforated draining spoon
fish slice
scissors
pastry or tartlet cutters
potato/vegetable peeler
can opener
grater
fruit juicer
sieves – 1 nylon, 1 metal
rolling pin
2 chopping boards
2 pastry brushes
scales
small whisk

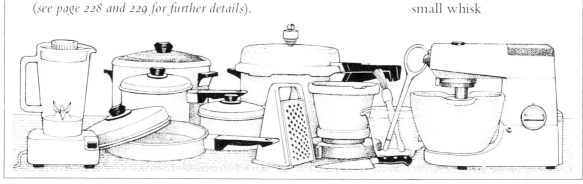

Glossary

Al dente (of pasta) cooked – but still firm to bite.

Aspic a clear savoury jelly used for setting and garnishing savoury dishes.

Au gratin used of cooked food when covered with a sauce, sprinkled with crumbs or grated cheese, dotted with butter and browned under the grill.

Bain-marie a large shallow dish or tin, containing 2.5–5 cm/1–2 inches hot water. Used for cooking delicate dishes. The food in its container sits in the bain-marie and the water maintains an even temperature during cooking.

Baking 'blind' to bake pastry cases without a filling. The raw pastry case is lined with foil or greaseproof paper and weighted with dried beans or stale bread crusts.

Basting moistening meat, poultry or game during roasting by spooning meat juices or melted fat from the tin over it, to prevent drying out and to add flavour and colour.

Béchamel sauce a well-seasoned white sauce. It is usually made with milk infused with onion, carrot, spices and herbs.

Binding adding a liquid, egg or melted fat to a dry mixture to hold it together.

Blanching boiling briefly either to loosen the skin from nuts, fruit and vegetables; or to set the colour of food and to kill enzymes prior to freezing; or to remove strong or bitter flavours.

Bouquet garni a bunch of flavouring herbs and spices, usually parsley, thyme, bay leaf, marjoram, cloves and peppercorns, tied in a piece of muslin, or bought in boxes of small muslin bags. It is added to savoury dishes and is easily removed after cooking.

Braising a way of cooking tougher cuts of meat in the oven or on the top of the cooker. Place the meat on a bed of flavourful chopped vegetables in a flameproof casserole or saucepan, with just sufficient liquid to cover the vegetables but not the meat. Cover tightly so that the meat cooks slowly in the steam.

Brining leaving food which is to be pickled or preserved in a salt and water solution.

Brochette a skewer used for grilling chunks of meat, fish and vegetables, as for kebabs.

Caramel sugar and water dissolved slowly and cooked until golden brown and syrupy.

Chaudfroid a béchamel-based sauce, set with aspic or gelatine and used to mask cold fish, poultry and game.

Chining to remove or cut through the chine bone at the base of the ribs to ease carving.

Clarify to clear fat or liquid of sediment and impurities. Fat is clarified by heating it with water, and allowing the cooled pure fat to rise to the surface. A stock or soup is clarified by boiling it with egg white and crushed egg shell, and straining when cool.

Court bouillon a seasoned savoury liquid containing lemon juice or vinegar, used for poaching pale food. It gives flavour and keeps the food's colour.

Crème fraiche cream that has matured but not turned sour.

Croquettes a mixture of meat, fish, poultry or potato bound together and formed into shapes. Usually coated in egg and crumbs before frying.

Croûte a large round of bread, toasted or fried, on which portions of meat are served.

Croûtons small pieces of bread, toasted or deep-fried, served as an accompaniment to soups or as a garnish.

Dariole a small mould which has straight sloping sides. Used for setting creams and jellies or for cooking puddings and cakes.

Devilled food which is cooked or served with a hot seasoning.

———————————•———————————

Right: Peach, lemon and kumquat conserve (see page 213)

Overleaf: Corn and pineapple pickle (see page 215); Mango and carrot chutney (see page 214); Marrow chutney (see page 215); Sweet tomato chutney (see page 215) and Garden pickle (see page 216)

Dress either to pluck, draw and truss as for poultry or game; or to arrange or garnish a cooked dish; or to prepare cooked shellfish in their shells as for crab and lobster.

Dripping the clarified fat of roast meat.

Dropping consistency the consistency of a cake or pudding mixture before cooking. The standard dropping consistency is when a spoonful of mixture falls from an upheld spoon within 5 seconds without shaking the spoon.

Duxelles a finely-chopped and minced mixture of mushrooms, onions, herbs and butter, used either as the base for a meat or poultry stuffing, or for stuffing vegetables.

Escalope a thin lean slice of meat, usually veal, which is beaten out to be large and very thin so it needs little cooking. Economical versions can be cut from pork, chicken or turkey.

Fines herbes a mixture of finely-chopped fresh parsley, chervil, tarragon and chives.

Flambé to flame food with brandy, or another spirit. The spirit is either set alight before it's poured over the food, or lit on the food.

Folding in mixing a light, whisked ingredient with another ingredient very gently without losing the lightness. This must be done with a large, flattish implement such as a metal spoon or spatula, by cutting through the mixture and folding it over the ingredient being incorporated.

Forcemeat (farce) a stuffing mixture often based on meat.

Fricassee a white stew or casserole with chicken, veal or rabbit.

Frying cooking foods in hot oil or fat, either shallow-frying in very little fat in a shallow pan, or deep-frying in about 5–6.5 cm/2–2½ inches fat so the food is completely immersed.

Galantine a dish of boned and stuffed poultry, game or meat glazed with aspic and served cold.

Whisky three-fruit marmalade (see page 211); Strawberry jam (see page 210); Lime and lemon marmalade (see page 210); Summer marmalade (see page 211) and Greengage jam (see page 210)

Garnish an edible savoury decoration for all types of savoury dish.

Genoese a very light sponge cake mixture. Eggs and sugar are whisked over hot water until thick and creamy. After cooling, melted fat and sifted flour are folded in to give a batter-type mixture which is then baked in a moderately hot oven.

Glaze used to make food look more appetising. A meat glaze is made from meat stock or gravy, boiled until reduced to a brown syrup and then cooled. A sweet glaze is jam softened with water, or a thickened arrowroot mixture. Egg yolks and whites are used to glaze baked dishes and pastries.

Glycerine a sweet, colourless, odourless, syrupy liquid. It retains moisture and is used in confectionery to prevent icings and fondants from hardening.

Infuse to steep herbs, spices or other flavourings in a very hot liquid until the liquid has absorbed the flavour.

Julienne a garnish for clear soups or consommés. Lightly-cooked vegetables, meats, or truffles, for example, are cut into matchsticks and added at the last moment. Fruit rind is used for desserts.

Kneading working a dough firmly with the knuckles for bread, or fingertips in the case of pastry, until smooth and well mixed.

Larding to add extra fat and flavour to less fatty meats such as game, poultry and offal. Strips of fat pork or bacon are threaded with a larding needle through the surface of a joint, or rashers of bacon are wrapped around.

Liaison a mixture used as a thickening agent, such as flour and water, or egg yolks and double cream, used to thicken sauces and stews.

Macedoine a mixture of vegetables or fruits of different colours, sliced or cut in shapes. Cooked or raw, used as a garnish, salad, or in a sauce.

Marinade a seasoned liquid in which foods are soaked to tenderise or increase their flavour. An acid base, wine or vinegar, softens tough fibres.

Masking covering or coating a cooked fish or meat with a savoury jelly, sauce or glaze.

Mirepoix a mixture of diced onions, carrots and celery that adds flavour to meat and fish dishes; it is also used as a base for soups and sauces.

Mull to warm ale or wine with spices and flavourings for serving hot.

Offal the edible internal organs of meat, poultry and game.

Panada a thick sauce made of flour or bread which is used to bind ingredients.

Par-boil to partly boil an ingredient in order to finish cooking by another process.

Paupiette a thin slice of meat rolled round a savoury filling.

Pectin a type of carbohydrate found to a greater or lesser extent in all fruits and vegetables. Used with sugar to set jams.

Pith in citrus fruit, the bitter white cellular lining to the rind covering the flesh.

Poaching to cook food in a small quantity of flavoured liquid in an open pan.

Raising agents substances such as baking powder and yeast, which, when heated or mixed with other ingredients, create a gas and force dough mixtures to rise.

Reducing concentrating a liquid by boiling and evaporation.

Rendering either slowly cooking meat tissues and trimmings to obtain fat; or clearing frying fat by heating it.

Rennet a substance extracted from the stomach lining of calves. Used to coagulate milk for junket (junket rennet) and for making cheese (cheese rennet).

Roasting traditionally this means cooking over direct heat as in a rotisserie or barbecue, as roasting in the oven is really a form of baking.

Roux a cooked paste mixture of butter and flour. A white roux, lightly cooked, is the basis for white sauces. For a brown roux it is cooked until golden brown, and is the basis for brown sauces.

Salmi a stew of game.

Sauté to fry food gently to bring out its flavour without colouring.

Scald either to heat milk or cream to just below boiling point; or to plunge fruit or vegetables in boiling water to remove the skins.

Sear to brown meat quickly in fat on all sides to seal in the juices.

Seasoned flour flour that has salt and pepper mixed in. Used to coat meat and fish.

Shortening a term applied to fats and oils used in making breads, cakes and pastries, because they make the mixture 'short', that is light, tender and crisp.

Simmering cooking in liquid which is heated to just below boiling point.

Skimming removing fat, scum or skin from the surface of hot foods with either absorbent kitchen paper or a large flat spoon.

Steaming to cook food in the steam from boiling water or stock.

Stewing cooking foods very slowly and gently in a flavoured liquid. The liquid is usually served with the food.

Truffles a rare mushroom-like fungus, black or white in colour, with a firm texture and delicate taste. Expensive delicacies, truffles are used mainly for garnishing.

Trussing tying a bird or joint of meat in a neat shape before cooking.

Yeast fungus cells used to produce alcoholic fermentation, or to cause dough to rise.

Zest coloured oily outer skin of citrus fruit which, when grated or peeled, is used to flavour foods and liquids.